Early Literacy Assessments and Teaching Strategies

Jerry L. Johns
Susan Davis Lenski
Laurie Elish-Piper

KENDALL/HUNT PUBLISHING COMPANY
4050 Westmark Drive   Dubuque, Iowa 52002

Books by Jerry L. Johns

Basic Reading Inventory (seven editions)
Secondary & College Reading Inventory (two editions)
Literacy for Diverse Learners (edited)
Handbook for Remediation of Reading Difficulties
Informal Reading Inventories: An Annotated Reference Guide (compiled)
Literacy: Celebration and Challenge (edited)
Spanish Reading Inventory

Books by Jerry L. Johns and Susan Davis Lenski

Improving Reading: A Handbook of Strategies (2nd edition)
Reading & Learning Strategies for Middle & High School Students (with Mary Ann Wham)
Celebrate Literacy! The Joy of Reading and Writing (with June E. Barnhart, James H. Moss, and
    Thomas E. Wheat)
Language Arts for Gifted Middle School Students

Book by Jerry L. Johns and Laurie Elish-Piper

Balanced Reading Instruction: Teachers' Visions and Voices (edited)

Author Addresses for Correspondence and Workshops

Jerry L. Johns
Northern Illinois University
Reading Clinic—119 Graham
DeKalb, IL 60115
E-mail: jjohns@niu.edu
815-753-8484

Susan Davis Lenski
Illinois State University
239 DeGarmo Hall
Normal, IL 61790-5330
E-mail: sjlensk@ilstu.edu
309-438-3028

Laurie Elish-Piper
Northern Illinois University
Reading Clinic—119 Graham
DeKalb, IL 60115
E-mail: laurieep@niu.edu
815-753-8487

Ordering Information
Telephone 800-228-0810
Fax 800-772-9165
Web Site www.kendallhunt.com

Photos by Susan Johns and Gary Meader

Copyright © 1999 by Kendall/Hunt Publishing Company

ISBN 0-7872-5619-6

Printed in the United States of America
10 9 8 7 6 5 4 3 2 1

Dedicated to Laurie and Michael Elish Piper

Laurie and son Michael at 2 months

In the middle of writing this book, Michael made an earlier than expected arrival into the world. We want to announce with joy a very special emergent reader.

Jerry & Sue

CONTENTS

SECTION 1

Overview of Emergent Literacy   1

SECTION 2

Early Literacy Pretests and Teacher's Directions   15

SECTION 3

Teaching Strategies and Activities   91

SECTION 4

Early Literacy Posttests   191

Appendices   247

References   265

Index   271

PREFACE

Purpose of This Book

The purpose of *Early Literacy Assessments & Teaching Strategies* is to assist teachers as they work with emergent readers and writers—children who are in the early stages of reading and writing development. These children are typically in preschool through grade two. Assessing children's development in reading and writing and then teaching to their strengths and needs have been identified as major concerns for teachers.

There are four major sections in this book.

Section 1. This section presents an overview of emergent literacy. Some of the important areas that extend beyond the scope of this book are highlighted along with general ideas to enhance literacy learning.

Section 2. This section consists of a group of 15 informal early literacy pretests. The assessments are informal in nature. The major areas covered by the assessments are:

- attitudes and experiences
- retelling
- literacy knowledge
- wordless picture reading
- auditory discrimination
- rhyme detection
- alphabet knowledge
- phonemic awareness
- writing
- spelling
- phonics
- decoding
- caption reading
- basic sight word knowledge
- passage reading

Also provided in Section 2 are all of the materials needed to assess children's knowledge, concise directions, and a reproducible Record Booklet.

Section 3. This section contains over 225 teaching strategies and activities in 15 different areas to aid teachers in assisting children with their literacy development. Many of these teaching strategies and activities parallel the assessments. Selected resources follow each of the 15 different areas containing teaching strategies.

Section 4. This section contains posttests for the informal literacy assessments. Similar to the pretests, these assessments can be used to help evaluate children's learning.

Appendices. The appendices contain resources to help teachers with emergent readers.

Appendix A: Professional organizations and agencies are listed as resources for teachers.
Appendix B: Word families are listed for reference and instruction.
Appendix C: Sight word lists are given for easy access to these words.
Appendix D: A continuum of children's development in early reading and writing is provided.

Word to the Wise Teacher

The assessments and teaching strategies in this book are intended to be both practical and easy to use. The assessments will inform you of a child's knowledge in some of the areas that contribute to literacy development. The teaching strategies and activities will help you advance children's literacy development.

As you apply and adapt these resources, you will improve your responsiveness to children's literacy growth.

ACKNOWLEDGMENTS

This book is the result of wide reading, research, reflection, experience, and lots of hard work. We are thankful that others have graciously assisted our efforts. Dorie Cannon, a talented, energetic teacher and assistant in the Reading Clinic, was helpful in developing and refining some of the assessments. Kristiina Montero, a Reading Clinic assistant, also helped refine the assessments and cheerfully assisted with numerous other tasks. She was also responsible for making many corrections in the manuscript and getting much of the final copy ready for the publisher. Kate McCabe, the Reading Clinic secretary, typed numerous drafts of the assessments.

Others who deserve special mention for their assistance with the assessments and teaching strategies are Dawn Andermann, Deb Augsburger, Jennifer Blair, Jennifer Bolander, Deborah Griswold, Judy LaShelle, Cheryl Mangione, Jennifer Mesko, and Kathleen Moriarty. A number of teachers in the Orland Park school district also shared comments on the assessments and offered ideas for the teaching strategies.

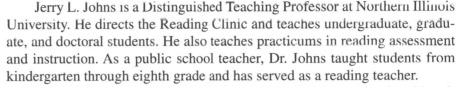

Jerry L. Johns is a Distinguished Teaching Professor at Northern Illinois University. He directs the Reading Clinic and teaches undergraduate, graduate, and doctoral students. He also teaches practicums in reading assessment and instruction. As a public school teacher, Dr. Johns taught students from kindergarten through eighth grade and has served as a reading teacher.

Dr. Johns has served on numerous committees of the International Reading Association and was a member of the Board of Directors. He was also president of the College Reading Association and the Illinois Reading Council.

Dr. Johns has been invited to consult, conduct workshops, and make presentations for teachers throughout the United States and Canada. He has also prepared nearly three hundred publications. His *Basic Reading Inventory* and *Improving Reading* (with Susan Davis Lenski) are widely used in undergraduate and graduate classes as well as by practicing teachers.

Susan Davis Lenski is an Associate Professor at Illinois State University where she teaches undergraduate and graduate courses in literacy. Professor Lenski brings 20 years of classroom experience to her university teaching, 11 of those years in the primary grades. During her years as a classroom teacher and reading specialist, Dr. Lenski focused her efforts on creating ways to implement developmentally appropriate instruction in elementary schools. Her efforts were recognized by the International Reading Association with an Exemplary Reading Program Award.

In addition to teaching at the university, Dr. Lenski currently consults with schools, writes for publication, and is researching the effects of teaching reading strategies in flexible groups in first-grade classrooms. This is her fifth book.

Laurie Elish-Piper is an Assistant Professor of Reading in the Department of Curriculum and Instruction at Northern Illinois University. She teaches a variety of reading courses for undergraduate, graduate, and doctoral students, including practicums in reading assessment and instruction. Prior to her current position, Dr. Elish-Piper worked as an elementary and middle school teacher and an educational therapist in a clinical setting. She has also developed and implemented family literacy programs for inner-city families and their young children.

Dr. Elish-Piper is active in many professional organizations where she serves on numerous committees, including the International Reading Association's Classroom Teacher Awards Committee. In addition, she is currently the Chair of the Illinois Reading Council's Parents and Reading Committee.

Dr. Elish-Piper has served as a consultant and presenter for teachers and parents throughout the Midwest. Her research, publications, and presentations focus on family literacy, reading and writing strategies, and authentic literacy assessment. She is co-editor of the book *Balanced Reading Instruction: Teachers' Visions and Voices* (with Jerry L. Johns) and has published articles in numerous professional journals.

SECTION I

Overview of Emergent Literacy

William Earl Smith

Three-year-old Spencer is sitting on his mother's lap as she reads to him from a favorite picture book. It is a familiar story, one that has been told, retold, read, and reread during Spencer's young life. As they read together, Spencer and his mother have an ongoing dialogue about the text. At the onset of the experience, Spencer insists that the reading begin on the right page rather than the left one. After the reading begins, he interrupts with comments and questions. He tells parts of the story just before they are read. He asks questions about

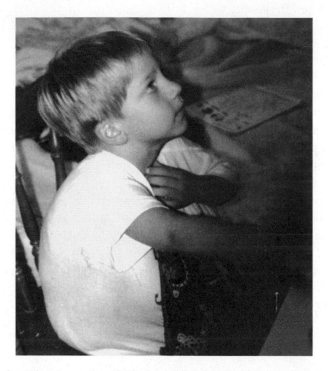

the print; pointing to different letters, he asks, "What's this? Is this an *S*? Are these two the same?" He points to words and wants to know what they are. He insists that his mother suspend reading the story to read words and phrases he indicates, including captions under pictures. At one point, he stops his mother, points to the picture of a man, and asks, "Mommy, why does that man look so mean?"

What is Spencer doing? Is there any value (other than entertainment) in this dialogue between Spencer and his mother? Actually, he is investigating text while he builds and confirms ideas about how text works, ideas that will develop into more sophisticated processes and strategies as he moves along the road to becoming a reader himself. The process of learning to read began long before this particular experience. Spencer has had many experiences reading with adults. By the time he enters school for the first time, he will have already developed a considerable amount of knowledge about print, books, and literacy.

༄

Developing Literacy Knowledge

As children are exposed to language and as they gradually become aware of how language works, they begin to experiment with it. Very early, this curiosity expands into an interest in the written forms of language, and, as a result, children are already on the road to literacy.

What are some of the important concepts of print and literacy that children develop? Some of the more obvious concepts are frequently taken for granted by adults; nevertheless, they are extremely important for young children. Some of these concepts are the ideas that books are for reading, that books have a front and a back, that books have a top and a bottom, that pages turn from right to left, and that reading is done from left to right and from top to bottom. To adults, these ideas seem so obvious that it is hard to realize that children do not always know them.

Children frequently develop these concepts of print quite naturally as they experience books, play with them, and—most importantly—hear them read aloud. Still, there may be children in your classroom who will not have developed these basic concepts; these children will need to be taught the concepts they have not learned at home.

Because it is necessary to talk about literacy knowledge in some sequence and because the different associated concepts are listed in an order of less complex to more complex, it appears that concepts about literacy knowledge are sequential—that one must be learned before another. Although this is somewhat true, it really isn't completely the case. The development of literacy knowledge is actually interactive. In other words, children learn a little about one concept and then some about another; learning one helps them learn the other.

Consider Spencer again; his conversation with his mother illustrates this point. He asked some interesting questions. Remember, he asked his mother to identify certain letters. He was becoming aware that letters exist as separate things. He was learning that these marks consistently have their own names. However, in this episode, he didn't indicate that he had learned that these letters represent sounds in words. Actually, at this time he had not yet indicated that he was beginning to be aware that words were made up of sounds. It wasn't too much longer after this experience that he indicated that he was becoming aware that the letter S was the first letter in his name and that it did stand for the sound beginning his name. He still did not know, however, the names of many of the other letters, nor did he recognize other sounds in words.

Learning the name of the letter S and its sound in his name provided background knowledge that made other significant letters and their sounds easier to learn. Learning that his name has a beginning sound was the onset of learning that words are made up of sounds. His question, "Mommy, why does that man look so mean?" is the beginning of his investigation of the relationships that exist between print and pictures. Spencer is working on a number of literacy concepts at the same time. He will continue to consider these different ideas, ask questions about them, and ask adults to do what may seem odd to them (such as to begin reading at the bottom of the page, to read captions under pictures first, or to begin reading on the right-hand page rather than the left). Over time, as he experiments and considers the results of these "odd" requests, he will develop the literacy knowledge necessary to be able to read.

Literacy knowledge also includes information that is more abstract and less obvious to the young child. For example, children need to become aware of the difference between print and pictures. During early emergent literacy, children will frequently "read" stories using the pictures. Later they learn that the pictures support the writing. They help the reader understand what the words mean. Becoming aware of the importance of print is the beginning of a second important set of concepts that is not always easy to develop. Children need to become aware of the nature of letters: they have particular shapes and names, they make up words, and they represent sounds.

As children are exposed to and use language, they become aware of two additional concepts that are essential to the development of the principles related to the alphabet. First, they develop phonological awareness, the understanding that language is made up of sounds. Children acquire the ability to recognize sounds of language as units of speech that are different from meaning. Second, children also develop phonemic awareness. Phonemic awareness is less inclusive than phonological awareness; it represents the child's ability to recognize that each word can be thought of as a sequence of distinct sounds or phonemes. An indication that children are beginning to develop an awareness of both of these concepts occurs when they begin to show that they recognize alliteration or the similarity of the beginning sounds in different words, they correct speech errors, and they develop an ability to play with words (Snow, Burns, & Griffin, 1998).

Adams, Foorman, Lundberg, and Beeler (1996) suggest that the acquisition of phonemic awareness is a necessary but rather difficult task for most children and that they do not develop it spontaneously. Nonetheless, the concepts involved in phonemic awareness are essential for children to be able to understand the alphabetic principle—the understanding that letters are used in writing to represent the individual sounds of words (Snow, Burns, & Griffin, 1998). The development of this understanding is most easily demonstrated as children begin to write letter-like shapes as well as letters to represent words and then later when they attempt to spell words, even though they may not be spelled correctly. It is not until the onset of this principle in literacy development that children are able to move on to the concepts associated with word recognition and reading. These early attempts to spell are often called developmental spelling and are an important indicator of the development of the alphabetic principle and the relationships that exist between letters and the sounds they represent. Children's development of the alphabetic principle can be seen as their spellings become more accurate in representing the sounds of language and as they come closer and closer to conventional spellings.

Children must have a basic understanding of the concepts of print if they are to be able to begin the process of learning to read; moreover, instruction directed toward teaching the phonological structure of words facilitates this process (Snow, Burns, & Griffin, 1998; Perfetti, Beck, Bell, & Hughes, 1987). Snow, Burns, and Griffin (1998, p. 57) summarize this relationship by saying, "In thinking about the process of learning to read, and about how best to frame early reading instruction, it is important to bear in mind these powerful reciprocal influences of reading skill and phonological awareness on each other."

The period of time during young children's lives when they are developing literacy knowledge, an understanding of print concepts, phonemic awareness, and alphabetic knowledge is usually referred to as emergent reading or emergent literacy. Emergent literacy begins, in some ways, "the moment the child is born" (Savage, 1994, p. 95). A good way to understand the meaning of emergent literacy is to compare emergent reading to the concept of reading readiness.

Reading Readiness vs. Emergent Reading

The terms *reading readiness* and *emergent reading* represent two quite different beliefs about what should happen early in instruction to help children become readers. The idea of readiness suggests that there is a time when a person is ready to begin a task. A child who has developed sufficient balance and strength may be thought of as ready to walk. An adult who has learned the necessary skills associated with a trade may be thought of as ready to begin to work in that trade. The idea of reading readiness is similar. It is built on the idea that a child who has acquired a number of skills is now ready to cross the threshold and begin to learn to read. Just as strength and balance suggest that a child is ready to walk, reading readiness suggests that the child now has the skills (typically things like visual discrimination, auditory discrimination, phonemic segmentation, listening comprehension, knowledge of the alphabet, and color recognition) to learn to read. The idea of reading readiness suggests that the necessary skills have been achieved, finished, or completed; the child has mastered those readiness skills that will support the new task of learning to read.

The fallacy here is that the idea of readiness assumes the beginning and completion of one task before starting the next one. It encourages instruction and drill on these "readiness" tasks to bring them to some recognized level of proficiency before beginning the task of learning to read. It fails to give credit to the interactive nature of literacy development. Remember Spencer's questions, the number of different literacy concepts with which he was experimenting, and the way each concept was a support to the learning of another? Think for a moment about young children you have seen using paper and pencils. The idea of readiness suggests that children learn to talk, then they learn to read, and then they learn to write. How can children write before they can read? Yet, you have seen children pick up a pencil, scribble something on a piece of paper, and proceed to read it. Long before he could read, Spencer was observed filling out checks, a task that he had seen his parents doing. Other prereading preschool children have filled out magazine inserts and put them in the mail. Often, the functions of writing are firmly established before children actually learn to read. The same is true for the development of the necessary concepts for successful reading. Consider the preschool child who says, "Look, that letter is the same one that starts my name," or the kindergartner who—after seeing and hearing the names of the day's helpers—exclaimed, "Look, teacher, all our class helpers' names begin with the same sound!"

Clay (1966) notes that emergent literacy is a progressive experience and that children pay attention to all aspects of print in their environment. Children are continuously developing concepts about language and print from the time they are born, not only after formal instruction begins. All forms of literacy (reading, writing, speaking, and listening) interact with each other. There is a strong relationship between them, and each influences the others during its development. The concept of emergent literacy assumes the development of literacy as a continuum that begins at birth and continues through life. Unlike the concept of reading readiness, it does not focus on reading alone. Reading, writing, speaking, and listening are all important aspects of a child's journey to literacy, each contributing its part to the child's understanding that will eventually lead to the ability to use print to receive and to express ideas.

While the concept of readiness is most often associated with direct instruction of specific prerequisite skills and the mastery of those skills, the concept of emergent literacy is frequently associated with a natural, functional development of language and reading. Emergent literacy is an approach frequently associated with the belief that children will develop reading skills when given the opportunity to use them in realistic ways for reasons they understand; in other words, instruction is placed in a context meaningful to the learner. Children are encouraged to play at reading, to look at books, to "write," to listen to stories read aloud, to retell stories, and to become involved in dramatic play in which pretend literacy activities are a part. Children enjoy activities that allow them to participate in literacy play centers. One example would be a space center in which children dress in a space suit, fill out flight plans before pretending to fly the spaceship, go over checklists to inspect the rocket, submit reports of their flight, and talk to each other over intercoms on the rocket. Another example is a center in which they fill out shopping lists, go to the store, select items, figure the cost, and write receipts for the sale of the items. Still another experience might be to have children go to a pretend restaurant, read the menu, and place their order. Waiters write orders, and receptionists take telephone calls and write dinner reservations. These are just three examples of how dramatic play provides opportunities for literacy tasks.

A comparison of two different classrooms in which young children were being taught illustrates the difference between the two approaches. In one class, a kindergarten teacher directly teaches the names and sounds of letters and helps children learn to sound out new words that they will later read in simple stories. The teacher teaches a number of vocabulary words through phonics, has children read text controlled for the vocabulary that had been previously taught, and helps children learn to answer various comprehension questions related to the text. The child's questions, "Why am I learning these letters? Why am I learning these words? Why am I reading this story that really doesn't sound like any language I have heard from the adults around me?" are never discussed. In other words, the context for the instruction makes little sense to the children.

In a different classroom, a second-grade teacher embraces the concept of emergent literacy. In this class, the children want to learn about space. They generate a number of questions about space that they are trying to answer. They work together for several days to find as many answers as they can. At the same time, the teacher teaches some of the same basic skills as those taught in the previous example. Children learn vocabulary words; they read those words in stories, and they write stories. Though the children answer many of their questions about space, they are left with a number of questions for which they cannot find answers. As a class, they decide they should write letters to the National Aeronautics and Space Administration. They divide the questions among each other; each child writes, revises, edits, and mails his or her own letter. Each child in that classroom is able to tell why he or she is writing these letters, why he or she is working on the words, and why it is important to spell them correctly. They all clearly understand the reasons for these literacy experiences and why they are doing what they are doing.

The second classroom example is a contrast to the first example. Both teachers teach new vocabulary that the children are expected to learn and be able to use. In the second example, however, those words and stories are introduced as they are being used in some purposeful way. The literacy knowledge and skills identified and developed from a meaningful context such as the children's speech, the use of language experience activities (Stauffer, 1970), discussion groups about what they are learning, the children's own oral language, and hands-on activities relate to the ideas they are reading about and that are being read to them by the teacher. The second example is more aligned with the concept of emergent literacy. It is couched in a social context of learning. Reading becomes a process that children develop through real experiences with print. Guided by adults, children begin to develop concepts of print and start to use print in their environment. As they begin to understand the function of print and are guided by skillful adults, the concepts of reading begin to emerge; reading becomes a very natural and real process. If meaningful reading and writing experiences are provided for children, reading begins to emerge.

Stages of Reading

Teaching children who are developing the concepts associated with emergent literacy is easier if there is a structure that provides benchmarks for a child's development. Good teaching requires knowing what the children in your classroom know and do not know. Such knowledge should be based on your assessment of a child's understanding of the identified concepts so that you know what to teach next. This assessment and instruction sequence needs to be based on an organization that is compatible with the ideas of emergent literacy. O'Donnell and Wood (1992) present an easy-to-follow, developmental sequence of learning to read that works very well for this purpose and is compatible with the assessments and teaching strategies in this book. This sequence represents a child's development from the early beginnings of literacy through proficient reading.

According to O'Donnell and Wood (1992, p. xi), literacy learning is "a language-learning process that is best acquired through functional, purposeful use of print." At the same time, they clearly talk about reading instruction. Although they would not recommend direct, intensive instruction of some of the specific skills of phonics and phonemic awareness, their descriptions of the developmental stages of learning to read plainly provide a framework for understanding the development of reading and the instructional strategies and practices that are appropriate for teachers to use to support this development.

This model of reading has five stages: emergent, initial, transitional, basic, and refinement. The first stage, emergent reading, is associated with children in preschool and kindergarten. The second stage, initial reading, is associated with children in grades one and two. The strategies and assessments in this book are primarily designed for children described in these first two stages. The third stage, transitional reading, is associated with children in grades two through four; but, because it is not unusual for some children in the second grade to be in the transitional stage of reading, this stage is also described.

Emergent Reading Stage

Preschoolers and children in kindergarten are usually in the emergent stage of reading development. This is the stage during which children are developing all of those emergent literacy behaviors that have been discussed earlier. It is during this stage that most children develop phonemic awareness and the alphabetic principle and build their receptive and expressive language skills. Children are expanding their concepts of the world around them, becoming familiar with the structure of stories, and experimenting with print concepts. In the emergent reading stage, children play at literacy tasks and often participate in pretend reading. Critical to this stage are the child's oral language development and an interest in print. Instruction is directed toward helping children develop an awareness of the purpose and nature of print, become familiar with the nature and structure of story, and further develop world knowledge.

In the emergent reading stage of development, it is particularly important that children be read to, thereby providing them with experiences about which they can talk and write. Their writing usually consists of scribbling, or it may be dictated to adults who do the actual writing. The language experience approach (Stauffer, 1970) and all of the teacher-directed activities that can accompany this approach are very important during this stage. Children should have many experiences that allow them to hear and retell stories. Some of the strategies discussed in Section 3 of this book that are appropriate for children in the emergent reading stage are Desire to Read (3.1), Background Knowledge (3.2), Reading as Meaning (3.3), Sense of Story (3.4), and Alphabet Knowledge (3.7). Children leave this stage knowing a few high frequency sight words, having begun to develop concepts of print, and being able to match some letters with their corresponding sounds.

Initial Reading Stage

Children in the initial stage of reading development are usually in first and second grades. They enter this stage with a very limited sight vocabulary and some awareness of print concepts. During this stage, children greatly expand the number of words that they recognize by sight; however, those sight words continue to be words that are generally in the child's spoken vocabulary. Children develop the awareness that print is meaningful and begin to predict what written text will be about. Looking at the cover of a picture book, children in the initial reading stage are able to make suggestions as to what they think the story may be about. When they hear the story, they can say whether they were correct in their predictions. They begin to develop strategies for word recognition or word identification. Again, most of the words that they are able to figure out will be words that are familiar to them in their oral language. Appropriate instructional goals for children in the initial reading stage are a continuation of the development of the concept that reading is a meaning-making process, various word-recognition strategies, and a sight vocabulary. Appropriate instructional strategies for children in the initial stage of reading development consist of a continuation of those strategies used with children in the emergent stage as well as the addition of follow-up activities to accompany read-alouds and shared reading that focus on helping children develop sight vocabulary, word recognition, and comprehension. A few of the strategies discussed in Section 3 of this book that would be appropriate in this stage of reading are all of those listed for the emergent stage, plus Writing (3.8), Phonics (3.10), and Sight Words (3.11). Indications that a child is leaving this stage and beginning to move into the transitional stage are his or her success in being able to read a large body of sight words, the ability to successfully use word-identification strategies, and the ability to select and independently read books appropriate to this level of reading.

Transitional Reading Stage

The expected grade range for children in the transitional stage of reading is somewhat broader than in the previous two stages. Children in the transitional stage are usually in the second through fourth grades. Probably the most representative characteristic of the transitional stage of reading is the child's ability to participate in independent reading activities. Because many children are able to figure out words that they have not seen in print before (although continued development of word-identification strategies is appropriate), they are able to spend longer sessions independently reading books of their own choosing. They improve their reading by reading. It is not that further instruction is inappropriate; but, at this stage, children begin to profit more from their personal, independent reading than they did in earlier stages.

In the transitional stage, children should develop automatic word-identification strategies. They should experience marked improvement in their ability to write. Strategies that are directed toward the achievement of these goals are appropriate, as are extensive opportunities to read independently and to discuss what they have read with other students. Children who have developed a large sight vocabulary, who read a variety of materials independently, and who are showing marked signs of fluent reading are those children who have moved out of the transitional stage. Strategies from Section 3 of this book that might be used during this stage are Desire to Read (3.1), Background Knowledge (3.2), Writing (3.8), Spelling (3.9), Phonics (3.10), Sight Words (3.11), Reading Comprehension (3.12), Cross Checking (3.13), Fluency (3.14), and Monitoring Reading (3.15). In all instances, the examples of suggested strategies in each of the stages of reading are only given to further help you understand the general nature of the reader in each stage. The most appropriate selection of strategies comes only after careful assessment of a child's background and needs.

O'Donnell and Wood (1992) recommend three instructional goals that are always appropriate, regardless of the stage of development, and that should always be a part of any reading program for children. They are 1) helping children develop positive attitudes about reading, 2) promoting extensive and varied reading experiences, and 3) fostering reading for meaning. Strategies to facilitate these goals can be found in Section 3 of this book, especially Desire to Read (3.1), Background Knowledge (3.2), Reading for Meaning (3.3), Writing (3.8), and Cross Checking (3.13).

Once again, Spencer provides an example of the reading development of a child who has moved from the emergent reading stage through the initial reading stage and on to the transitional reading stage. Throughout his preschool years, Spencer continued to develop literacy knowledge. He learned the names of the letters of the alphabet, he came to realize that these letters represented speech sounds in written words, print took on more and more meaning for him, pictures became important in helping him to understand the story, and he developed a few sight words that he recognized in varying print environments (his first and last name, "George" from reading the *Curious George* books, a few words that were used in Sunday School, and some street signs). As he moved on to first grade, Spencer began to recognize that he could sound out words by applying the sounds of the letters to the words.

Spencer spent quite a long time in the initial stage of reading development. Sounding out words was difficult for him. Spencer spent a number of months in first grade sounding out words. Even when it seemed certain that he knew the words, he would sound them out, often sounding out the same word a number of times on the same page. Spencer is a child who likes rules, and he likes them to apply consistently. But the pronunciation of words does not always follow the rules. For example, when he was in the first month of first grade, he completely understood and could use Roman numerals after one simple explanation. One night after his father completed reading one of the Boxcar Children books to him, Spencer commented that in second grade he would have to be able to read chapter books by himself. He was beginning to realize that he needed to change the way he was currently reading. With time, he began to read more fluently. As he became a more fluent reader, Spencer developed a larger sight vocabulary and stronger word-identification strategies. However, he was a child who needed much more instruction and guidance through the initial and transitional stages than many other children. Lessons dealing with background knowledge, reading as meaning, sense of story, sight words, and cross checking (strategies described in Section 3 of this book) were necessary for him to move along the road toward proficient reading.

Helping Children Develop Literacy Skills at Home

Literacy does not just burst onto the scene. It takes time and preparation, beginning at birth. A child's success at school with literacy activities, instruction, and development depends a great deal on what happens in the child's home from the time of birth. Parents and guardians interact with children, talking and playing with them, changing, bathing, and feeding them, putting them to bed, and reading to them. Parents or care givers may approach these tasks in a rather perfunctory way, accepting them as necessary parts of their roles without realizing just how significant these times with the child can be. However, the interactions that take place between adults and the child can have a profound influence on the child's preparation for a successful school experience and the development of reading and writing skills. It is not just the interaction that makes the difference but also the nature of that interaction; there must be a quality of enjoyment and engagement on the part of both the adults and the child. According to Leichter (1984), the productivity of these interactions depends on literacy experiences shared between the adults and the child, the literacy materials available in the home, and the quality and nature of the relationship that exists between the adults and the child.

Adults who can turn mundane tasks such as diapering and bathing into play times and who approach getting ready for bed, bedtime reading, and other daily interactions as play times are more successful in helping children develop the necessary skills associated with emergent literacy and later success in learning to read and write at school. During these times, activities such as reciting nursery rhymes, singing fun songs, making silly noises, babbling, and making up silly words all contribute to the child's development of many of the skills that later will become very important in learning to read and write. These events are usually intended as fun and play, but they lay important groundwork for literacy development. Literacy events are most successful when parents approach them as play rather than as teaching experiences. The interactions that children initiate during these times are the real secret of successful literacy development during such parent-child interactions. Though all of the types of activities mentioned above are important, probably the most important thing that parents or care givers can do for their children is to read to them at regular times, such as at bedtime and also when the child asks to be read to.

When Spencer's mother, Kimberly, was very young, it became a nightly ritual for her father to read stories and sing nursery rhymes at bedtime. It took very little time, but it was a special time for the two of them. Years later, when Kimberly became a mother, she asked her father about the stories they used to read and the rhymes they used to sing. She asked him to sing the same nursery rhymes to her boys that he had sung to her. This experience had made a lasting impression on her young mind while helping her develop an early sense of language as well as a sense of how to interact with her own children.

Reading aloud to children from birth through the school years is vitally important to the development of literacy. Research by Chomsky (1972), Cullinan (1992), Huck (1976), and Morrow (1997) supports reading aloud to children. Reading aloud provides a language model for children to imitate, it builds an interest in books, it presents positive and fun experiences with reading, and it teaches that reading is an appropriate recreational activity. Reading aloud supports and strengthens background information, and it builds a sense of story structures. Bromley (1998, p. 134) says, "besides being pleasurable, enjoyable, soothing, and energizing," reading aloud also:

- Builds general knowledge
- Expands vocabulary
- Develops concepts of print
- Reveals different language patterns
- Reveals different writing styles
- Encourages visual imagery
- Inspires writing

- Increases achievement
- Boosts comprehension
- Extends knowledge of literary elements
- Broadens genre knowledge
- Improves listening skills
- Fosters curiosity and imagination
- Promotes motivation to read and learn

Providing support with other literacy activities in which children may participate while playing is an important function of both the home and the school. If a child is independently looking at a book, parents or care givers should take the time to answer questions about the book, listening and responding to comments. If the child wants help writing something, parents should take the time to provide that help. When a child comes to parents or care givers with a scribbled note, they should "read" and discuss it together.

Parents or care givers should reinforce children's attempts at literacy activities. Rather than trying to point out how to correct children when shown a piece of writing, parents and care givers should take the opportunity to find something positive to say about the child's attempts. Such behavior communicates to the child that his or her literacy tasks are valued, and it establishes an environment in which the child feels comfortable enough to continue to share his or her writing with others. In this type of environment, children come to recognize the parents or care givers as a resource for information, help, and support.

Parents or care givers can provide a wide variety of experiences, such as trips to the zoo, airport, shopping malls, amusement parks, fire stations, and animal parks. They can take their children to libraries and bookstores not only to get books but also to make the event an outing, an opportunity to look for books, and a chance to read together. Children can choose books they like or look for books on special topics. They learn how to use the library when they see other adults and children doing the same things. Trips to the bookstore become opportunities to examine the thousands of available children's books and give children an opportunity to develop strategies for selecting books.

If these times with young children are approached by parents and care givers with the idea of making them instructional experiences, both the child and the adults are likely to become frustrated and fail to achieve their goals. Silvern and Silvern (1990, p.14) give the following suggestions for such times:

- Let the child decide when to stop the activity.
- Watch for signs of tiring.
- Never force the activity.
- Let the child's interest dictate the activity.
- Don't push a reading game if the child is not responding—just read.
- Pick short readings for sleepyheads.
- Skip reading altogether if the child is too tired.
- Let the child pick the story.
- Read your child's favorites, not your own; children like books for reasons different from those of adults.
- Be prepared to read favorite books often.

Snow, Burns, and Griffin (1998, p. 138) write, "Adults who live and interact regularly with children can profoundly influence the quality and quantity of their literacy experiences." Parents or care givers do this by sharing their literacy experiences with children by providing books, pencils, crayons, markers, paper, magazines, and other literacy tools in the home for use by children. Parents and care givers build positive, supportive relationships and create emotionally safe environments in which children can examine and practice literacy events.

Helping Children Develop Literacy Skills at School

Literacy activities provided by parents and care givers are much like those provided by teachers at school. When children come to school having had many experiences with literacy, there is a greater likelihood that they will be successful at school. Parents or care givers are partners with schools in the development of children's literacy skills. Without exposure to literacy activities in the home and the support of activities such as those previously discussed, it is much more difficult for children to be successful with the experiences and instruction that teachers provide to build excited, interested, and motivated readers. Reading is a way of life; it is something that most adults do as naturally as breathing. Reading provides entertainment. It is a primary source of information gathering. It is a daily activity. And though schools can overcome the lack of good literacy experiences in the home and teach children to be readers when they have not had the advantages of literacy activities in the home, doing so is much harder. Success at school in literacy development is greatly facilitated by the partnership between the school and the home.

Teachers have the responsibility to build on the literacy knowledge children bring to school. To build effectively on the child's background, it is essential that teachers are able to answer three questions about each student's literacy development.

1. What literacy knowledge does the child have? Knowing what your students know and don't know is essential to good teaching. It suggests which areas you should focus on next, and it is necessary in order to prevent children from being instructed in areas that are really repetitions of what they already know.

2. What needs to be taught next? Though literacy learning is interactive and not necessarily learned one skill at a time, it is important for a teacher to be able to make decisions about which literacy skills to emphasize with which children. It may be necessary to provide more experiences during which children will become more familiar with the names or sounds of the letters of the alphabet, work on sight words, learn about books, develop background knowledge, learn to read for meaning, develop a desire and motivation to be a reader, develop a sense of story, work on writing stories, develop fluency, and better monitor their reading.

3. How do you know when each child is ready to move on to different literacy skills? Teachers are constantly making decisions about and evaluating children's progress. Good assessment should help a teacher know what children know as well as what needs to be worked on next.

Answering these questions is a circular process: assess to see what children know and determine what to teach next, teach selected strategies, assess to see what children have learned, and decide what to teach next. Good assessment is central to good teaching. It should inform you and determine instruction. Where good assessment is lacking, you take the chance either of teaching something that is too easy or of teaching over the children's heads. If activities are too simple, children continue to do what they can already do and have no opportunity for growth. If activities are too difficult, children become frustrated and are unable to grow because there is too much that is new. Good teachers are able to plan instruction based on children's needs.

This instruction needs to take place in a meaningful context that provides opportunities to use the literacy skills that are being developed in the classroom. Systematic, explicit instruction designed to teach literacy skills can be prepared, but explicit instruction should always be taught in some authentic, meaningful activity.

Providing Meaningful Literacy Experiences

Classroom activities are not the sole prerogative of the teacher. Teachers should invite student ownership so that children have some say in planning what will be studied; teachers should provide some activities that permit voluntary participation and students' choices, such as activities that allow children to choose topics for writing or the self-selection of materials for free reading. Classroom activities and instruction should be based on the idea that children become literate by participating in literacy activities that engage them in purposeful language used in social settings. At the same time, students are not expected to reinvent the support skills that are needed to participate in such activities. Teachers should capitalize on children's natural developmental stages to teach the skills they need to read.

To illustrate a way to integrate instruction in a meaningful way, consider the earlier example of the primary teacher and the study of space. When the decision to write letters to ask their unanswered questions was made, the children were not left on their own to figure out how to do the task. They were given examples of letters that had been written for similar purposes. They read *The Jolly Postman* by Janet and Allan Ahlberg (1986). Time was spent in class talking about how to compose their letters so that they were polite and gave the reader some information about the writer and why he or she was writing. They learned how to ask the question and how to thank the receiver ahead of time for his or her attention to the request. Specific lessons were taught on the form of a business letter as well as how to address envelopes. Attention was paid to learning how to spell the words that were needed in the letter. There were lessons on how to revise and edit the letters, paying attention to content and to the form of the text with such things as periods at the end of sentences, appropriate use of capital letters, good handwriting, and the spacing of words. Every day for several days, the teacher planned specific, systematic instruction on a number of literacy skills that would support the quality of the students' letters that were to be mailed.

At the same time, it was apparent that children knew why they were participating in every lesson. After a lesson on editing, children were asked why they thought the teacher had taught the lesson. Each child was able to respond with answers that clearly indicated that he or she understood the purpose of editing their letters. It wasn't because the children were told why editing was important. Rather, it was because the children were participating in a broader science unit that they had helped choose and design, one that they were interested in and had been reading and writing about, one they were sharing with parents and students in other classrooms. It was because the letter writing was a part of a bigger, more important, and contextualized activity. Writing the letters had been the children's idea. They knew that what they were doing would help accomplish goals that they had helped establish.

Good literacy instruction is contextualized and meaningful to children. It provides opportunities for children to participate in all of the language forms and to take part in literacy activities. It allows them to be literate while they are learning literacy skills.

Developing Motivational Literacy Experiences

Teachers are not only responsible for helping children develop literacy; they are also obligated to do this in a way that builds in the motivation to learn. Motivation is demonstrated as children choose to read during free choice time, when they read on a regular basis, when they read for varied purposes, and when they show a willingness to spend a sustained period of time with a task. It doesn't take extensive research to realize that motivation is important. If motivation is a willingness to participate in a task over a sustained period of time and to willingly return to that task with some sort of commitment, then it only seems reasonable that motivation is essential. One cannot learn to read without spending long periods of time with print and reading.

Another way to help children develop the motivation to read is by reading yourself. Teachers need to let children see them reading. Children need to realize that their teacher not only reads but also enjoys it. When you let children see you reading for pleasure as well as to learn, you become a reading role model who provides a much needed example to children. Being a role model is often thought of as an important characteristic for the home. However, it is equally important at school. Teachers should model reading and writing for children. This is easily and naturally done when meaningful, contextualized units of study are part of the reading/writing curriculum.

Beyond providing good models, teachers should provide help to children as they participate in reading and writing activities. If children are independently looking at books, teachers must take time to answer any questions about the books that children may have. Teachers should listen and respond to children's comments. If children need help writing something, teachers should take the time to respond. Children will come to recognize the classroom as a safe place to experiment with literacy and as a resource for information or help. Good teachers provide classroom environments that reinforce children's attempts at literacy activities. This is most easily accomplished when the children are participating in projects or broader units of study for which the literacy tasks are not just drill and practice of skills but are designed to help children learn more about the topic of the unit.

Final Thoughts

The literacy goals of a classroom are to help children become efficient and effective readers, writers, and speakers. Children who are motivated to read and write, who have the word-identification strategies to deal with written text, and who not only understand what they read but are also able to apply this information are fluent readers. The reading of fluent students has expression related to the meaning of the text, and it flows without interruption. Such readers are able to relate their experiences in life to what they read.

A look at Spencer's development of literacy is a good example of the development of a young reader. He began by being read to and talked to at home, by being a part of the home's literacy environment. Later, at school, his teachers contributed to his development as they considered what he knew and could do and, through good assessment, planned further instruction. At school Spencer began to learn the phonics skills he needed for beginning word identification. Through home and school experiences, he came to realize that he would eventually be expected to read more like the adults around him. This would require fluency and more proficient word-identification strategies. These understandings prepared Spencer to better respond to the instructional strategies his teacher had planned. With Spencer, motivation was often sustained as he came to realize that reading was a good way to find information about topics of interest to him. The combination of reading activities at home, thoughtful assessment and instruction at school, and Spencer's own desire to read made Spencer's development as a reader an ongoing process.

Spencer is not an exception. All children come to school with literacy experiences. Every child is an emergent reader. The development of reading begins as young children notice the print in their environments and continues as they experience literacy activities at home and at school. To facilitate the literacy development of a child, parents, care givers, and teachers need to become aware of what the child knows and can do. Such knowledge can usually be gained through informal assessment. Instructional activities should build on what the child can do and nudge the child into new areas of learning. Using the assessment-instruction cycle, parents, care givers, and teachers can help emergent readers develop into motivated, facile readers and writers.

Early Literacy Pretests and Teacher's Directions

OVERVIEW
of Early Literacy Pretests and Teacher's Directions

Section 2 contains 15 Early Literacy Assessments to help teachers assess children's emerging and developing abilities in reading. The major purpose of each assessment is presented below.

2.1   **Interviews About Reading:**   Helps determine a child's understanding of the nature of reading, the purposes for reading, and the child's attitude toward reading.

2.2   **Retelling a Story:**   Sheds light on how well a child comprehends a story. The ability to listen to a story being read, remember the story's content, and retell the story are important precursors to reading comprehension.

2.3   **Literacy Knowledge:**   Contains questions to ask while sharing a book with the child. The questions will help assess the child's knowledge of print directionality, letters, words, punctuation, and the like.

2.4   **Wordless Picture Reading:**   Assesses the child's ability to tell a story using pictures.

2.5   **Auditory Discrimination:**   Helps evaluate the child's ability to distinguish words that differ in one phoneme (sound).

2.6   **Rhyme Detection:**   Assesses the child's ability to hear whether words rhyme. This skill is often helpful in learning phonics and is usually taught in early phonemic awareness instruction.

2.7   **Alphabet Knowledge:**   Contains upper-case and lower-case letters of the alphabet in nonsequential order to help assess the child's letter-naming ability.

2.8   **Phoneme Segmentation:**   Helps to assess the child's ability to segment phonemes or sounds in speech.

2.9   **Writing:**   Provides an opportunity for the child to demonstrate his or her ability to write letters, words, and sentences.

2.10   **Developmental Spelling:**   Assesses the stages a child goes through prior to conventional spelling and provides windows into a child's thinking about letter-sound relationships.

2.11   **Consonant Phonic Elements:**   Helps assess the child's knowledge of the beginning and ending sounds of words.

2.12   **Decoding:**   Helps assess the child's ability to decode new words. This assessment is most useful for a child who is able to read simple texts.

2.13   **Caption Reading:**   Assesses the child's ability to read a brief story with helpful picture clues.

2.14   **Basic Sight Word Knowledge:**   Contains 10 words to help assess the child's ability to identify the most common words in English.

2.15   **Passage Reading:**   Helps determine how well the child can read connected text. Four passages are available and range from pre-primer through second-grade level.

For each assessment on the following pages, you will find a page containing a brief overview of the assessment, the materials you will need, the procedures and directions for administration, and guidelines for scoring and interpretation. Whenever assessment materials are needed for a particular test, you will find them immediately following the directions. These are the materials you will use with the child. At the very end of this section is a Record Booklet (pp. 63–89) you can use to record and summarize the child's responses to the assessments administered. Teachers have found this arrangement easy to use based on a similar plan in the *Basic Reading Inventory* (Johns, 1997).

Take a few minutes and survey the assessments to see how they are arranged. For example, if you begin with assessment 2.1 (Interviews About Reading), you will see the page containing the overview, materials needed, procedure, and scoring and interpretation information. (We refer to this page as Teacher's Directions in the Contents.) The actual interview sheets containing the questions you will use with the child are found in the Record Booklet (pp. 63–89) at the very end of this section. Take a minute and locate the two interview forms in the Record Booklet. There are several other assessments organized like the Interviews About Reading. See assessments 2.2, 2.5, 2.6, 2.8, and 2.9.

When an assessment has something the child needs to look at during the administration, it can be found directly after the Teacher's Directions. Take a moment and look at assessment 2.3 to see the child's copy of the story that you will use with the child during the Literacy Knowledge assessment. Then look at the very back of this section and find the Record Booklet. Go to assessment 2.3 in the Record Booklet and you will see the sheets you use to ask questions and note the child's responses. Assessments 2.4, 2.7, 2.10, 2.11, 2.12, 2.13, 2.14, and 2.15 are organized in a similar manner.

Choosing Assessments to Administer

The assessments were designed to help you assess areas of interest or concern for children in your classroom. There is a wide range of reading ability among children in primary classrooms, and there is no simple way to tell you what assessments to use. We honor and embrace your professionalism as you decide which assessments will help you explore your students' emergent reading so that instruction can be more responsive to their needs. The chart below is intended to give you a general idea of the range of assessments for children who are not yet reading (novice) to those who read at a second-grade level (facile). As you can see from the chart, some assessments are likely to be more useful at the early stages of reading acquisition (e.g., Literacy Knowledge, Wordless Picture Reading) while others will be helpful for students who are already reading (Decoding, Passage Reading). In some instances, an assessment can be useful for a wide range of readers (e.g., Interviews About Reading, Retelling a Story, and Developmental Spelling).

Assessments for Emergent Readers

Early Literacy Assessments	Continuum of Assessment Recommendations	
	Novice	Facile*
Interviews About Reading	——————————————————————————————	
Retelling a Story	——————————————————————————————	
Literacy Knowledge	———————————————	
Wordless Picture Reading	———————————————	
Auditory Discrimination	———————————————	
Rhyme Detection	———————————————	
Alphabet Knowledge	———————————————	
Phoneme Segmentation	————————————————————	
Writing	————————————————————	
Developmental Spelling	——————————————————————————————	
Consonant Phonic Elements	———————————————	
Decoding	———————————————	
Caption Reading	——————————	
Basic Sight Word Knowledge	——————————————————	
Passage Reading	———————————————	

*Grade 2 Reading Level

18

The critical consideration in selecting assessments is what you want to learn about the child's literacy development. The box below contains some skills and abilities related to reading and the assessments that correspond to these areas. You can use this information as a point of departure for selecting assessments; however, you should also carefully evaluate the specific assessments to ascertain their appropriateness for the child. As you use the assessments over a period of time, you will learn which ones are most helpful for enhancing the literacy development of children in your classroom.

If you're interested in the child's	You might want to use assessment
oral language ability/comprehension	2.2, 2.4
general notions about reading and literacy	2.1, 2.3, 2.7, 2.9, 2.10
writing and spelling	2.9, 2.10
ability to work with sounds orally	2.5, 2.6, 2.8
phonics and decoding abilities	2.9, 2.10, 2.11, 2.12
word knowledge	2.4, 2.9, 2.10, 2.13, 2.14
story knowledge or sense of story	2.2, 2.4, 2.15
ability to read independently	2.13, 2.14, 2.15

2.1 Interviews About Reading

🦝 Overview

Interviews About Reading are designed to determine the child's understanding of the nature of reading, the purposes for reading, and the child's attitude toward reading.

✔ Materials Needed

The pages in the Record Booklet containing the interview questions and a tape recorder (if desired).

🔤 Procedure

1. Duplicate the appropriate section of the Record Booklet. If the child does not yet read, choose the Emergent Reader Interview. If the child is beginning to read, use the Early Reading Interview.

2. You may decide to tape record the interview rather than write the child's responses on the page in the Record Booklet during the interview. If you tape record the interview, set up the tape recorder and test it to make sure it is working properly.

3. With the child, say, **"Today we're going to talk about reading and your ideas about reading. There are no right or wrong answers. I'm going to ask you some questions. To answer the questions, just tell me what you are thinking."**

4. If you are tape recording the interview, say, **"I'm going to turn on the tape recorder so that I can remember what you say. Do you mind?"** (Teacher: Be sure to test the tape recorder.)

5. If you are writing the child's responses, say, **"I will be writing down what you say so that I can remember your comments. Is that all right with you?"**

6. Begin asking the interview questions in the order they are written. If the child does not answer, prompt with easy questions such as "Do you have any brothers or sisters? and What animals do you like?" Once the child feels comfortable answering the questions, proceed with the interview.

✍ Scoring and Interpretation

Record the child's responses as accurately as possible. Then read the responses looking for overall patterns. Informally determine whether the child views himself or herself as learning to read and whether the child has a positive or negative attitude toward reading. Record your qualitative judgment of the child's attitude and understanding about reading with an X on the continuum located on the front page of the Record Booklet. Areas of concern can be strengthened by using the instructional strategies and activities in Section 3 of this book, especially 3.1.

2.2 Retelling a Story

Overview

A retelling assessment sheds light on how well a child comprehends stories. The ability to listen to a story being read, remember the story's contents, and retell the story are important precursors to developing reading comprehension.

✓ Materials Needed

An age-appropriate story that is new to the child and the page in the Record Booklet.

Procedure

1. Choose a short book that is new for the child. The book should have an obvious plot with named characters. You may choose to use props or puppets with the story if you think visual aids could help the child. Some examples of books that would be appropriate for young children are:

   • Carle, E. (1969). *The very hungry caterpillar.* Cleveland: Collins-World.
   • Galdone, P. (1986). *Over in the meadow.* New York: Simon & Schuster.
   • Numeroff, L.J. (1985). *If you give a mouse a cookie.* New York: HarperCollins.
   • Sendak, M. (1975). *Seven little monsters.* New York: Harper & Row.
   • Wood, A. (1984). *The napping house.* San Diego: Harcourt Brace Jovanovich.

2. Before reading the book say, **"I'm going to read a story to you. After I am finished reading, I will ask you to tell me the story as if you were telling it to someone who has not read the story. As you listen, try to remember as much of the story as you can."**

3. Read the book aloud to the child.

4. After you have read the book say, **"Now tell me as much of the story as you can."** If the child hesitates, ask probing questions such as **"What was the story about?"** or **"Who was in the story?"** or **"What happened next?"** You may want to tape record the retelling for future reference.

5. Using the page in the Record Booklet, indicate with Xs the extent to which the child includes or provides evidence of the information on the list.

Scoring and Interpretation

To interpret the Retelling, look at where the Xs have been placed. If the child has Xs predominantly on the right side of the page, you can consider the child to have good comprehension. If the Xs are mostly on the left, you may want to refer to Section 3 of this book, especially 3.4 and 3.12. If you find that there is no pattern for the Xs, read another story and engage the child in a second retelling. If you find the same pattern, informally identify specific comprehension strengths and weaknesses by noting which areas were marked some degree or none and which ones were marked high or moderate degree. Then record your qualitative judgment of the child's retelling by marking an X on the continuum located on the front of the Record Booklet.

2.3   Literacy Knowledge

Overview

Literacy Knowledge contains questions to ask while sharing a book with the child. These questions will help assess the child's knowledge of print directionality, letters, words, punctuation, and the like.

✓   Materials Needed

A book (*Friends* or *Animals*), two 3″ × 5″ cards, and the Record Booklet.

Procedure

1. Duplicate the appropriate section of the Record Booklet.

2. Remove the book *Friends* for the pretest or *Animals* for the posttest. Staple or bind the book.

3. Prepare by reading the assessment items in the Record Booklet in conjunction with the child's book.

4. For the assessment, say, **"I'd like you to show me some of the things you know about reading. You won't have to read."**

5. Begin with the first item in the Record Booklet and proceed through the assessment.

6. Stop if the child seems frustrated.

7. Note any relevant observations in the Record Booklet.

Scoring and Interpretation:

Circle plus (+) for correct responses and minus (−) for incorrect responses. Count the number of pluses and record the total in the box on the record sheet and on the front of the Record Booklet. The maximum score is 20. Informally judge the child's knowledge of literacy concepts on the Literacy Knowledge page in the record sheet by marking Xs on the continuums. Then record your qualitative judgment of the child's overall literacy knowledge by marking an X on the continuum located on the front of the Record Booklet. Areas of concern about literacy knowledge can be strengthened by the instructional strategies and activities in Section 3 of this book, especially 3.5 and 3.7.

Note:
Remove and bind the following
Friends **booklet for use with the**
Literacy Knowledge Assessment (2.3).

Friends

by Dorie Cannon & Cheryl Mangione

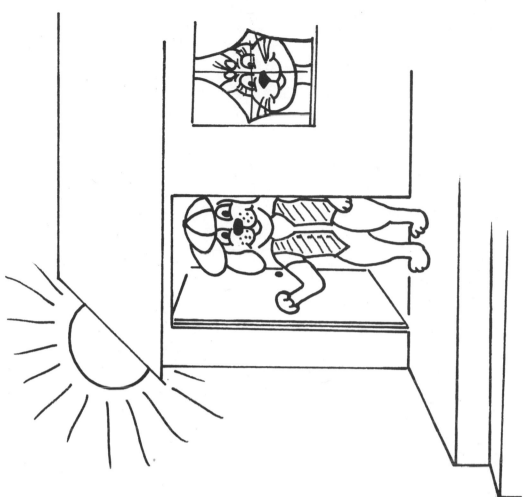

It is Saturday.

Dog and Cat have been waiting all week for this day.

1

First they go running.

It makes them

feel good.

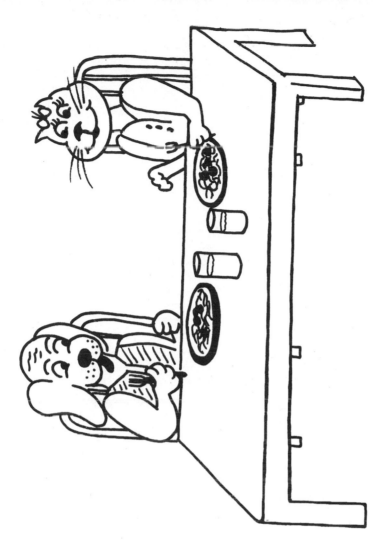

Wow, are they

hungry now!

3

Dog and Cat go
to the park.
They like riding
their bikes.

4

They play ball.

This is fun!

Cat says, "Where can
we read? Let me see.

How about under
that tree?"

"Great idea," says Dog.

6

Cat and Dog sing.

They laugh.

Being friends is
a lot of fun.

7

It is time to go
home now.

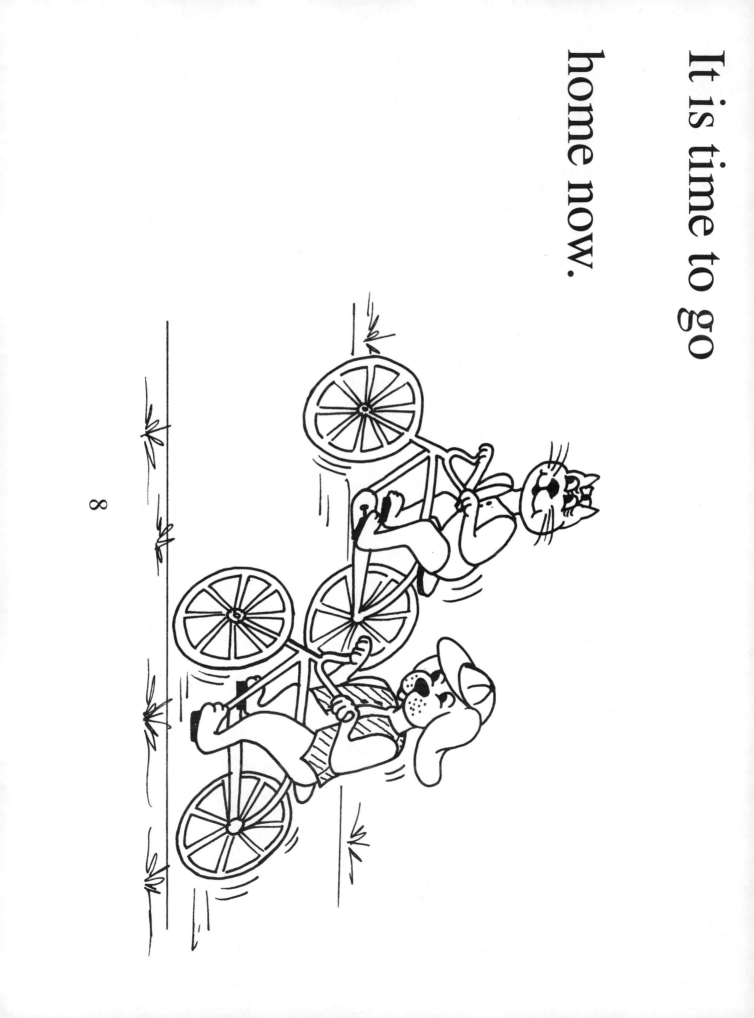

It has been

a long day.

Dog and Cat are

very tired.

They are so happy!

The two friends

dream about what

will happen

tomorrow.

10

2.4 Wordless Picture Reading

🐛 Overview

Wordless Picture Reading will help assess the child's ability to tell a story using pictures.

✓ Materials Needed

The wordless picture story, the Record Booklet, and a tape recorder.

🔠 Procedure

1. Show the child the entire page containing the wordless picture story.

2. Invite the child to look at each frame in order. Point to each frame in order as you say, **"I think you can use these pictures to tell me a story. Think about the story that the pictures tell."** Give the child time to study the pictures.

3. Then ask the child to look at the pictures again and when ready, begin telling the story with the first picture (point to it). Say, **"Tell me your story from the pictures. Begin here."**

4. After the child tells the story, you may want to ask the child to tell you the story while you write it. As the child tells the story, write the child's dictation on a copy of the record sheet for the wordless picture story or on a separate piece of paper. This is similar to what teachers do in a language experience activity. You may also want to tape record the child's story for in-depth analysis.

5. After the child has finished dictating, have him or her read it aloud while pointing to the words. If the reading is similar to the text, mentally note miscues. If the "reading" is quite different from the text, you may wish to write or tape record what the child says.

6. Following the child's reading, ask the child to point to several words in the text and to find where a particular sentence begins and ends.

✍ Scoring and Interpretation

Make qualitative judgments regarding the student's ability to follow directions and the level of language used in telling the story. Look for evidence that the story connects to the pictures and the degree to which the student has a sense of story. Additionally, look for any evidence that the student uses book language. Then record an X on the continuum located on the front of the Record Booklet. To help the child gain a better sense of story, refer to Section 3 of this book, especially 3.4.

Pretest — Wordless Picture Reading — Child's Copy

2.5 | **Auditory Discrimination**

Overview

Auditory Discrimination will help evaluate the child's ability to distinguish between words that differ in one phoneme (sound).

✔ Materials Needed

The page in the Record Booklet containing the Auditory Discrimination assessment and the Record Booklet.

Procedure

1. Practice the words on the list, saying them clearly in a normal voice.

2. Do not rush the child during the assessment.

3. If the child misses a pair of items or asks for one to be repeated, move on to the next item and return to any such items at the conclusion of the test. If the child responds correctly, give credit.

4. Face the child and say:

   "Listen to the words I am about to say: fair-far.

   Do they sound exactly the same or are they different? (For young children, the teacher may prefer the words "alike" and "not alike" in place of the words "same" and "different.")

   Yes, they are different.

   Listen to these two words: cap-cap.

   Are they the same or different?

   Now I am going to read you pairs of words. I want you to tell me if they are the same or different. Do you understand what you are to do? Please turn your back to me and listen very carefully."

5. Say all the words distinctly but in a normal voice.

6. Mark + for correct responses and − for incorrect responses.

Scoring and Interpretation

Note the number of correct "same" and "different" responses and enter the total on the record sheet and on the front of the Record Booklet. Based on the error scores, make a judgment about the child's auditory discrimination ability and record an X on the continuum located on the summary page of the Record Booklet. A child who misses two or more of the "same" pairs may not have understood the concepts "same" and "different." Such results may mean that the test was not valid.

Areas of concern can be strengthened by the instructional strategies and activities in Section 3 of this book, especially 3.6.

2.6 Rhyme Detection

Overview

Rhyme Detection will help assess the child's ability to hear whether words rhyme. This skill is helpful in learning phonics. It is also often taught early in phonemic awareness instruction.

✓ Materials Needed

The page in the Record Booklet containing the Rhyme Detection assessment and the Record Booklet.

Procedure

1. Duplicate the appropriate page of the Record Booklet.

2. Practice saying the words on the list.

3. Say the following to the child, **"I want you to tell me if two words rhyme. When words sound the same at the end, they rhyme. *Hat* rhymes with *cat*. Does *look* rhyme with *book*? Yes. Does *mat* rhyme with *bat*? Yes. But not all words rhyme. *Mice* does not rhyme with *soon* because *mice* ends with *ice* and *soon* ends with *oon*. Does *cat* rhyme with *pig*? No. Does *sick* rhyme with *pick*? Yes. Now, listen carefully. I'm going to say some words, and I want you to tell me if they rhyme."**

4. Say all the words distinctly but in a normal voice.

5. Place a ✓ in the appropriate column to indicate whether the child's response was correct or incorrect.

Scoring and Interpretation

Count the number of items correct and record the total on the record sheet and on the front of the Record Booklet. Informally judge the child's ability to detect rhymes and record an X on the continuum located on the front of the Record Booklet. If the child could profit from additional instruction in rhyme detection, refer to the instructional strategies and activities in Section 3 of this book, especially 3.6.

2.7 Alphabet Knowledge

Overview

The Alphabet Knowledge assessment contains upper-case and lower-case letters of the alphabet in non-sequential order to help assess letter-naming ability. Lower case *a* and *g* appear in both manuscript and print form.

Materials Needed

The child's page in this book containing upper-case and lower-case letters, two 5″ × 8″ cards, and the Record Booklet.

Procedure

1. Duplicate the appropriate page of the Record Booklet.

2. Place the alphabet page before the child. Use the 5″ × 8″ cards to block off everything but the line being read. If necessary, point to each letter. Say, **"Here are some letters. I want to see how many you know."** Encourage the child to say "pass" or "skip it" if a particular letter is not known. Stop if the child becomes frustrated or has little or no knowledge of the letters.

3. As the child responds, use the Record Booklet to note correct (+) and incorrect responses. When responses are incorrect, record the actual response or *DK* (child doesn't know) above the stimulus letter. If the child self-corrects, write *s/c*; self-corrections can be made at any time. Some sample markings are given below.

Marking	Meaning of Marking
+ O	Identified correctly
DK O	Don't know
C O	Said C for O
C s/c O	Said C for O but self-corrected

Scoring and Interpretation

Count the correct number of responses for the upper-case letters and the lower-case letters. Self-corrections are counted as correct. Note the scores in the boxes on the record sheet and on the front of the Record Booklet. Based on the number of correct responses, make a judgment about the child's alphabet knowledge and record Xs on the continuums located on the summary page of the Record Booklet. Unknown letters or incorrect responses may help form the basis for instructional interventions. Refer to Section 3 of this book, especially 3.7.

B T R Z F N

X V I M J D K

Y Q W C U A L

O H S E G P

s d o a k w g

l u r t q h y

i p v f n z g

b x e c j m a

Pretest — Alphabet Knowledge — Child's Copy

2.8 Phoneme Segmentation

Overview

Phonemic awareness refers to the child's ability to segment phonemes or sounds in speech. Phonemic awareness is strongly related to success in reading and spelling acquisition. This assessment was designed for use with English speaking kindergartners. It may also be used with older children experiencing difficulty in literacy acquisition.

✓ Materials Needed

The page in the Record Booklet containing the assessment and the Record Booklet.

Procedure

1. Duplicate the appropriate section of the Record Booklet.

2. Say to the child, **"Today we're going to play a word game. I'm going to say a word, and I want you to break the word apart. You are going to tell me each sound in the word in order. For example, if I say** *old,* **you should say** */o/-/l/-/d/.*" (Teacher: Be sure to say the sounds, not the letters, in the word.)

3. Then say, **"Let's try a few together."** The practice items are *ride, go,* and *man.* If necessary, help by segmenting the word for the child. Encourage the child to repeat the segmented sounds.

4. Provide feedback after each response. You can nod or say "Right" or "That's right." If the child is incorrect, correct him or her, and provide the appropriate response.

5. Proceed through all of the items. Circle those items that the child correctly segments. Incorrect responses may be recorded on the blank line following the item.

Scoring and Interpretation

The child's score is the number of items he or she correctly segments into all constituent phonemes. No partial credit is given. For example, *she* (item 5 on the pretest) contains two phonemes /sh/-/e/; *grew* (item 7 on the pretest) contains three phonemes /g/-/r/-/ew/; and *three* (item 4 on the posttest) contains three phonemes /th/-/r/-/ee/. If the child says letter names instead of sounds, code the response as incorrect and note the type of error in the Record Booklet. Such notes are helpful in understanding the child's literacy development. Some children may partially segment, simply repeat the stimulus item, provide nonsense responses, or give letter names.

Total the number of correct responses. Place the score in the box on the record sheet and on the front page of the Record Booklet. Then make an overall judgment of the child's phoneme segmentation abilities and record an X on the continuum located on the front page of the Record Booklet. A wide range of scores is likely. Yopp (1995) reported that two samples of kindergartners achieved mean scores of 11.78 and 11.39 when all 22 words were administered.

The child's responses may help form a basis for instructional interventions. Refer to Section 3 of this book, especially 3.6.

2.9 Writing

Overview

In the Writing assessment, the child is asked to demonstrate his or her ability to write words, letters, and sentences.

✔ Materials Needed

A pencil or pen, paper (lined and unlined), and the Record Booklet.

Procedure

1. Give the child lined and unlined paper and a pencil or pen. If possible, have choices of paper and writing instruments.

2. Depending on the child's age or ability, you may want to give separate directions for each task: **"Write some letters for me."** Then say, **"How many words can you write?"** Finally **"Write a sentence."** For an older child, you could say, **"I'd like you to write some letters, words, and sentences."** Be patient and encouraging. You might ask the child to begin by writing his or her first name. If there is some success, try the last name.

3. After the child has finished, invite him or her to share what was written. Make mental notes or use the Record Booklet.

4. For children who say, "I can't write," you might want to ask him or her to use "kid writing" or to print an X. Continue with a few other letters and perhaps names and numbers that the student may know. You might also suggest general categories of words: pets, colors, foods, and things you can do.

Scoring and Interpretation

Informally evaluate the child's writing using the areas on the Writing page in the Record Booklet. Record an X on the continuum located on the front page of the Record Booklet that represents your overall judgment. Strategies to encourage writing are found in Section 3 of this book, especially 3.8.

2.10 Developmental Spelling

Overview

Developmental spelling refers to the stages of spelling that children go through prior to conventional spelling. Developmental spelling provides windows into children's thinking about letter-sound relationships. This assessment consists of challenging words that most emergent readers and writers cannot spell. For this reason, it requires them to use their knowledge of letter-sound relationships to spell the words they hear. The children's spellings are not scored as correct or incorrect; rather they are analyzed by using a developmental scale. This assessment can be administered individually, to a small group, or to an entire class of children.

✓ Materials Needed

The child's page in this book and the Record Booklet.

Procedure

1. Duplicate the appropriate number of copies of the child's page in this book.

2. Duplicate the appropriate section of the Record Booklet.

3. Tell the child(ren), **"Today we are going to spell some words. Some of the words will be hard but don't worry. Just spell them the best you can by making good guesses about the sounds and letters you hear in the words."**

4. Distribute the child's copy from the Record Booklet to each child taking the assessment.

5. Dictate the list of ten words. After saying each word, use it in a simple sentence. For example, for the first word in the list (drop), say, **"drop...Do not drop the dish when you dry it."** Continue through the entire list of words. Repeat words and sentences, as necessary.

   1. drop
   2. faster
   3. liked
   4. back
   5. monster
   6. mess
   7. packed
   8. make
   9. earn
   10. greet

Scoring and Interpretation

The child's general developmental spelling stage is determined by analyzing the child's spelling for each word on the list and then identifying the stage that appears most frequently. Follow these steps when analyzing the child's developmental spelling.

1. Look at the child's spelling for each word on the list. Analyze the child's spelling using the Developmental Spelling Stage Scoring Chart. The child's spelling may not match exactly, but it should be the best match on the chart.

2. Write the appropriate developmental spelling stage label (e.g., precommunicative, semiphonetic, etc.) next to each of the ten words on the child's copy.

3. To determine the child's general developmental spelling stage, look for the label that appears most frequently.

4. Record the child's stages for each word and the general developmental spelling stage on the record sheet. Then record your qualitative judgment of the child's overall developmental spelling stage by marking an X on the front of the Record Booklet.

To help developmental spelling, refer to the instructional strategies and activities in Section 3 of this book, especially 3.9.

Developmental Spelling Stage Scoring Chart

Precommunicative (Pre.)	Semiphonetic (Semi.)	Phonetic (Phon.)	Transitional (Trans.)	Conventional (Conv.)
1. random letters or symbols	dp	dop	dropp	drop
2. random letters or symbols	ft	fasr	fastr	faster
3. random letters or symbols	lt	likt	licked	liked
4. random letters or symbols	bk	bak	backe	back
5. random letters or symbols	mtr	mostr	monstur	monster
6. random letters or symbols	ms	mss	mes	mess
7. random letters or symbols	pt	pkt	paked	packed
8. random letters or symbols	mk	mak	macke	make
9. random letters or symbols	en	ern	earnn	earn
10. random letters or symbols	gt	gret	grete	greet

2.11 Consonant Phonic Elements

Overview

Consonant phonic elements will help assess the child's knowledge of the beginning and ending sounds of words. The tasks are of the recognition (not writing) type.

✓ Materials Needed

The child's pages in this book containing the pictures and letters, two 5″ × 8″ cards, and the Record Booklet.

Procedure

Part 1 (p. 49 in Pretest and p. 209 in Posttest)

1. Show the child the page containing the pictures and letters. Cover everything but the first row of pictures.

2. Point to the pictures and say, **"Look at the pictures and tell me what they are."** If the child does not say *ball, cat, leg,* and *wagon,* say the correct words. Be sure the child knows the names of the pictures before continuing.

3. Then say, **"I will say a word, and I want you to point to the picture that begins with the same beginning sound as the word I say."** Then say the words one at a time and circle the child's responses on the appropriate page of the Record Booklet. The correct responses are in bold type. The words for the pretests are *came, wolf, box, look,* and *went.* The words for the posttest are *coat, wood, book, leaf,* and *wet.* After the last word, cover the pictures with one of the 5″ × 8″ cards.

Part 2 (p. 49 in Pretest and p. 209 in Posttest)

4. Cover the letters except the first row *(o, x, d, n, k).* Then say, **"I will say a word. I want you to point to the letter that you hear at the beginning of the word I say. Be sure to listen for the sound at the beginning of the word."** Then say the word and circle the child's response on the appropriate page of the Record Booklet. The correct response is in bold type. Then cover the line of letters, expose a new line of letters, and say the next word. If necessary, repeat the basic instruction: **"Point to the letter you hear at the beginning of _____."** The words for the pretest are *duck, hand, kitten, mouse,* and *table.* The words for the posttest are *door, head, keep, mother,* and *toy.*

Part 3 (p. 50 in Pretest and p. 210 in Posttest)

5. Cover everything but the picture of the sun (pretest) or man (posttest) and the row of letters following it. Say, **"Now I want you to name the picture and then point to the letter that begins the first sound of the picture. What's this picture? Good, now point to the letter that begins the first sound of the picture."** Circle the child's response on the appropriate page of the Record Booklet. The correct response is in bold type. Continue to the next item. If the child does not say the correct name for the picture, say the correct word and repeat the directions: **"Point to the letter that begins the first sound of the picture."** Continue giving the remaining items in a similar fashion. The pictures for the pretest are *sun, fish, giraffe, net,* and *pen.* The pictures for the posttest are *man, fork, giraffe, nose,* and *pencil.*

Part 4 (p. 49 in Pretest and p. 209 in Posttest)

6. Return to the top of the page and cover everything but the first row of pictures. Then say, **"You probably remember the names of these pictures. Please say them for me."**

7. Then say, **"This time I want you to listen to the ending sound of the word I say. Then I want you to point to the picture with the same ending sound as the word I say."** Say the words one at a time and

circle the child's responses on the appropriate page of the Record Booklet. The correct responses are in bold type. The words for the pretest are *flat, pen, bag, street,* and *tall.* The words for the posttest are *hat, hen, log, feet,* and *call.* The basic direction is, **"Point to the picture that ends with the same ending sound as _____."** When the last item is completed, cover the pictures with one of the 5″ × 8″ cards.

8. Then cover the letters except for the first line. Say, **"I will say a word. I want you to point to the letter that has the same ending sound as the word I say."** The basic direction is, **"Point to the letter that ends with the same sound as _____."** The words for the pretest are *duck, band, went, house,* and *win.* The words for the posttest are *truck, land, bent, mouse,* and *pin.* Then say the words one at a time and circle the child's responses on the appropriate page of the Record Booklet. The correct responses are in bold type. Then cover that line of letters, expose a new line of letters, and say the next word.

✐ Scoring and Interpretation

1. Count the number of initial sounds recognized and record the total on the record sheet and on the front of the Record Booklet.

2. Count the number of ending sounds recognized and record the total on the record sheet and on the front of the Record Booklet.

Informally judge the child's knowledge of initial and final sounds recognized and record Xs on the continuums located on the front of the Record Booklet. If the child's initial and final phonic skills need to be strengthened, refer to the instructional strategies and activities in Section 3 of this book, especially 3.10 and 3.15.

o	x	d	n	k
n	d	a	g	h
f	k	r	x	t
m	s	p	t	h
l	v	t	j	n

d   s   r   o   g

h   y   f   b   c

f   k   g   s   t

w   c   r   d   n

r   h   j   n   p

Pretest — Consonant Phonic Elements — Child's Copy

50

2.12 Decoding

Overview

Decoding contains a list of names to help assess the child's ability to decode new words. This assessment is most useful for children who have some reading ability.

✓ Materials Needed

The child's page in this book containing the list of names, a 5″ × 8″ card, and the Record Booklet.

Procedure

1. Duplicate the appropriate page of the Record Booklet.

2. Place the list of names before the child and say something like, **"I'd like you to pretend to be a teacher who must read the names of students in a class — just as I have done in our class. Do the best you can and make a guess if you're not sure."** Use a 5″ × 8″ card to expose one name at a time and say, **"Begin with this one."**

3. Encourage the child to read the entire list but be sensitive to a child who may find the task too difficult or frustrating after several names. Be supportive and encouraging; however, use your professional judgment to decide whether to discontinue the assessment.

4. As the child responds, use the Record Booklet to note correct (+) and incorrect responses. When responses are incorrect, write phonetic spellings (e.g., Rit for Rite, Chook for Chuck, Prestin for Preston) for names that are mispronounced.

Scoring and Interpretation

Count the number of names that were pronounced correctly. Each first and last name is counted separately. A name is considered correct regardless of where the student places the accent. For names where the vowel pronunciation depends on which syllable the consonant is placed (e.g., Ho/mer or Hom/er), count them correct for either pronunciation. The source for the names (except one) was Cunningham (1990).

Record the number of correct names on the record sheet and on the front of the Record Booklet. Based on the number of correct responses, make a judgment about the child's decoding ability. Then record an X on the continuum located on the summary page of the Record Booklet. Analyze the mispronounced names looking for patterns that suggest particular strengths or weaknesses in decoding. Refer to Section 3 of this book for ideas for strengthening decoding, especially 3.10 and 3.13.

Bee Rite

Tim Cornell

Yolanda Clark

Roberta Slade

Gus Quincy

Ginger Yale

Patrick Tweed

Wendy Swain

Fred Sherwood

Dee Skidmore

Ned Westmoreland

Troy Whitlock

Zane Anderson

Source: Cunningham, P. (1990). The names test: A quick assessment of decoding ability. *The Reading Teacher, 44,* 124–129.

Pretest — Decoding — Child's Copy

2.13 Caption Reading

🌈 Overview

Caption Reading will help assess the child's ability to read a brief story with helpful picture clues.

✓ Materials Needed

The page in this book containing the story and the Record Booklet.

🔤 Procedure

1. Show the child the page containing the story.

2. Invite the child to look at frames of the story (pictures and text) in order as numbered.

3. Then ask the child to read the story aloud. Say, **"I want you to read the story to me."** As the student reads, mentally note any miscues or record them on the appropriate page of the Record Booklet.

4. If the child has difficulty reading the story, have the child listen while you read it aloud. Say, **"Listen to me read the story. Then I will want you to read it to me."** After your reading, invite the child to read.

5. Encourage the child to talk about the story with you.

✍ Scoring and Interpretation

Informally note the miscues the child made, the degree of fluency, and other behaviors on the record sheet of the Caption Reading. Record your overall qualitative judgment of the reading with an X on the continuum located on the front page of the Record Booklet. If the child was able to read the story, you can informally analyze fluency, miscues, and overall engagement with the task.

If you read the story first, evaluate the degree to which the child was able to memorize and repeat the text. Be alert for how the child uses language as you talk about the story.

Based on the behaviors the child exhibits, refer to Section 3 of this book, especially 3.3, 3.4, and 3.11.

1

The cat sleeps.

2

The dog sleeps.

3

The bird sleeps.

4

The baby sleeps.

Pretest — Caption Reading — Child's Copy

2.14 Basic Sight Word Knowledge

Overview

The Basic Sight Word Knowledge assessment contains ten words to help assess the child's ability to identify the most basic words in English.

✓ Materials Needed

The child's page in this book, a 4″ × 6″ card, and the Record Booklet.

Procedure

1. Duplicate the appropriate page of the Record Booklet.

2. Place the page containing the words before the child with the words covered. Say, **"I want you to say some words for me. Let's begin with this one."**

3. Move the card below each word and ask the child to say the word. If the child says the number, cover it up and point to the word. Then proceed to the next word.

4. Encourage the child to say "pass" or "skip it" for any unknown words. Say, **"Just do the best you can."** Stop if no response is given to the first four words.

5. As the child reads, note correct responses with a plus (+) in the appropriate place of the Record Booklet. Record any incorrect responses by using the following markings (or your own system):

Marking	Meaning of Marking
+ men	Pronounced correctly
man men	Word mispronounced
man s/c men	Said man for men but self-corrected
DK men	Don't know
m — men	Partial pronunciation

6. Proceed until you observe anxiety, frustration, or reluctance on the part of the child.

Scoring and Interpretation

Count the number of words pronounced correctly and record the score in the box on the record sheet and on the front of the Record Booklet. Self-corrections are counted as correct. The words occurring in the pretest and posttest are the most frequently occurring words in printed English. Based on the correct responses, make a judgment about the child's word knowledge and record an X on the continuum located on the front of the Record Booklet. An informal analysis of incorrect responses should help you develop tentative instructional interventions for word identification. For instructional ideas, refer to Section 3 of this book, especially 3.11.

1. the

2. and

3. a

4. is

5. it

6. for

7. he

8. as

9. they

10. be

2.15   Passage Reading

Overview

The four passages will help determine how well the child is able to read connected text. The passages are based in part on Gunning's (1998) work and descriptions of beginning reading levels. The table below gives some basic information about each of the reading passages.

Passage	Grade Level	Reading Level Code	Words	Approximate Reading Recovery Level
Easy Sight Word	Pre-primer	EE	25	4–8
Beginning	Primer	E	50	9–11
Grade 1	1	E7141	100	12–20
Grade 2	2	E8224	100	—

✓ Materials Needed

The pages in this book containing the passages, a 5″ × 8″ card, and the Record Booklet.

Procedure

1. Duplicate the appropriate section of the Record Booklet.

2. Choose a passage that you think the child can read. Place the passage before the child and cover everything but the illustration and the title.

3. Activate the child's background knowledge by saying, **"Read the title to yourself and look at the pictures. Then tell me what you think this story will be about."** Informally judge the extent of the child's background knowledge and record an X along the continuum on the record sheet.

   Then say, **"Read the story to me. I'll ask you to answer some questions when you are finished."** As the child reads, note any miscues in the appropriate place of the Record Booklet using the following markings (or your own system):

Marking	Meaning of Marking	Marking	Meaning of Marking
man men	Substitution	*m —* men	Partial pronunciation
man s/c men	Self-correction	men	Repeated word
~~men~~	Omitted word	*small* ^men	Insertion

Also, note other behaviors, such as finger pointing, ignoring punctuation, engagement, and strategies used to pronounce words not known at sight. Count the *total* number of miscues or the number of *significant* (those that affect meaning) miscues. Self-corrections need not be included in counting miscues.

4. When the child has finished reading, ask the comprehension questions or invite a retelling of the story. Record a + for correct responses and a − for incorrect responses. You may also give half credit. The letter beside the comprehension questions indicate the following types of questions:

Letter	Type of Question
T	Topic
F	Fact
E	Experience/Evaluation
I	Inference
V	Vocabulary

5. If the child was successful, present the next passage. Continue administrating graded passages until the child has many word recognition miscues (i.e., frustration level) or is unable to answer more than half of the comprehension questions. If the initial passage was too difficult, try an easier passage or proceed to Caption Reading.

✍️ Scoring and Interpretation

1. Use the scoring guides on the record sheet to evaluate word recognition and comprehension. For word recognition, count the *total* number of miscues or the number of *significant* (those that affect meaning) miscues. Record the number of miscues in the appropriate box on the record sheet. Then find and circle the level (Independent, Ind./Inst., Instructional, Inst./Frust, or Frustration) on the scoring guide at the bottom of the passage corresponding to the number of total or significant miscues.

2. For comprehension, count the number of comprehension questions missed, and record this number in the appropriate box on the record sheet. Then find and circle the level on the scoring guide at the bottom of the questions. If retelling is used to assess comprehension, circle *excellent* for independent level, *satisfactory* for instructional level, and *unsatisfactory* for frustration level.

3. There are also areas of word recognition and comprehension at the bottom of some record sheets that you can evaluate on a scale of 1 to 5. Then make an overall qualitative judgment of the child's word recognition and comprehension abilities on the summary page of the Record Booklet.

4. Throughout the assessment, watch for behaviors often associated with frustration: lack of expression, word-by-word reading, excessive anxiety, and so on. Note such behaviors in the margins of the record sheet.

5. Estimate the child's oral reading rate by timing the reading and inserting the seconds required for reading as the divisor in the formula at the bottom of the record sheet. Perform the necessary division. The resulting numeral will be an estimate of the child's rate in words per minute (WPM). An example of rate determination is shown below. See Johns (1997, p. 35) for further information about reading rate.

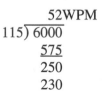

An informal analysis of the child's word recognition and comprehension abilities should help you identify areas for instruction. Refer to Section 3 of this book, especially 3.2., 3.3, 3.10, 3.11, 3.12, 3.13, and 3.14.

My Dog

I have a dog.

My dog is Spark.

Spark is a big dog.

He plays ball.

I play with Spark.

Spark is a fun dog.

The Small Fish

There are two small fish. One is red and the other is blue. They live in the sea. They like to play.

One day a big green fish came to the sea. It did not want to play. It wanted to eat the small fish. The big fish was mean.

Paws Visits School

Fred has a big black cat. The cat is named Paws. Fred took Paws to his small school. All of the children loved Paws. They all tried to pet Paws at one time. Paws was very afraid. She jumped out of Fred's arms and ran away. Fred looked all around but could not find Paws. Fred's friend, Anne, looked under the little table. Anne saw Paws under the table. Anne ran and told Fred where she saw Paws. Paws came out when she saw Fred. Fred hugged Paws tightly. Fred took Paws home and gave her some food to eat.

The Lost Babies

It was getting dark outside. All the animal mothers were looking for their children. Mrs. Turtle found her babies near a tree. Mrs. Toad jumped in the weeds after she found her hungry children. Mrs. Fish found her babies by the rocks in the river. They were safe and happy.

Mrs. Rabbit was very scared. She could not find her babies anywhere. She was afraid that a fox might find her babies first. She looked all over the forest.

Mrs. Mouse helped Mrs. Rabbit look for her lost babies. Mrs. Mouse found them. The lost babies were safe at home.

RECORD BOOKLET FOR EARLY LITERACY ASSESSMENTS

Jerry L. Johns, Susan Davis Lenski, & Laurie Elish-Piper

Child _____ Grade/Age _____ Sex M F   Date of Test _____

School _____ Examiner _____ Date of Birth _____

Profile of Emergent Reader

	Low or Not Evident	Some		High or Always Evident
2.1 Interviews About Reading Attitude and Interest				
2.2 Retelling a Story				
2.3 Literacy Knowledge _____ /20				
2.4 Wordless Picture Reading				
2.5 Auditory Discrimination _____ /12				
2.6 Rhyme Detection _____ /10				
2.7 Alphabet Knowledge				
_____ /26 upper case				
_____ /28 lower case				
2.8 Phoneme Segmentation _____ /11				
2.9 Writing				
2.10 Developmental Spelling				
2.11 Consonant Phonic Elements				
_____ /15 initial				
_____ /10 final				
2.12 Decoding _____ /26				
2.13 Caption Reading				
2.14 Basic Sight Word Knowledge _____ /10				
2.15 Passage Reading				
word recognition				
comprehension				

If you're interested in the child's	You might want to use assessment
oral language ability/comprehension	2.2, 2.4
general notions about reading and literacy	2.1, 2.3, 2.7, 2.9, 2.10
writing and spelling	2.9, 2.10
ability to work with sounds orally	2.5, 2.6, 2.8
phonics and decoding abilities	2.9, 2.10, 2.11, 2.12
word knowledge	2.4, 2.9, 2.10, 2.13, 2.14
story knowledge or sense of story	2.2, 2.4, 2.15
ability to read independently	2.13, 2.14, 2.15

Teacher's Directions   20
Child's Copy   None

1. Do you like to have someone read to you? _____ Yes _____ No

   Who do you like to read to you? _____

2. What kinds of stories do you like?

   _____

3. Tell me the name of a favorite story.

   _____

4. Do you have many books at home? _____ Yes _____ No

   Where do you keep the books? _____

5. Who do you know that likes to read? _____

6. Are you learning to read? _____ Yes _____ No

   Tell me more about that. _____

7. Do you want to learn how to read better? _____ Yes _____ No

   Tell me more about that. _____

8. Do you think you will be a good reader? _____ Yes _____ No

   Tell me more about that. _____

9. What makes a person a good reader? _____

   _____

10. What is reading? _____

   _____

Qualitative Judgments of Interviews About Reading
EMERGENT READER (PREK–K)

	Not Evident Low Seldom Weak Poor		Some		Evident High Always Strong Excellent
Overall interest in reading	├	┼	┼	┼	┤
Familiarity with specific stories	├	┼	┼	┼	┤
Availability of books	├	┼	┼	┼	┤
Knowledge of reading role models	├	┼	┼	┼	┤
Confidence in learning to read	├	┼	┼	┼	┤
Motivation to learn to read	├	┼	┼	┼	┤
Knowledge of purpose of reading	├	┼	┼	┼	┤

Observations, Comments, Notes, and Insights

From Johns, Lenski, and Elish-Piper, *Early Literacy Assessments & Teaching Strategies*

Teacher's Directions   20
Child's Copy   None

1. Do you like to have someone read to you? _____ Yes   _____ No

   Who do you like to read to you? _____

2. What kinds of stories do you like? _____

   _____

3. Tell me the name of a favorite story. _____

4. Do you have many books at home? _____ Yes _____ No

   How many books do you think you have? _____

5. Who do you know that likes to read? _____

   _____

6. Do you think you are a good reader? _____ Yes _____ No

   Why or why not? _____

7. What makes a person a good reader? _____

   _____

8. When you are reading and come to a word you don't know, what do you do?

   _____

9. What do you do when you don't understand what you are reading?

   _____

10. What is reading?

   _____

Qualitative Judgments of Interviews About Reading
EARLY READER (GRADES 1–2)

	Not Evident Low Seldom Weak Poor		Some		Evident High Always Strong Excellent
Overall interest in reading	├──────┼──────┼──────┼──────┤
Familiarity with specific stories	├──────┼──────┼──────┼──────┤
Availability of books	├──────┼──────┼──────┼──────┤
Knowledge of reading role models	├──────┼──────┼──────┼──────┤
Confidence in learning to read	├──────┼──────┼──────┼──────┤
Motivation to learn to read	├──────┼──────┼──────┼──────┤
Knowledge of word-identification strategies	├──────┼──────┼──────┼──────┤
Knowledge of comprehension strategies	├──────┼──────┼──────┼──────┤
Knowledge of purpose of reading	├──────┼──────┼──────┼──────┤

Observations, Comments, Notes, and Insights

From Johns, Lenski, and Elish-Piper, *Early Literacy Assessments & Teaching Strategies*

Teacher's Directions   21
Child's Copy   None

BRIEF DIRECTIONS

Say to the child: **"I'm going to read a story to you. After I am finished reading, I will ask you to tell me the story as if you were telling it to someone who has not read the story. As you listen, try to remember as much of the story as you can."** Read an age-appropriate book that is new to the child. After reading, say, **"Now tell me as much of the story as you can."** If the child hesitates, ask probing questions such as **"What was the story about?"** or **"Who was in the story?"** or **"What happened next?"**

Qualitative Judgments of Retelling a Story

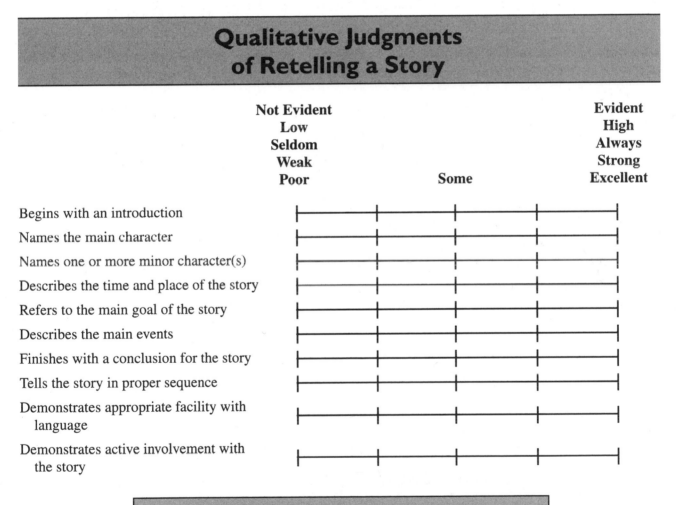

	Not Evident / Low / Seldom / Weak / Poor		Some		Evident / High / Always / Strong / Excellent
Begins with an introduction					
Names the main character					
Names one or more minor character(s)					
Describes the time and place of the story					
Refers to the main goal of the story					
Describes the main events					
Finishes with a conclusion for the story					
Tells the story in proper sequence					
Demonstrates appropriate facility with language					
Demonstrates active involvement with the story					

Observations, Comments, Notes, and Insights

Teacher's Directions   22
Child's Copy   *Friends*

BRIEF DIRECTIONS

Show the book *Friends* to the child. Say, **"I'd like you to show me some of the things you know about reading. You won't have to read."** Ask the following questions as *you* read the book to the child. Circle correct (+) or incorrect (−) responses. Total correct responses.

PAGE

+ −   1. Hand the book to the child and say, **"Show me the front of this book."**

1   + −   2. Say, **"Point to where I should start reading."** *Read page 1.*

2   + −   3. Ask, **"Which way should I go?"** Check for knowledge of left to right. *Read first line of page 2.*

2/3   + −   4. Ask, **"Where should I go after that?"** Check for knowledge of a return sweep to the left. *Read rest of page 2 and page 3.*

3   + −   5. On page 3, point to the comma and ask, **"What's this or what's this for?"**

4   + −   6. *Read text on page 4.* Point to a period and ask, **"What's this or what's this for?"**

5   + −   7. *Read text on page 5.* Point to the exclamation mark and ask, **"What's this or what's this for?"**

6   + −   8. *Read text on page 6.* Point to the question mark and ask, **"What's this or what's this for?"**

6   + −   9. Point to a lower-case letter (w, g, c) and say, **"Find a capital letter like this, find an upper-case letter like this, or find the big one like this."**

7   + −   10. *Read text on page 7.* Say, **"Show me one letter."** (Two 3″ × 5″ cards may be useful for items 10–19.)

+ −   11. Say, **"Show me two letters."**

+ −   12. Say, **"Show me only one word."**

+ −   13. Say, **"Show me two words."**

+ −   14. Say, **"Show me the first letter of a word."**

+ −   15. Say, **"Show me the last letter of a word."**

+ −   16. Say, **"Show me a long word."**

+ −   17. Say, **"Show me a short word."**

+ −   18. Say, **"Show me a sentence."**

8/9   + −   19. *Read text on pages 8 and 9.* Point to a capital letter (I, D, T) and say, **"Find a small letter like this or find a lower-case letter like this."**

10   + −   20. *Read text on page 10.* Close the book and hand it to the child with back cover showing and say, **"Show me the title or show me the name of the book."**

☐   **Total Correct**

From Johns, Lenski, and Elish-Piper, *Early Literacy Assessments & Teaching Strategies*

Qualitative Judgments of Literacy Knowledge

	Not Evident Low Seldom Weak Poor		Some		Evident High Always Strong Excellent
Overall engagement	├─────	──┼─────	──┼─────	──┼─────	──┤
Understanding of print directionality	├─────	──┼─────	──┼─────	──┼─────	──┤
Knowledge of punctuation	├─────	──┼─────	──┼─────	──┼─────	──┤
Correspondence of upper-case and lower-case letters	├─────	──┼─────	──┼─────	──┼─────	──┤
Knowledge of letter and letters	├─────	──┼─────	──┼─────	──┼─────	──┤
Knowledge of word and words	├─────	──┼─────	──┼─────	──┼─────	──┤
Ability to frame a sentence	├─────	──┼─────	──┼─────	──┼─────	──┤

Observations, Comments, Notes, and Insights

| Teacher's Directions | 37 |
| Child's Copy | 38 |

Qualitative Judgments
of Wordless Picture Reading

	Not Evident Low Seldom Weak Poor		Some		Evident High Always Strong Excellent
Overall engagement					
Connects pictures to story					
Language use					
Sense of story					

Reading Dictation (check one if used)

_____ Child was unable to read what was dictated.

_____ Child pointed to words but only read a few words.

_____ Child pointed to words and read about half of the words.

_____ Child read what was dictated practically verbatim.

Observations, Comments, Notes, and Insights

Teacher's Directions 39
Child's Copy None

				Same	**Different**
1.	though	—	show		☐
2.	moss	—	moth		☐
3.	jump	—	jump	☐	
4.	luck	—	lock		☐
5.	sing	—	sing	☐	
6.	light	—	sight		☐
7.	set	—	sit		☐
8.	rap	—	rack		☐
9.	bed	—	bad		☐
10.	sit	—	sick		☐
11.	duck	—	duck	☐	
12.	can	—	tan		☐

Total Correct ☐

Observations, Comments, Notes, and Insights

2.6 Rhyme Detection

Teacher's Directions   40
Child's Copy   None

BRIEF DIRECTIONS

Say to the child: **"I want you to tell me if two words rhyme. When words sound the same at the end, they rhyme.** *Hat* **rhymes with** *cat.* **Does** *look* **rhyme with** *book*? **Yes. Does** *mat* **rhyme with** *bat*? **Yes. But not all words rhyme.** *Mice* **does not rhyme with** *soon* **because** *mice* **ends with** *ice* **and** *soon* **ends with** *oon.* **Does** *cat* **rhyme with** *pig*? **No. Does** *sick* **rhyme with** *pick*? **Yes. Now, listen carefully. I'm going to say some words, and I want you to tell me if they rhyme."** Place a ✓ in the appropriate column, total correct responses, and record the score in the box.

			Correct	Incorrect
1. bee	—	see	_____	_____
2. tall	—	call	_____	_____
3. jet	—	dog	_____	_____
4. can	—	man	_____	_____
5. him	—	gym	_____	_____
6. hen	—	bag	_____	_____
7. rat	—	sat	_____	_____
8. room	—	zoom	_____	_____
9. back	—	sing	_____	_____
10. bake	—	rake	_____	_____

Total Correct ☐

Observations, Comments, Notes, and Insights

From Johns, Lenski, and Elish-Piper, *Early Literacy Assessments & Teaching Strategies*

2.7 Alphabet Knowledge

Teacher's Directions 41
Child's Copy 42

BRIEF DIRECTIONS

Present the alphabet sheet to the child. Use 5″ × 8″ cards to block off everything but the line being read. If necessary, point to each letter with a finger. Then say, **"Here are some letters. I want to see how many you know."** Place + above correctly identified letters. Record the child's responses for incorrect letters. Total correct responses and record the score in the boxes. Note that lower case a and g appear in both manuscript and print form.

B	T	R	Z	F	N	
X	V	I	M	J	D	K
Y	Q	W	C	U	A	L
O	H	S	E	G	P	

☐ **Total Correct**

s	d	o	a	k	w	g
l	u	r	t	q	h	y
i	p	v	f	n	z	g
b	x	e	c	j	m	a

☐ **Total Correct**

Observations, Comments, Notes, and Insights

2.8 Phoneme Segmentation

Teacher's Directions   43
Child's Copy   None

BRIEF DIRECTIONS

Say to the child: **"Today we're going to play a word game. I'm going to say a word, and I want you to break the word apart. You are going to tell me each sound in the word in order. For example, if I say** *old,* **you should say** */o/-/l/-/d/."* *(Teacher: Be sure to say the sounds, not the letters, in the word.)* **"Let's try a few together."**

PRACTICE ITEMS

ride, go, man *(Assist the child in segmenting these items as necessary.)*

TEST ITEMS

(Circle those items that the child correctly segments; incorrect responses may be recorded on the blank line following the item.) The correct number of phonemes is indicated in parentheses.

1. dog (3) _____   7. grew (3) _____

2. keep (3) _____   8. that (3) _____

3. fine (3) _____   9. red (3) _____

4. no (2) _____   10. me (2) _____

5. she (2) _____   11. sat (3) _____

6. wave (3) _____

Total Correct ☐

Observations, Comments, Notes, and Insights

The author, Hallie Kay Yopp, California State University, Fullerton, grants permission for this test to be reproduced. The author acknowledges the contribution of the late Harry Singer to the development of this test. Adapted from Yopp, H.K. (1995). A test for assessing phonemic awareness in young children. *The Reading Teacher, 49,* 20–29.

From Johns, Lenski, and Elish-Piper, *Early Literacy Assessments & Teaching Strategies*

Teacher's Directions	44
Child's Copy	None

BRIEF DIRECTIONS

Give the child paper and pencil. Ask the child to do some writing. Record qualitative judgments, observations, and insights below.

Qualitative Judgments of Writing

	Not Evident / Low / Seldom / Weak / Poor		Some	Evident / High / Always / Strong / Excellent

Directionality

Left to right

Top to bottom

Child's Name

Knowledge of first (F) and last (L) name

Letter-Sound Relationships

Represents sounds heard at word beginnings

Represents sounds heard at word endings

Represents sounds heard in word middles

Uses vowels

Writing Conventions

Use of word boundaries

Use of punctuation

Writing (check one)

_____ Scribbles or "cursivelike" scribbles

_____ Letterlike formations

_____ Repeated letters, numbers, words

_____ Variety of letters, numbers, words

Overall Message Intent (check one)

_____ Child indicated no message intent or did not communicate a message.

_____ Child talked about but did not read or pretend to read what was written.

_____ Child was able to read what was written.

Teacher could make sense of writing independently.   yes   no

2.10 Developmental Spelling

Teacher's Directions 45–46
Child's Copy 79

BRIEF DIRECTIONS

Provide each child with a copy of the child's sheet. Tell the child(ren), **"Today we are going to spell some words. Some of the words will be hard but don't worry. Just spell them the best you can by making good guesses about the sounds and letters you hear in the words."** Dictate each word and use it in a short sentence. The words are listed below. Use the Developmental Spelling Stage Scoring Chart on page 46 to analyze the child's spelling for each word. Then determine each child's general developmental spelling stage by noting the stage that appeared most frequently.

1. drop
2. faster
3. liked
4. back
5. monster
6. mess
7. packed
8. make
9. earn
10. greet

Circle the child's developmental spelling stage for each word.

1. **drop**	Precommunicative	Semiphonetic	Phonetic	Transitional	Conventional
2. **faster**	Precommunicative	Semiphonetic	Phonetic	Transitional	Conventional
3. **liked**	Precommunicative	Semiphonetic	Phonetic	Transitional	Conventional
4. **back**	Precommunicative	Semiphonetic	Phonetic	Transitional	Conventional
5. **monster**	Precommunicative	Semiphonetic	Phonetic	Transitional	Conventional
6. **mess**	Precommunicative	Semiphonetic	Phonetic	Transitional	Conventional
7. **packed**	Precommunicative	Semiphonetic	Phonetic	Transitional	Conventional
8. **make**	Precommunicative	Semiphonetic	Phonetic	Transitional	Conventional
9. **earn**	Precommunicative	Semiphonetic	Phonetic	Transitional	Conventional
10. **greet**	Precommunicative	Semiphonetic	Phonetic	Transitional	Conventional

GENERAL DEVELOPMENTAL SPELLING STAGE (CHECK ONE)

☐ Precommunicative ☐ Semiphonetic ☐ Phonetic ☐ Transitional ☐ Conventional

From Johns, Lenski, and Elish-Piper, *Early Literacy Assessments & Teaching Strategies*

Child's Name _____

Stage

1. _____   _____

2. _____   _____

3. _____   _____

4. _____   _____

5. _____   _____

6. _____   _____

7. _____   _____

8. _____   _____

9. _____   _____

10. _____   _____

Pretest — Developmental Spelling — Child's Copy

2.11 Consonant Phonic Elements

Teacher's Directions   47
Child's Copy   49–50

INITIAL CONSONANT SOUND RECOGNITION

PART 1

1. came	ball	**cat**	leg	wagon
2. wolf	ball	cat	leg	**wagon**
3. box	**ball**	cat	leg	wagon
4. look	ball	cat	**leg**	wagon
5. went	ball	cat	leg	**wagon**

PART 2

6. duck	o	x	**d**	n	k
7. hand	n	d	a	g	**h**
8. kitten	f	**k**	r	x	t
9. mouse	**m**	s	p	t	h
10. table	l	v	**t**	j	n

PART 3

11. sun	d	**s**	r	o	g
12. fish	h	y	**f**	b	c
13. giraffe	f	k	**g**	s	t
14. net	w	c	r	d	**n**
15. pen	r	h	j	n	**p**

Total Correct ☐

From Johns, Lenski, and Elish-Piper, *Early Literacy Assessments & Teaching Strategies*

FINAL CONSONANT SOUND RECOGNITION

PART 4

1. flat   ball   **cat**   leg   wagon
2. pen   ball   cat   leg   **wagon**
3. bag   ball   cat   **leg**   wagon
4. street   ball   **cat**   leg   wagon
5. tall   **ball**   cat   leg   wagon

6. duck   o   x   d   n   **k**
7. band   n   **d**   a   g   h
8. went   f   k   r   x   **t**
9. house   m   **s**   p   t   h
10. win   l   v   t   j   **n**

Total Correct ☐

Observations, Comments, Notes, and Insights

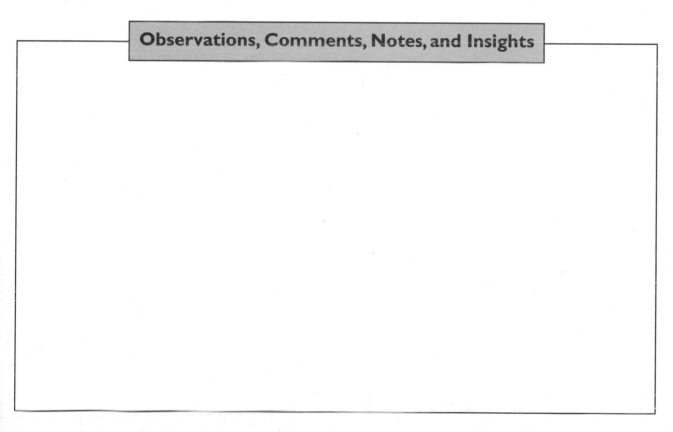

2.12 Decoding

(based on Cunningham, 1990)

Teacher's Directions	51
Child's Copy	52

BRIEF DIRECTIONS

Present the sheet with the names to the child. Say, **"I'd like you to pretend to be a teacher who must read the names of students in a class—just as I have done in our class. Do the best that you can and make a guess if you're not sure."** Use a 5″ × 8″ card to expose one name at a time and say, **"Begin with this one."** Note correct responses with a + and use phonetic spellings for names that are mispronounced. Total correct responses and record the score in the box.

	First Name	Last Name
Bee Rite	_____	_____
Tim Cornell	_____	_____
Yolanda Clark	_____	_____
Roberta Slade	_____	_____
Gus Quincy	_____	_____
Ginger Yale	_____	_____
Patrick Tweed	_____	_____
Wendy Swain	_____	_____
Fred Sherwood	_____	_____
Dee Skidmore	_____	_____
Ned Westmoreland	_____	_____
Troy Whitlock	_____	_____
Zane Anderson	_____	_____

☐ **Total Correct**

From Johns, Lenski, and Elish-Piper, *Early Literacy Assessments & Teaching Strategies*

| Teacher's Directions | 53 |
| Child's Copy | 54 |

The cat sleeps.

The dog sleeps.

The bird sleeps.

The baby sleeps.

Qualitative Judgments of Reading

If the child read the story, check the most characteristic statement of the child's reading.

_____ The child's reading is an exact match with the text.

_____ The child's reading closely matches the text.

_____ The child's reading is somewhat related to the text but is based on the illustrations.

_____ The child's reading is related mostly to the illustrations.

If you read the story first, check the statement most characteristic of the child's reading.

_____ The child used memory to read the text with high accuracy.

_____ The child used memory and illustrations to read the text with fair accuracy.

_____ The child did not seem to remember your reading and relied almost entirely on the illustrations to read the text.

	Not Evident Low Seldom Weak Poor	Some	Evident High Always Strong Excellent

Other Reading Behaviors

Retelling

Reads left to right

Reads top to bottom

Demonstrates letter-sound
relationships

Uses monitoring (rereads, corrects)

Points to correct words (if
requested by you)

Engagement

Confidence as a reader

Observations, Comments, Notes, and Insights

From Johns, Lenski, and Elish-Piper, *Early Literacy Assessments & Teaching Strategies*

Teacher's Directions   55
Child's Copy   56

BRIEF DIRECTIONS

Present the list of words for the pretest. Ask the child to identify the words. Say, **"I want you to say some words for me. Let's begin with this one."** Use a plus (+) for correct responses. Record the child's responses for incorrect words. Total correct responses and put the score in the box.

1. the _____

2. and _____

3. a _____

4. is _____

5. it _____

6. for _____

7. he _____

8. as _____

9. they _____

10. be _____

Total Correct ☐

Observations, Comments, Notes, and Insights

Easy Sight Word Passage Reading

Teacher's Directions 57–58
Child's Copy   59

Background: Low |———|———| **High**

My Dog

I have a dog.

My dog is Spark.

Spark is a big dog.

He plays ball.

I play with Spark.

Spark is a fun dog.

EE (Pre-Primer) Activating Background:
Read the title to yourself and look at the pictures. Then tell me what you think this story will be about.

T   1. ___   What is the story mostly about?
(a dog; Spark)

F   2. ___   What is the dog's name?
(Spark)

F   3. ___   What does Spark do?
(play ball)

E   4. ___   Why do you think Spark is a fun dog?
(any logical response; because he likes to play ball)

I   5. ___   What other things might Spark like to do?
(any logical response)

V   6. ___   What is a dog?
(any logical response; an animal; a pet)

Total Miscues [ ]   **Significant Miscues** [ ]   **Questions Missed** [ ]

Word Recognition Scoring Guide		
Total Miscues	Level	Significant Miscues
0	Independent	0
1	Ind./Inst.	—
2	Instructional	1
—	Inst./Frust.	—
3	Frustration	2

Retelling
Excellent
Satisfactory
Unsatisfactory
_____ WPM
) 1500

Comprehension Scoring Guide	
Questions Missed	Level
0	Independent
1	Ind./Inst.
1½	Instructional
2	Inst./Frust.
2½+	Frustration

Qualitative Analysis of Word Identification and Comprehension (1 = not evident; 5 = evident)											
Word Identification						**Comprehension**					
Uses graphophonic information	1	2	3	4	5	Makes predictions	1	2	3	4	5
Uses semantic information	1	2	3	4	5	Seeks to construct meaning	1	2	3	4	5
Uses syntatic information	1	2	3	4	5	Understands topic and major ideas	1	2	3	4	5
Knows basic sight words automatically	1	2	3	4	5	Remembers facts or details	1	2	3	4	5
Possesses sight vocabulary	1	2	3	4	5	Evaluates ideas from passages	1	2	3	4	5
Possesses numerous strategies	1	2	3	4	5	Makes and supports appropriate inferences	1	2	3	4	5
Uses strategies flexibly	1	2	3	4	5	Stays focused on reading	1	2	3	4	5

From Johns, Lenski, and Elish-Piper, *Early Literacy Assessments & Teaching Strategies*

Teacher's Directions 57–58
Child's Copy 60

E (Primer) Activating Background:
Read the title to yourself and look at the picture. Then tell me what you think this story will be about.

Background: Low |———|———| High

The Small Fish

There are two small fish. One is red and the other is blue. They live in the sea. They like to play.

One day a big green fish came to the sea. It did not want to play. It wanted to eat the small fish. The big fish was mean.

T 1. ___ What is this story about?
(fish; two fish who almost got eaten by a big green fish)

F 2. ___ What size was the green fish?
(big)

F 3. ___ What do the red fish and the blue fish like to do in the sea?
(play)

E 4. ___ What do you think the small fish will do to get away from the green fish?
(any logical response; swim fast)

I 5. ___ What do you think the red fish and the blue fish did when they saw the green fish?
(any logical response; they swam away quickly)

V 6. ___ What does "play" mean?
(any logical response)

Total Miscues ☐ **Significant Miscues** ☐ **Questions Missed** ☐

Word Recognition Scoring Guide		
Total Miscues	Level	Significant Miscues
0	Independent	0
1–2	Ind./Inst.	—
3	Instructional	1
4	Inst./Frust.	2
5+	Frustration	3

Retelling
Excellent
Satisfactory
Unsatisfactory

WPM
) 3000

Comprehension Scoring Guide	
Questions Missed	Level
0	Independent
1	Ind./Inst.
1½	Instructional
2	Inst./Frust.
2½+	Frustration

Qualitative Analysis of Word Identification and Comprehension
(1 = not evident; 5 = evident)

Word Identification						Comprehension					
Uses graphophonic information	1	2	3	4	5	Makes predictions	1	2	3	4	5
Uses semantic information	1	2	3	4	5	Seeks to construct meaning	1	2	3	4	5
Uses syntactic information	1	2	3	4	5	Understands topic and major ideas	1	2	3	4	5
Knows basic sight words automatically	1	2	3	4	5	Remembers facts or details	1	2	3	4	5
Possesses sight vocabulary	1	2	3	4	5	Evaluates ideas from passages	1	2	3	4	5
Possesses numerous strategies	1	2	3	4	5	Makes and supports appropriate inferences	1	2	3	4	5
Uses strategies flexibly	1	2	3	4	5	Stays focused on reading	1	2	3	4	5

2.15 Grade 1 Passage Reading

Teacher's Directions 57–58
Child's Copy 61

Background: Low |———|———| **High**

Paws Visits School

Fred has a big black cat. The cat is named

Paws. Fred took Paws to his small school. All

of the children loved Paws. They all tried to

pet Paws at one time. Paws was very afraid.

She jumped out of Fred's arms and ran away.

Fred looked all around but could not find

Paws. Fred's friend, Anne, looked under the

little table. Anne saw Paws under the table.

Anne ran and told Fred where she saw Paws.

Paws came out when she saw Fred. Fred

hugged Paws tightly. Fred took Paws home

and gave her some food to eat.

E 7141 (Grade 1) Activating Background:
Read the title to yourself and look at the picture. Then tell me what you think this story will be about.

T 1. ___ What is this story about?
(Paws; a cat; a boy who takes his cat to school)

F 2. ___ What color was the cat?
(black)

F 3. ___ What was the cat's name?
(Paws)

F 4. ___ Why did the cat run away?
(she was afraid)

F 5. ___ Who helped Fred find his cat?
(Anne)

F 6. ___ Where did Anne find Paws?
(under the table)

I 7. ___ How do you think Anne felt when she found Paws?
(any logical response; happy; excited; glad)

I 8. ___ Why do you think Fred took Paws to school?
(any logical response; to show the other children)

E 9. ___ Do you think Fred will take Paws to school again? Why?
(any logical response)

V 10. ___ What does "afraid" mean?
(scared)

Total Miscues ☐ **Significant Miscues** ☐ **Questions Missed** ☐

Word Recognition Scoring Guide		
Total Miscues	Level	Significant Miscues
0–1	Independent	0–1
2–4	Ind./Inst.	2
5	Instructional	3
6–9	Inst./Frust.	4
10+	Frustration	5+

Retelling
Excellent
Satisfactory
Unsatisfactory

WPM

)6000

Comprehension Scoring Guide	
Questions Missed	Level
0–1	Independent
1½–2	Ind./Inst.
2½	Instructional
3–4½	Inst./Frust.
5+	Frustration

From Johns, Lenski, and Elish-Piper, *Early Literacy Assessments & Teaching Strategies*

Teacher's Directions 57–58
Child's Copy   62

Background: Low |———|———| **High**

The Lost Babies

It was getting dark outside. All the animal mothers were looking for their children. Mrs. Turtle found her babies near a tree. Mrs. Toad jumped in the weeds after she found her hungry children. Mrs. Fish found her babies by the rocks in the river. They were safe and happy.

Mrs. Rabbit was very scared. She could not find her babies anywhere. She was afraid that a fox might find her babies first. She looked all over the forest.

Mrs. Mouse helped Mrs. Rabbit look for her lost babies. Mrs. Mouse found them. The lost babies were safe at home.

E 8224 (Grade 2) Activating Background:
Read the title to yourself and look at the picture. Then tell me what you think this story will be about.

T 1. ____ What is this story about?
(Mrs. Rabbit looking for her lost babies; lost babies)

F 2. ____ Where did Mrs. Turtle find her babies?
(by a tree)

F 3. ____ Where were the baby fish?
(by the rocks in the river)

F 4. ____ Who couldn't find her babies?
(Mrs. Rabbit)

F 5. ____ What was Mrs. Rabbit afraid of?
(that a fox might find her babies)

F 6. ____ Who found the baby rabbits?
(Mrs. Mouse)

I 7. ____ What time of day did the story take place? Why?
(any logical response; night)

I 8. ____ What do you think Mrs. Rabbit did when she heard Mrs. Mouse's news?
(any logical response; went right home)

E 9. ____ Why would Mrs. Rabbit be afraid of a fox?
(any logical response; it might eat her babies)

V 10. ____ What does "safe" mean?
(any logical response; no danger; no harm; protection)

Total Miscues [ ] **Significant Miscues** [ ] **Questions Missed** [ ]

Word Recognition Scoring Guide		
Total Miscues	Level	Significant Miscues
0–1	Independent	0–1
2–4	Ind./Inst.	2
5	Instructional	3
6–9	Inst./Frust.	4
10+	Frustration	5+

Retelling
Excellent
Satisfactory
Unsatisfactory

____ WPM
) 6000

Comprehension Scoring Guide	
Questions Missed	Level
0–1	Independent
1½–2	Ind./Inst.
2½	Instructional
3–4½	Inst./Frust.
5+	Frustration

SECTION 3

Teaching Strategies and Activities

OVERVIEW
of Teaching Strategies and Activities

Section 3 consists of 15 areas of instruction for children who are at the emergent through facile reading stages that correspond to beginning reading to an instructional level of second grade. The 15 areas for instruction are presented in a semi-hierarchical order as illustrated in the chart on page 18. Section 3 provides areas of instruction for children as they progress from the emergent through facile reading stages.

The instructional areas in Section 3 are organized in the following way. Each instructional area has a teaching goal. The teaching goal is the foundation for your instruction; it's your main objective. The assessments from Sections 2 and 4 that relate to the instructional area follow the teaching goal. As you learn about the abilities of the children you teach through administering and interpreting the assessments, you can tailor your teaching by using the instructional strategies in Section 3.

Each instructional area begins with a background section that defines the instructional area and summarizes the research base. It provides the reasons for your instruction. Following the background, two or more teaching strategies are presented. Each teaching strategy provides a step-by-step method that explains how to use the strategy to accomplish the teaching goal. After the teaching strategies, several ideas and activities are presented. These brief ideas and activities support the teaching strategies and provide additional ways to accomplish your teaching goal. Concluding each instructional area is a list of selected resources. Each list provides the names of children's books, media and technology, and/or professional references to support your teaching.

3.1   Desire to Read

Goal   To help children develop positive attitudes, interest, and motivation toward reading.

Assessments   Interviews About Reading 2.1 and 4.1

BACKGROUND

Children are born with a desire to learn. They are interested in the people, things, and events around them. When young children come to school, they still have a strong drive to learn. One of the things most children want to learn when they come to school is to read and write (Cochrane, Cochrane, Scalena, & Buchanan, 1988).

The desire to read and write is an important foundation for all literacy learning. If children view reading and writing as interesting, exciting, and meaningful, they will be more likely to engage in reading and writing. As with any skill, additional practice and engagement with reading and writing leads to improved competence.

You can capitalize on young children's natural interest and curiosity by providing a classroom environment that invites children into literacy. Classroom environments that contain many types of print, offer easy access to reading and writing materials, provide for choice, and immerse children in literacy activities motivate and support children's literacy development (Sulzby & Teale, 1991).

There are simple strategies and activities you can use in your classroom to arouse and build on children's natural curiosity and interest in literacy. The teaching strategies and activities set forth below provide suggestions to assist you with creating a classroom environment and literacy program that will help children develop positive attitudes, interest, and motivation toward reading.

TEACHING STRATEGY 1	**Morning Message**

The Morning Message is a daily classroom routine that provides a meaningful context for reading and writing in the classroom. The teacher writes the Morning Message to the students to share important information about the upcoming day and concludes by asking the children a related personal question. Children may try to read the message on their own, and then the teacher engages in shared reading to guide the children through the reading. Finally, children discuss, draw, or write a response to the question.

DIRECTIONS

1. Write a short message on the chalkboard or on chart paper. The message should include important information about the upcoming day. The message then concludes by asking the children a related personal response question. A sample message is shown on the next page.

Dear Boys and Girls,

Today is art day. We will be painting pictures. We will use blue, green, red, and yellow paint. I like to use many colors in my paintings. What colors will you use when you paint today?

Your friend,
Mrs. Jones

2. Post the message prior to the children's arrival in the classroom. Provide time for the children to look at the message and informally discuss it among themselves.

3. Gather the children around the message. Read the message aloud to the children.

4. Reread the message. Invite the children to join in with the reading if they would like to do so.

5. Discuss the ideas in the message. Discuss the question in the message. Provide time for students to informally discuss their responses to the question.

6. Ask children to record their responses to the question by either drawing or writing a response in their journals.

7. Provide time for children to share their responses.

| TEACHING STRATEGY 2 | Shared Reading |

Shared Reading replicates the bedtime story sharing situation with an individual, a small group, or a classroom of children. This strategy allows children to participate in and enjoy books they cannot read on their own (Mooney, 1990). The emphasis of this strategy is on enjoyment of the story as a whole. Teachers can introduce new, exciting books to children through Shared Reading.

DIRECTIONS

1. Select a predictable children's book with engaging illustrations. If you are reading with a large group of children, a Big Book will work well.

2. Gather the children into a circle so they all can hear the story and see the illustrations.

3. Show the children the cover of the book and read the title. Ask them to make predictions about the contents of the book. Provide time for volunteers to share their ideas.

4. Read the story aloud to the children inviting them to read along if they would like to do so.

5. Provide time for the children to share their personal responses and favorite parts of the book.

6. Reread the book inviting the children to read along if they would like to do so.

7. Place the book in the classroom library so the children can read it during their free time.

Ideas and Activities

1. Provide daily class time for self-selected reading. Consider using a fun acronym as a name for this activity (e.g., DIRT: Daily Independent Reading Time or DEAR: Drop Everything And Read). Provide access to varied types of reading materials and allow children to find a comfortable place to read in the classroom. During this time, you should also be reading to serve as a good reading model for the children. You can also provide a short sharing time after children have completed their reading.

2. Model your enthusiasm and love for reading. Bring in your favorite books and share them with the children. Discuss how and why reading is important to you. Provide a special display of your favorite books in the classroom. Update the display on a regular basis.

3. Create a print-rich classroom environment that includes access to and displays of various types of print. Possible types of print are listed below.

   - labels for important classroom locations and materials
   - lists of children's names (e.g., who lost a tooth, birthdays)
   - sign-in sheet
   - message board
   - posters with captions
   - displays of the children's work and writing
   - announcements
   - classroom rules and procedures
   - chart and language experience stories
   - children's books and magazines

4. Read aloud to the children at least once a day, more often if possible. Focus on the children's enjoyment of and personal reactions to the story. Consider using different voices and sound effects to make the read-aloud experience highly motivating for the children. Provide time for children to ask questions and discuss their responses to the story.

5. Create literacy play centers so children can explore literacy through meaningful play situations. A list of literacy play centers and suggested materials is provided in the box below.

Literacy Play Centers

Post Office Center
mailboxes
envelopes
paper
stationery
stickers or stamp pads
address labels
boxes
packages
cash register
play money

Restaurant Center
menus
order pad and pencil
tablecloth
dishes
glasses
silverware
napkins
list of daily specials
cash register
play money

Office Center
phone
computer or typewriter
message pad
pens and pencils
paper
calculator
note pads
file folders
rubber stamps and stamp pad

Grocery Store Center
grocery cart
food packages
price stickers
advertisements
coupons
cash register
play money
shopping lists
grocery bags

---

6. Schedule time for children to share the books they are reading and stories they are writing with their classmates. Learning what their peers are reading and writing often serves as a motivator for students to pursue similar reading and writing tasks. Consider using a special chair such as a rocking chair to make the sharing experience more special. Provide options so children can share with a small group of children or the entire class.

7. Implement a home-school reading program through the use of reading backpacks. Fill several small backpacks or book bags with children's books on specific topics or by particular authors. Include construction paper, markers, crayons, pencils, and a small notebook in the backpack. Attach a short note explaining that parents and children are invited to share the books and write or draw about their favorite parts. When children return the backpack to school, provide time for them to share their responses. Post their responses on a bulletin board or in the classroom library. Change the contents of the backpacks frequently and rotate them around the classroom so all children can take home a reading backpack on a regular basis.

8. Arrange the classroom so children have easy access to literacy materials. For example, consider establishing a writing center that contains different types of paper, markers, pencils, pens, a computer, a children's typewriter, letter stamps, picture dictionaries, scissors, glue, tape, letter tiles, magnetic letters, and other writing supplies. Label storage areas for materials in the center so children can find and put away materials themselves.

9. Implement a message board in the classroom. Consider using a bulletin board with a pocket or envelope for each child. To introduce the message board, write a personalized message to each student in the classroom. Provide daily time for children to write messages to their classmates. To keep the message board going, you may want to write messages to several children each day.

10. Invite children to engage in artistic responses to literature. Provide opportunities for children to explore creative dramatics, art, music, dance, and movement activities after reading a book. These types of responses actively involve children in learning and literature.

11. Introduce children to various genres of literature by doing brief book talks. During book talks, focus on enticing children to want to read the books without giving away the stories. After conducting book talks, make the books available in the classroom library.

12. Develop a cross-age reading buddy program. This type of program pairs a younger child and an older child so they can read together. The focus of this type of activity is on enjoying the stories and making reading fun.

13. Introduce poetry, rhymes, jingles, and jump-rope rhymes to children. Display these materials on chart paper so children can read them on their own during free time. Encourage children to engage in word play by developing their own verses or modifications of the poems, rhymes, jingles, and jump-rope rhymes.

14. Develop a classroom listening center so children can follow along as they listen to a tape-recorded version of a book. Rotate the books and tapes in the listening center on a regular basis.

15. Establish a well-stocked classroom library and provide daily time for children to browse through the library and select materials. Suggestions for creating a classroom library are detailed in the following list.

☞ Creating a Classroom Library

Specific, named location:	The classroom library is in a highly visible area, and it has a specific name.
Partitioned and private:	The classroom library is separated from other areas in the classroom by book shelves, book carts, or other partitions.
Comfortable:	The library contains comfortable seating such as bean bag chairs, carpet squares, or pillows.

Number of books:	Provide a minimum of five to eight books per child in the classroom.
Assortment of books:	Provide books from varied genres and reading levels. Be sure to include other reading materials such as magazines, pamphlets, materials written by the children, and class books.
Organization:	Organize books and provide labels to show the organization (e.g., genres, themes, topics, authors, or reading levels).
Shelving:	Include some open shelving so students can see book covers. Shelve other books with the spines facing out to provide room for more books in the available space.
Literature Displays:	Include displays with posters, puppets, felt boards, stuffed animals, and puppets that are related to children's books.

Selected Resources
DESIRE TO READ

Predictable Books

Ahlberg, J., & Ahlberg, A. (1978). *Each peach pear plum.* New York: Scholastic.

Barracca, D., & Barracca, S. (1990). *The adventures of Taxi Dog.* New York: Dial.

Brett, J. (1985). *Annie and the wild animals.* New York: Houghton Mifflin.

Kimmel, E.A. (1994). *Anansi and the talking melon.* New York: Holiday House.

Kimmel, E.A. (1988). *Anansi and the moss-covered rock.* New York: Holiday House.

Slobdkina, E. (1968). *Caps for sale.* New York: Scholastic.

Walsh, E.S. (1993). *Hop jump.* San Diego, CA: Harcourt Brace Jovanovich.

Rhyme and Jump-Rope Rhyme Books

Cole, J. (1989). *Anna Banana: 101 jump rope rhymes.* New York: Morrow.

Cole, J. (1987). *Norma Jean, jumping bean.* New York: Random House.

Cole, J., & Calmenson, S. (1990). *Miss Mary Mack and other children's street rhymes.* New York: Morrow.

Jorgensen, G. (1989). *Crocodile beat.* New York: Bradbury Press.

Wescott, N.B. (1987). *Peanut butter and jelly: A play rhyme.* New York: Dutton.

Professional Resources for Locating Children's Books

Bishop, R.S. (Ed.). (1994). *Kaleidoscope: A multicultural booklist for grades K–8.* Urbana, IL: National Council of Teachers of English.

Jensen, J.M., & Roser, N.L. (Eds.). (1993). *Adventuring with books: A booklist for pre-K – grade 6* (10th ed.). Urbana, IL: National Council of Teachers of English.

McClure, A.A., & Kristo, J.V. (1996). *Books that invite talk, wonder, and play.* Urbana, IL: National Council of Teachers of English.

Silvey, A. (Ed.). (1995). *Children's books and their creators.* Boston: Houghton Mifflin.

3.2 Background Knowledge

Goal To help children expand their experiences and build background knowledge.

Assessments Wordless Picture Reading 2.4 and 4.4

BACKGROUND

Children can learn more effectively when they can relate new learning to something they already know. This type of previous knowledge is often referred to as background knowledge or schema (Anderson, 1994), and it is an important foundation for constructing meaning in reading and writing. Some children come to school with a wealth of experiences that help them connect school learning to their life experiences. Other children come to school with limited experiences and exposure to events, objects, and books (Salinger, 1996).

The concept of building background knowledge focuses on providing new experiences to children. Building background knowledge is greatly supported by providing children with concrete experiences and opportunities to use their senses to examine materials and objects. Because young children learn by doing, playing, and being actively involved, hands-on experiences are essential for building background knowledge.

Activating background knowledge refers to the process of helping children remember what they already know about a topic. You can help children activate their background knowledge by making connections between what they already know and what they will learn. Simple techniques such as making predictions, discussing, or drawing what is already known about a topic, or brainstorming how two topics are alike are examples of strategies you can use to help activate children's background knowledge.

By planning simple experiences related to a topic of study or book, you can build and activate children's background knowledge, thus increasing the likelihood that they will understand and learn the new concepts. Specific suggestions for building and activating children's background knowledge are provided below.

TEACHING STRATEGY 1	Object Exploration

The Object Exploration strategy provides children with concrete experiences related to an upcoming area of study. Young children learn through active involvement and hands-on experiences, and this strategy provides them with opportunities to personally explore and examine materials before they begin a new unit of study. In addition, related vocabulary and concepts are introduced in relation to the concrete objects, thereby providing a useful framework for children to understand and learn the new words and ideas related to the topic of study.

DIRECTIONS

1. Identify an upcoming unit of study and gather concrete objects related to the unit. For example, if you are studying eggs, gather raw eggs, cracked eggs, hard-boiled eggs, brown eggs, duck eggs, and magnifying glasses.

2. Tell the children you will be starting a new unit. Inform them of the topic for the new unit. Show them the concrete objects you have gathered and tell them they will be examining these materials to prepare for the unit.

3. Provide exploration time for the children to use their senses to explore and examine the objects. Share magnifying glasses so the children get a closer look at the objects.

4. Ask the children to brainstorm words that describe the objects they have explored. Write the words on the chalkboard, a piece of chart paper, or an overhead transparency. Make a separate list for each object. For example, if children explored eggs as described in step 1, make lists of the describing words on chart paper labeled *raw egg, cracked egg,* and *hard-boiled egg.*

5. Discuss the words on the lists and what the children learned about the objects. Inform the children that they will be learning many things about the topic in the new unit.

6. Display the brainstorming lists in the classroom. Add new words to the lists as children participate in additional activities related to the unit.

TEACHING STRATEGY 2	Book Boxes

Book Boxes are collections of artifacts related to a story, poem, or informational book. A Book Box is decorated according to the focus of the book, and it contains at least three important objects related to the book. Teachers can use Book Boxes to introduce a book to children by sharing the objects, discussing why the objects are included, and inviting the children to make predictions about the book.

DIRECTIONS

1. Identify a story, poem, or informational book that you will be sharing with children.

2. Read the book to identify at least three important objects that are mentioned in the book.

3. Gather these objects or pictures of the objects and place them in a box.

4. Decorate the box according to the focus of the book. Also, write the title and author of the book on the box.

5. Prior to reading the book with the children, show them the Book Box. Discuss the decorations on the box and the title and author of the book.

6. Remove one object from the box. Discuss what the object is and why it is included in the Book Box. Invite the children to make predictions about what other objects might be in the Book Box and why.

7. Share the objects in the Book Box. Invite the children to make predictions about what the book will be about based on the objects in the Book Box.

8. Introduce the book to the children and read it with them as a teacher read aloud, shared reading activity, or guided reading activity.

Knowledge Chart

A Knowledge Chart focuses on children's prior knowledge about a topic and their new knowledge about a topic after reading (Macon & Macon, 1991). This strategy invites children to share their knowledge about the topic of a book they will be reading by brainstorming words and ideas related to the topic. After the book is read, children then focus on the new knowledge they learned about the topic, thus connecting their background knowledge with new learning.

DIRECTIONS

1. Select an informational book the children will be reading or that you will be reading to them. Identify the topic of the book.

2. Create a Knowledge Chart on the chalkboard, a piece of chart paper, or an overhead transparency. A sample Knowledge Chart is shown below.

Knowledge Chart

Prior knowledge about _____	New knowledge about _____

3. Tell the children they will be reading a book about a specific topic. Show them the Knowledge Chart and ask them to brainstorm what they already know about the topic. Write their ideas on the Knowledge Chart.

4. Explain to the children that they should think about the ideas on the Knowledge Chart as they read or listen to the book. Tell them that you will be asking them to share their new knowledge about the book after they have read or listened to the book.

5. Read the book with the children as a teacher read aloud, shared reading activity, or guided reading activity. Discuss the book with the children.

6. Ask the children to share the new knowledge they learned about the topic. Add this information to the Knowledge Chart.

7. Engage the children in a discussion about how their prior knowledge compared to their new knowledge. Remind them that thinking about what they already know about a book or topic is an important strategy that good readers use to prepare for reading.

Ideas and Activities

1. Take frequent field trips to locations in the community such as the library, grocery store, dairy, fire station, farm, post office, veterinarian's office, hospital, and restaurant. Exposure to these locations will help to build children's background knowledge about important locations, people, jobs, and things in their communities.

2. Invite guest speakers into the classroom to share information and artifacts related to their jobs, hobbies, or travels. Provide time for children to examine the artifacts and ask questions. Consider speakers with interesting jobs or hobbies and be sure to contact children's parents, community members, and school

personnel when looking for guest speakers. Consider the concrete artifacts that a guest speaker will be able to bring to share with children during a presentation. A list of possible guest speakers is provided in the box.

Guest Speaker Ideas

Banker	Farmer	Photographer
Musician	Cook	Artist
Receptionist	Nurse	Painter
Dentist	Veterinarian	Gardener
Weather forecaster	Store clerk	Doctor
Traveler	Florist	Secretary
Bus driver	Dog trainer	Astronomer
Mechanic	Computer professional	Construction worker
Hobbyist	Collector	Sports enthusiast

---

3. Help children develop a picture of a place, event, or person by sharing photos or videos with children prior to reading about the new topic of study. This technique works well when you cannot bring real objects or speakers into the classroom.

4. Create jackdaws to introduce a new topic of study. A jackdaw is a collection of artifacts related to a topic or book. Jackdaws may contain concrete objects, photographs, a list of related words, a time line of events, clothing or personal items related to a character, and various other materials. A jackdaw is displayed like a mini-museum in the classroom, and it serves as an excellent introduction to a new area of study (Rasinski & Padak, 1996). You and the children can also add materials to the jackdaw throughout the unit.

5. Invite children to bring in interesting artifacts and collections to share during Show and Tell time. Encourage other children to ask questions about the Show and Tell objects. Provide time for several children to Show and Tell each day. Create a classroom area to display Show and Tell materials for the students to explore during their free time.

6. Read to children on a daily basis to expose them to new ideas, experiences, and information. Vary the types of books you read to include poetry, fiction, nonfiction, fairy tales, folk tales, and other genres. Provide time to discuss the books after reading them. After sharing the books, place them in the classroom library so the children can explore or reread them during their free time.

7. Engage children in filling out a K-W-L chart for a new topic of study (Ogle, 1986). The chart focuses on What I **K**now, What I **W**ant to Learn, and What I **L**earned. Before the children read a nonfiction book, the teacher introduces the K-W-L chart and asks the children to brainstorm what they already **K**now about the topic of the book. Next, the children list the things they **W**ant to learn about the topic. After reading the book or listening to the book, the children list the things they **L**earned about the topic. This strategy works best as a teacher-guided activity for a group of children. The teacher serves as a scribe who writes the children's ideas on the various sections of the chart. A blank K-W-L chart is provided below.

K-W-L Chart for _____

K	W	L
What I already know:	What I want to learn:	What I learned:

8. Provide access to appropriate reference materials so children can look up information on topics about which they want to learn more. For example, create a classroom research center that contains children's dictionaries, children's encyclopedias, easy-to-read nonfiction books, computer resources, children's magazines, and informational posters.

9. Invite children to complete a Quickdraw or Quickwrite about a new topic of study. In a quickdraw or quickwrite, children are told about a new topic they will be studying. Children then draw or write what they already know about that topic. After two to three minutes of drawing or writing time, provide an opportunity for children to share their ideas. Discuss their knowledge about the topic as an introduction to the new topic of study.

10. Ask children to make predictions about a book based on the title and cover illustration to activate their background knowledge before reading or listening to a book. Follow up on children's predictions by asking them to explain how they made their predictions.

11. Supply interesting hands-on materials and place them in the classroom discovery center so children can explore them during their free time. Change the materials in the discovery center on a regular basis. Suggestions for the discovery center are in the following list.

☞ **Suggested Materials for Classroom Discovery Centers**

Science Materials	Art Materials
Rocks	Paints
Shells	Brushes
Plants	Assorted papers
Magnifying glasses	Markers
Magnets	Glue
Scales	Scissors
Leaves	Crayons
Pine cones	Hole punch
Fossils	Ribbons
Children's microscopes	Cloth scraps
Nonfiction books on science topics	Posters showing various styles of art
Music Materials	Math Materials
Rhythm sticks	Counters
Drums	Graph paper
Materials to make simple instruments	Number lines
Triangles	Calculators
Recorders	Adding machines
Tape recorders	Number blocks
Tapes of various types of music	Math manipulatives
Song books	Abacus
Charts with song lyrics	Pencils
Conductor's baton	Paper

Informational Magazines for Children

Chickadee Magazine
25 Boxwood Lane
Buffalo, NY 14227-2780
Topics: Science, nature, and technology
Ages: 8 and under

Zoobooks
Wildlife Education Limited
9820 Willow Creek Rd.
Suite 300
San Diego, CA 92131
Topics: Wildlife
Ages: 5 and up

Let's Find Out
Scholastic, Inc.
2931 E. McCarty Street
P.O. Box 3710
Jefferson City, MO 65102-9957
(800-651-1586)
Topics: Science, social studies, theme-centered
Ages: Pre-K to K

Sesame Street Magazine
P.O. Box 52000
Boulder, CO 80301
Topics: Games and real-life activities
Ages: 3–7

Your Big Backyard
National Wildlife Federation
8925 Leesburg Pike
Vienna, VA 22184
(800-432-6564)
Topics: Nature, conservation
Ages: 3–6

Crayola Kids Magazine
P.O. Box 37198
Boone, IA 50037-7968
(800-846-7968)
Topics: Art, fact-based activities
Ages: 4–8

Media and Technology

Busytown CD-ROM (readiness skills and activities)
UPDATA (800-882-2844)

Richard Scarry's Best Neighborhood Ever CD-ROM (creative play activities in the neighborhood).
UPDATA (800-882-2844)

Richard Scarry's Busiest Neighborhood Ever CD-ROM (life skills and creative play in the
    neighborhood)
UPDATA (800-882-2844)

Thinkin' Things Collection 1 CD-ROM (thinking skills for young children).
UPDATA (800-882-2844)

3.3 Reading as Meaning

Goal To help children learn that meaning is the purpose of reading.

Assessments Interviews About Reading 2.1 and 4.1

BACKGROUND

An important foundation for early literacy development involves children's awareness that reading is the process of constructing meaning from text. Children learn that stories make sense when parents and teachers read and discuss stories with them. They also develop an understanding that environmental print provides useful information or directions (Purcell-Gates, 1989). For example, children learn that menus help them know what foods are served in a restaurant; letters and greeting cards help them "stay in touch" with friends and family members; and package labels help them identify and use the contents properly (Tompkins, 1997).

During the early stages of literacy development, children also develop an understanding that spoken language can be written down and that the purpose of written language is to communicate a message to the reader. Clay (1979) describes this awareness of the communication function of print as the intentionality principle. In this phase of literacy development, children understand that print communicates meaning.

When teachers engage children in many authentic reading and writing activities, children will develop an understanding that print makes sense and carries a message. Suggestions to help teachers foster children's understanding of the purpose and function of reading are provided below.

TEACHING STRATEGY 1 Language Experience Approach

The Language Experience Approach (LEA) helps children make connections between spoken and written language (Stauffer, 1970). Children's dictation serves as the foundation for the LEA. The main premises behind the LEA are that children can talk about what they have experienced; their words can be written down; and they can read what they say. The language experience approach begins with the children's experiences and own language; therefore, it provides a personalized connection between learning about spoken and written language.

DIRECTIONS

1. Provide a hands-on experience for children such as a field trip to an apple orchard or a cooking activity.

2. Invite the children to tell about their experiences with the hands-on activity by dictating a story. This can be done with individual children, small groups, or with a class of children.

3. Inform the children that you will record their ideas in writing.

4. Write the children's dictations on chart paper. Be sure to write exactly what the children say. Do not make corrections for grammar or usage unless you have been teaching a specific writing convention, such as using capital letters at the beginning of sentences or periods at the end of sentences.

5. When the children have completed the story, read it aloud to them.

6. Reread the story, inviting the children to share in the reading if they would like to do so. Reread the story several times. Discuss ideas contributed by specific students. Ask the children how you knew what to write for the story.

7. Guide the children to understand that the story's ideas came from their words and ideas. Discuss how their words can be spoken, written, and then read.

8. Have the children illustrate the story and then bind it into a Big Book. Place the Big Book in the classroom library so the children can read and reread it during their free time.

TEACHING STRATEGY 2	Scrambled Story

The Scrambled Story strategy helps focus children's attention on the idea that print and stories carry meaning. By presenting children with a story that is missing important information, children will conclude that stories should make sense.

DIRECTIONS

1. Select a simple story and delete two to three important pieces of information such as the setting, main character's name, or an important plot event.

2. Recopy the story onto chart paper and read it to the children.

3. As you read the story aloud, pause several times to ask the children, "Does this make sense?" and "Are we missing any information?"

4. Tell the children that you have the original copy of the book and you will read them the page from the book to help them figure out what the story should sound like. Add the missing information to the chart paper version of the story.

5. Continue with this pattern until you have identified and added all of the missing information.

6. Discuss with the children that reading and stories should always make sense.

Ideas and Activities

1. Read to children daily and engage them in discussions about what you are reading. Read from stories, environmental print, and other forms of print. Focus on helping children understand the meaning of what you are reading by using prompts such as "What was the story about?" and "What is the sign telling us?"

2. Engage the children in shared reading using Big Books. Discuss the stories with the children. Place the Big Books in the classroom library and encourage children to read or pretend read the stories to their classmates, classroom visitors, and even dolls and stuffed animal friends.

3. Share the book *Hey, I'm Reading* (1995) by Betty Miles. Engage the children in a discussion of the purposes and goals of reading based on ideas presented in the book.

4. Share the book *Oh, How I Wished I Could Read!* (1995) by John Gile. Engage the children in a discussion of the functions and goals of reading based on ideas presented in the book. Encourage children to discuss how they use and see others use reading in their daily lives.

5. Create a fractured fairy tale by removing at least one important part of a familiar fairy tale. Read the fairy tale to the children and ask them what is missing. Ask them how the missing information affected their understanding and enjoyment of the story. Lead the children to the conclusion that reading should make sense.

6. Play the game *What's Silly?* while reading to the children. As you are reading a story, leave out a phrase, sentence, or important word. Then ask the children, "What's silly about what I just read?" Discuss what was wrong with what you read. Then discuss how reading should make sense.

7. Write simple directions on the chalkboard. An example follows.

   Hang up your coat.
   Sign in.
   Go to bed.

   Ask the children to read the directions with you. Ask the children if they have any questions about the directions. Ask them if the directions make sense. Discuss how writing should make sense to the reader.

8. Gather several food packages and their contents (e.g., several different types of cereal, crackers, or cookies that are familiar to the children). Take the contents out of the food packages and ask children to help you identify which foods belong in which packages. Discuss the strategies you can use to match the food with the package. Focus the children's attention on the print on the packages. Discuss how the print on packages communicates important information.

9. Engage the children in a reading scavenger hunt by posting several simple messages around the classroom. An example follows.

   1. Go to the library center.
   2. Check out a book.
   3. Return to your table.
   4. Read the book to yourself.

   After the hunt, discuss how the children knew what they should do during the activity.

10. Take a walking tour of the classroom and school and point out important signs that are posted. Discuss the purpose and message that each sign carries. Ask the children how and why the signs are important and helpful.

Children's Books with Simple Story Lines for Scrambled Stories

Asch, F. (1982). *Milk and cookies.* New York: Parents Magazine.

Bennett, J. (1985). *Teeny tiny.* New York: Trumpet.

Brett, J. (1989). *The mitten.* New York: Putnam.

Carle, E. (1990). *The very quiet cricket.* New York: Philomel.

Fox, M. (1986). *Hattie and the fox.* New York: Bradbury.

Galdone, P. (1973). *The little red hen.* New York: Seabury.

Havill, J. (1993). *Jamaica and Brianna.* Boston: Houghton Mifflin.

Lobel, A. (1970). *Frog and Toad are friends.* New York: Harper & Row.

Children's Books for Creating Fractured Fairy Tales

Brett. J. (1987). *Goldilocks and the three bears.* New York: Sandcastle.

Galdone, P. (1974). *Little Red Riding Hood.* New York: McGraw-Hill.

Galdone, P. (1970). *The three bears.* New York: Clarion Books.

Galdone, P. (1970). *The three little pigs.* New York: Seabury.

Huck, C. (1989). *Princess Furball.* New York: Greenwillow.

Lobel, A. (1978). *The pancake.* New York: Greenwillow.

Professional Resources

Avery, C. (1993). *And with a light touch: Learning about reading, writing, and teaching with first graders.* Portsmouth, NH: Heinemann.

Frasier, J., & Skolnik, D. (1994). *On their way: Celebrating second graders as they read and write.* Portsmouth, NH: Heinemann.

Slaughter, J.P. (1993). *Beyond storybooks: Young children and the shared book experience.* Newark, DE: International Reading Association.

3.4   Sense of Story

Goal   To help children develop a sense of story.

Assessments Retelling a Story 2.2 and 4.2; Wordless Picture Reading 2.4 and 4.4

BACKGROUND

Young children need to develop background knowledge about how stories are structured and what characteristics and components stories possess. This knowledge is important to emergent readers because it allows them to anticipate and understand stories and how they work. A sense of story provides children with a framework for understanding the stories that are read to them and the stories they read to themselves (Lukens, 1995).

Children who come to school with many home reading experiences typically possess a good sense of story because of the many stories that have been read to them by their families or care givers. Children who have not been read to on a regular basis prior to coming to school will need to be immersed in stories and reading experiences so they too can develop a sense of story (Edwards, 1986).

Story selections for emergent readers should focus on simple stories with related illustrations and large, clear print. Story sharing should be an interactive process with many opportunities for children to discuss, ask questions, and note observations about the stories (Salinger, 1996). If you share stories with children on a daily basis in the classroom, you will notice that children will develop an understanding of the characteristics and components of stories as well as an interest in reading.

TEACHING STRATEGY 1	**Simple Story Elements**

The Simple Story Elements strategy helps children verbalize what they know about how stories are structured. This strategy focuses on the places, people and animals, and things that happen in a story (Johns & Lenski, 1997). This strategy will help children develop a foundation about the components all stories possess. After children understand this strategy, story mapping and other story element activities can be introduced.

DIRECTIONS

1. Select a familiar children's book with a clear, simple story line. Using a familiar story such as a fairy tale works well when introducing this strategy. If possible, select a story that all or at least most of the children already know.

2. Ask the children to tell you what they know or remember about the story. List these ideas on the chalkboard.

3. After the children have had a chance to share their ideas, group their responses into the following three columns on the chalkboard: places, people and animals, and things that happen. For example, if you were using *The Three Little Pigs,* the children might list the following ideas:

Places	People and Animals	Things That Happen
in the woods	three little pigs	Wolf blows down houses.
pigs' houses	Big Bad Wolf	

4. Explain to the children that all stories include information on the places, people and animals, and things that happen in the story. Go on to discuss that a story must have all of these parts.

5. Read the familiar story to the children. Ask them to listen carefully to see if the ideas listed on the chalkboard are correct or if changes need to be made. For example, if you were using *The Three Little Pigs,* the revised list might contain the ideas listed below:

Places	People and Animals	Things that Happen
in the woods	three little pigs	Wolf blows down straw house.
straw house	Big Bad Wolf	Wolf blows down wood house.
wood house		Wolf can't blow down brick house.
brick house		

6. Ask children to make suggestions about ideas that need to be added, removed, or changed. Be sure to ask children to support and explain their responses.

7. Repeat this strategy with other stories, including stories that are new to children.

TEACHING STRATEGY 2	Plot Relationships Chart

The Plot Relationships Chart helps children understand and identify the major plot elements in fictional stories. This strategy uses the clue words *Somebody, Wanted, But,* and *So* to help children develop an understanding of how the main character, goal, problem, and solution of a story fit together (Schmidt & Buckley, 1991).

DIRECTIONS

1. Select a children's book that has clear plot elements: main character, goal, problem, and solution.

2. Read the story aloud to the children. Provide time for the children to discuss the story and their reactions to the story.

3. Place a blank copy of the Plot Relationships Chart on the chalkboard, an overhead transparency, or a piece of chart paper. A sample chart is provided below.

Plot Relationships Chart

Somebody	Wanted	But	So

4. Tell the children they will be using the chart to learn about the important parts of stories and how they fit together.

5. Guide the children through identifying the main character of the story by asking them, "Who is the important *Somebody* that the story is about?" Discuss the children's responses and, when agreement is reached, write the main character's name in the *Somebody* column on the chart.

6. Use this pattern to guide the children through identifying and discussing the other plot elements.

7. Explain to children that all stories have these important parts. Provide additional opportunities to work with the Plot Relationships Chart and other stories. A modification of the Plot Relationships Chart is the Plot Relationships Frame. A sample frame is provided below.

_____ wanted _____
        Somebody

but _____ so _____.

TEACHING STRATEGY 3	Story Star

The Story Star is a variation of a story map. Story maps provide visual representations of the major elements in a story. Story maps help children see and understand how the elements of a story fit together so they can understand what they are reading. There are many variations of story maps that can be used to help children develop an understanding of story elements, but those that have a simple format and focus on a limited number of elements are most appropriate for emergent and beginning readers. The Story Star is a very basic type of story map that is appropriate for use with young children.

DIRECTIONS

1. Select a children's book with a simple story line and clear story elements: main character, setting, events, problem, and solution.

2. Introduce the book to the children and invite them to make predictions about the book based on its title and cover illustration.

3. Read the book aloud to the children. Provide time for them to discuss the story and their personal reactions to it.

4. Display a blank Story Star on the chalkboard, an overhead transparency, or a piece of chart paper. Explain to the children that you will use the Story Star to identify the important parts of the story. A sample Story Star is provided below.

5. Begin with the main character from the story and ask the children, "Who was the story about?" Discuss their responses and explanations. Write the main character's name on the Story Star. If desired, a picture of the main character can also be added to this part of the Story Star.

6. Continue with this pattern by asking children the following questions to guide their thinking.

   - When and where did the story happen?
   - What important events or things happened in the story?
   - What was the problem that the main character had in the story?
   - What was the solution for the problem in the story? or How did the story end?

7. If desired, include a drawing inside each point of the star for each of the elements listed on the Story Star.

8. Discuss with children that all stories have the elements listed on the Story Star. Provide additional opportunities for the children to use the Story Star strategy with other children's books.

Ideas and Activities

1. Read to children on a daily basis. Expose them to a variety of good stories. During and after story reading activities, provide time for children to ask questions, note observations, and discuss the stories. Place books you have read to the children in the classroom library so they can read and look at the books during their free time.

2. Use storytelling to expose children to stories and to develop a sense of story through oral language. Select a simple story and collect several props to help you tell the story. Provide discussion time after telling the story. Encourage the children to retell the story to a classmate.

3. After reading a story with the children, invite small groups of children to retell the story using simple props, puppets, or a felt board. Place these materials in a classroom literacy center so children can engage in retelling activities during center time or their free time.

4. Have children complete simple story boards for the important elements of stories. For example, divide a piece of construction paper into four equal sections. Label the sections *Who, When, Where,* and *What.* Ask the children to draw and label *Who* the story was about, *When* the story took place, *Where* the story happened, and *What* the important events in the story were. Provide time for children to share and discuss their story boards. A sample story board format is provided below.

Who?	When?
Where?	What?

5. Invite children to use creative dramatics to act out favorite stories. If possible, supply simple props and costumes for children to use in their story dramas. Provide time for children to share their story dramas with other children.

6. Have children illustrate major events from a story. These illustrations can then be sequenced to match the events in the story. Stories such as Eric Carle's *The Very Hungry Caterpillar* (1969) work well for this type of story sequencing activity.

7. Provide access to a well-stocked classroom library so children can look at and read books on a daily basis. Schedule a daily time for children to read and discuss self-selected books.

8. Use wordless picture books to engage children in talking about the story and discussing the important components of the story. For a list of wordless picture books with clear, simple story lines, see Selected Resources: Sense of Story.

9. Encourage parents to read stories to and with their children on a daily basis. Provide access to appropriate books by sharing books from the classroom and school library.

Wordless Children's Books with Simple Story Lines

Bang, M. (1980). *The gray lady and the strawberry snatcher.* New York: Four Winds.

Carle, E. (1971). *Do you want to be my friend?* New York: Crowell.

Day, A. (1995). *Carl's birthday.* New York: Farrar Straus Giroux.

DePaola, T. (1981). *Pancakes for breakfast.* New York: Harcourt.

Ormerod, J. (1981). *Sunshine.* Wooster, OH: Lathrop.

Turkle, B. (1976). *Deep in the forest.* New York: Dutton.

Media and Technology

Goldilocks and the Three Bears CD-ROM (interactive storybook with comprehension activities).
UPDATA (800-882-2844)

Talking Classic Tales CD-ROM (interactive stories with sound effects and animation).
UPDATA (800-882-2844)

The Cat Came Back CD-ROM (interactive storybook).
Sanctuary Woods (415-578-6340)

Professional Resources

Brooks, E. (1996). *Just-right books for beginning readers: Leveled booklists and strategies.* New York: Scholastic Professional Books.

Macon, J.M., Bewell, D., & Vogt, M. (Eds.) (1991). *Responses to literature: Grades K–8.* Newark, DE: International Reading Association.

Opitz, M. (1998). *Getting the most from predictable books: Strategies and activities for teaching with more than 75 favorite children's books.* New York: Scholastic Professional Books.

Tarlow, E. (1987). *Teaching story elements with favorite books: Creative and engaging activities to explore character, plot, setting, and theme that work with any book.* New York: Scholastic Professional Books.

3.5 Literacy Knowledge

Goal To help children learn concepts about print in books.

Assessments Literacy Knowledge 2.3 and 4.3

BACKGROUND

As children grow, they learn about the world around them and gradually develop literacy skills. Knowledge about reading and writing begins early in children's lives (Teale & Sulzby, 1989). Very young children begin to notice that reading and writing are part of their world. For example, young children learn that their environment is full of print. They see print material such as newspapers and magazines in their homes, they see print on television, and they recognize signs and logos on products and in stores. As children begin to notice print, they are progressing toward literacy (Clay, 1985). Regardless of their backgrounds, all children are learning about their worlds and how literacy fits into their lives (Taylor, 1983).

Even though all children have important background experiences, they have had various degrees of exposure to books. Some children have participated in thousands of hours of shared reading with caring adults. Other children have had very little experience with books. The amount of experience children have had with books is important in their acquisition of literacy. Most children who have been read to have learned some of the basics of literacy knowledge. They may know that books are for reading, that books open from right to left, where the pictures in books are, what print is used for, and so on. Children need to understand the purpose of books and concepts about print in order for instruction to be effective.

Many young children have learned that print carries meaning, and they know how to open a book and turn the pages. However, many children still do not know the terminology of reading—the concept of a letter, a word, a sentence, or sounds (Johns, 1980). As children begin to learn to read, they need to learn how language operates, that a written word matches a spoken word, that spaces are used between words, and that sentences are set off with punctuation. This literacy knowledge is an important precursor to independent reading.

When children do not know concepts about print, they need instruction in those concepts. Children need a solid base of literacy knowledge in order to firmly grasp other aspects of the reading process. The following teaching strategies, ideas, and activities provide suggestions that promote children's literacy knowledge.

TEACHING STRATEGY 1   Book Demonstrations

The object of Book Demonstrations is to introduce children to concepts about print. Many children are unfamiliar with book parts, how books are read, and the relationship between words and speech. Providing children with explicit instruction about the parts of books can help them increase their literacy knowledge.

DIRECTIONS

1. Choose a Big Book to read to children. Before reading, identify some concepts about print that you want to introduce. Some of the concepts that children need to learn are the following:

   • a book is for reading
   • the front and the back of a book
   • the top and the bottom of a book
   • pages turn from right to left
   • the difference between print and pictures
   • print carries meaning
   • pictures on a page are related to what the print says
   • print is read from left to right
   • print is read from top to bottom
   • where one begins reading on a page
   • what a title of a book is
   • what an author is
   • what an illustrator is

2. Introduce the concept. For example, you might show children where the top of the book is and where the bottom of the book is. Read the story. After reading, reinforce the concept you introduced by asking children to point to the top of the book and the bottom of the book.

3. Spend several sessions each week introducing concepts about print. At each session, review the previous lesson that you taught. Some children require many exposures to print before they increase their literacy knowledge.

TEACHING STRATEGY 2	What Can You Show Us?

What Can You Show Us? (Richgels, Poremba, & McGee, 1996) is a strategy that uses story reading with children's exploration of text to help them increase their literacy knowledge. When children use meaningful text to discover concepts about print, they are apt to be engaged in personal learning. What Can You Show Us? allows teachers to reinforce children's discoveries and guide them into learning about books, words, and print.

DIRECTIONS

1. Select a Big Book to read to the children or write a dictated story on the chalkboard or on chart paper. Preview the story by telling the children that there is a new story on the chalkboard or on the easel. Tell them to look at the story during the day.

2. After children have had time to look at the story, direct their attention to the text by asking them to talk with each other about what they see. Then point out the title of the story, the author's name, and the cover illustration.

3. Before reading the story, ask the children, "What Can You Show Us?" Invite a child to come to the front and show the class something about the text. After the first child has identified something about the story, have other children repeat the process. Children may identify letters, words, or pictures, or they may tell the other children something about the book. Encourage all responses.

4. Read the story to the children. Then reinforce what the children noticed by repeating things they have said. For example, if a child points to the title of the story *Where the Wild Things Are* (Sendak, 1963), point to the title and repeat it. If a child has pointed to a letter, have the children identify that letter in other words or on other pages of the story. If there is a concept that you want the children to notice, an excla-

mation point, for example, tell children that you also have noticed something. Show children the element you want to introduce.

5. Tell children that there are many things about stories that they can notice on their own. Have the story available so that children can look at it after you have finished the lesson. Repeat this strategy often until children become familiar with concepts related to books.

Ideas and Activities

1. Sit with a small group of children. Hand little books to each of the children. Explain that the spines of books are on the left and that books open from the right. Have children identify their left hand. You might do this by showing them that the thumb and index finger on their left hand form an L shape. Have them place the spine of the book in the curve of their left thumb and index finger. Then have them open the book.

2. Explain that when you read a book you turn pages from right to left. After children have placed a book with the spine to the left, have them practice turning pages of the book. Encourage them to turn one page at a time. Show children that each page is different and that they will need to look at each page when reading.

3. Give children books to read. Tell them that most books begin with a word. Have them identify the first word in the book. Then explain that books have an ending word. Have children identify the last word in the book.

4. Help children identify the top and bottom of books by giving them picture books. Arrange several picture books on a table. Ask children to pick up a book and open it to a picture. Tell them that they should be able to identify the subject of the picture. Have them tell you what the picture shows. Explain that when a book is held correctly, they will be able to tell what the picture is about.

5. Gather together paper, pencils, and crayons. Staple the paper so that it is in book form. Sit with a small group of children. Explain that you will be showing the children how to write a book. Have one child dictate a title. Show children where to place the title on the cover of the book. Then open to the first page and have another child dictate a sentence. Write the sentence on the first page. Show children where the sentence belongs and discuss where they could draw a picture. Continue writing several sentences. Show children how to turn the pages and write the book from beginning to end. Then have children illustrate the pages. When the book is complete, read it to the children.

6. Print children's names on index cards and show one of them to the children. Point to a child's first name, say it, and then point to the child's last name and say it. Show the children the space that separates the first and last names by pointing to them. Tell the children that there are two words on the card. Frame each word with your hands. Have children frame their first name and then their last name on their index card. Give each child the index card with his or her name on it.

7. Have children dictate a story or use a sentence from a Big Book. Write the sentence on heavy paper or tagboard. Read the sentence aloud. Then cut the sentence apart at each word. Have children put the words together and place them in a pocket chart to make up the sentence. Read the sentence together noting how the words make up a sentence.

8. Write a sentence on the chalkboard or on chart paper. Make word cards that match the words in the sentence. Give the word cards to several children. Ask children to find the word in the sentence that matches their word card. Tell children that they have a word and that the words together make up a sentence. Point to the beginning capital letter and the ending punctuation mark. Then have children read the entire sentence.

9. Read books to children several times each day. With each reading, remind children of one of the concepts about print.

10. Read a story to the children. Write all of the words from a sentence in the story on sentence strips. Then cut them apart so that each word and punctuation mark is separate. Have each child hold one of the words or punctuation cards. Have children rearrange themselves to make up the sentence.

11. Explain that after each word there should be a space to show where the word stops and the next word begins. Use a book to show children how spaces are used between words in stories. Explain that spaces between words should be the same size. Have children write their own stories. Their writing will probably use developmental spelling. After children write, have them place their index finger or a pencil after each word to determine whether they have included spaces in their writing.

12. Practice counting words (Cunningham, 1995). Give children 10 counters (plastic disks, paper squares, raisins, or anything similar) in a paper cup. Start by counting some familiar objects in the room such as bulletin boards, doors, or plants. Have children place one of their counters on their desks as you point to each object. Be sure children return their counters to their cup at the end of each count. Then tell children that you can also count words by putting down a counter for each said word. Model the process with the sentence "Today is Tuesday." First, say the sentence naturally. Then say the sentence slowly, pausing after each word, so children can put down a counter for each word. Ask children how many words you said. Proceed to other sentences, capitalizing on children's interests. As children begin to understand that words can be counted, invite them to offer their own sentences. They should say the sentence twice, once in the normal way and then one word at a time.

13. When reading from a Big Book or from sentences on the chalkboard, move your hand from left to right underneath the print. Explain that when reading you need to read the words at the left first, then read to the right one word at a time. Show children how to move to the next line of print. Slowly show children how to track print. After you have modeled the left to right progression of print, help children track their own reading from left to right by guiding their hands as they read. Encourage young children to read with a moving hand until they no longer need to physically track words.

14. Write a sentence on the chalkboard or on chart paper. Read the sentence to the children, moving your hand under the words as you read. Explain that the sentence is made up of words. Read the sentence slowly. Then have the children clap their hands one time for every word you say.

Picture Books

Baker, J. (1991). *Window.* New York: Greenwillow.

Carle, E. (1974). *My very first book of shapes.* New York: Crowell.

Collington, P. (1995). *The tooth fairy.* New York: Knopf.

Eastman, P.D. (1960). *Are you my mother?* New York: Random House.

Keats, E.J. (1962). *The snowy day.* New York: Viking.

Rohmann, E. (1994). *Time flies.* New York: Crown.

Sendak, M. (1963). *Where the wild things are.* New York: Harper & Row.

Sis, P. (1992). *Ocean world.* New York: Greenwillow.

Media and Technology

Electro Dog CD-ROM (words for children to match as they read).
UPDATA (800-882-2844)

Lion King Animated Storybook CD-ROM (interactive story of Lion King).
UPDATA (800-882-2844)

Stickybear's Reading Room CD-ROM (bilingual program with activities in word matching and word finding).
UPDATA (800-882-2844)

The Little Turtle CD-ROM (interactive story with audiovisual effects).
UPDATA (800-882-2844)

Professional Resources

Clay, M.M. (1985). *The early detection of reading difficulties* (3rd ed.). Portsmouth, NH: Heinemann.

Holdaway, D. (1979). *The foundations of literacy.* Sydney: Ashton Scholastic.

McGee, L.M., & Richgels, D.J. (1996). *Literacy's beginnings: Supporting young readers and writers* (2nd ed.). Boston: Allyn and Bacon.

3.6 Phonemic Awareness

Goal To help children become aware of the sounds in spoken words.

Assessments Auditory Discrimination 2.5 and 4.5; Rhyme Detection 2.6 and 4.6; Phoneme Segmentation 2.8 and 4.8

BACKGROUND

Phonemic awareness is the ability to segment and manipulate sounds in words. Children who have phonemic awareness skills are able to recognize when words rhyme, can hear isolated sounds of words, can segment words into their sounds, and can blend the sounds together into words. Phonemic awareness is strongly related to success in reading and is a powerful predictor of reading achievement (Adams, 1990). In order to benefit from phonics instruction, students require a basic level of phonemic awareness. However, some children do not naturally learn how sounds form words.

Because phonemic awareness is the ability to hear the sounds in words, phonemic awareness activities generally should precede formal instruction in phonics. Children who are unable to identify words that rhyme, for example, may be hindered in learning the sound-symbol relationships that are a foundation of phonics instruction. In addition, children who do not understand that words are made up of sounds can often profit from instruction in phonemic awareness.

The activities that are necessary to teach children how to become aware of the sounds in language may not seem like real teaching. Instead, they may just seem fun. However, these types of activities are appropriate and necessary for children to learn how to decode words and read independently. When you provide children with instruction in phonemic awareness skills, they will most likely improve their ability to hear sounds in words, which is a foundation for later reading development (Gillam & van Kleeck, 1996).

The teaching strategies, activities, and ideas that follow emphasize oral language activities that support phonemic awareness. As you teach children how to hear the sounds in our language, you should be aware of children's progress. Through informal assessment, you can judge whether children are able to hear sounds and rhymes. As you notice children's proficiency with hearing rhymes, sounds in isolation, and blended sounds, teach transition strategies that emphasize sounds but begin to introduce letters. After you introduce letters with phonemic awareness activites, you can begin the teaching of phonics so that children will begin to associate letters with sounds.

TEACHING STRATEGY 1	I Spy Rhymes

One of the foundational skills for establishing how language works is the ability to identify rhyming words. Being able to hear word rhymes helps children develop an understanding that word families can represent the same sound in different words. The strategy I Spy Rhymes helps children listen for and identify rhyming words.

1. Read a book or poem aloud that contains several rhyming words. Tell children that they should be listening for words that rhyme. Remind children that rhyming words will sound alike. Say a rhyming word pair such as *bike* and *like*. Tell children that *bike* and *like* rhyme because they have the same ending sound.

2. Reread the story or poem. Draw children's attention to the words that rhyme.

3. Read a second story or poem. Tell children that when they hear a rhyming word pair, they should stand and say, "I spy _____ and _____." The children should say the rhyming word pair as in "I spy *bike* and *like*."

4. Most stories or poems that you read will have several different rhyming words. Allow children to say all of the rhymes. If they miss some, reread the story or poem emphasizing the rhymes that were not heard.

5. Repeat the activity several times each week until the children are able to identify rhyming words.

TEACHING STRATEGY 2	**Sound Boxes**

Sound Boxes help children segment the sounds in a word. Sound Boxes were originally developed by Elkonin (1973) and can be used to help young children develop phonemic awareness. When children use Sound Boxes, they learn that words are made up of phonemes, or sounds, and that most words contain more than one sound.

DIRECTIONS

1. Select words that are familiar to children. Prepare cards with simple illustrations along with a matrix that contains a box for each sound in the word. Note that the boxes represent each sound, not necessarily each letter. Secure sufficient counters (plastic, chips, pennies, beans) for each child. An example of a picture with sound boxes follows.

2. Slowly say the word represented by the picture and push the counters one sound at a time into the boxes. Model the process a second time. Invite the children to say the word as you move the counters. For example, if you are using the sound box for the word *duck,* say the word and then the sounds as in this example: "Duck. /d/ /u/ /k/." As you say the first sound, /d/, move a counter into the first box. Then say /u/ and move a second counter into the second box. Finally, say the sound /k/ and move the counter into the third box. Remember to say the sounds, not the letters, of the word.

3. Provide another example and begin to transfer the responsibility of identifying the sounds to the children. Encourage children to identify the picture and to pronounce the word carefully and deliberately. The goal is to emphasize each sound without distorting the word and to put a counter in each box while saying each sound.

4. After children have learned how to use sound boxes, eliminate the boxes below the pictures and have children move the sound counters to the bottom of the picture.

TEACHING STRATEGY 3	Put It Together

Children who are able to sound out words successfully are usually able to blend the sounds associated with the letters into a word. Blending sounds is one of the components of phonemic awareness and is an important skill for beginning readers (Ericson & Juliebo, 1998). The strategy Put It Together helps children learn how to blend sounds into words.

DIRECTIONS

1. Explain that you will be saying a word by its sounds. If you have a puppet available, say that the puppet only likes to say whole words. Tell children that you will be saying the sounds of the word and that the puppet will say the whole word.

2. Tell children to listen carefully as you say the sounds of the word. Then say the sounds of a word such as /l/ /u/ /n/ /ch/ for the word *lunch.* Have the children put the word together by blending the sounds into a whole word. If the children say the word correctly, have the puppet repeat the word.

3. After children are able to blend sounds, try the strategy with other words.

TEACHING STRATEGY 4	Break and Make

Another phonemic awareness component is the ability to manipulate sounds by substituting one sound for another in a word. The strategy Break and Make gives children practice making new words from an initial word and hearing the difference between the words. Children are asked to break up a word and make a new word. As children break and make words, they hear the sounds in word families. You can use letter tiles with the Break and Make strategy if the children are ready to begin the transition from hearing sounds in words to understanding that the sounds they hear are associated with letters. In this activity, however, emphasize sound substitution, not the letter-sound correspondence.

DIRECTIONS

1. Identify a word from a word family that has easily identifiable sounds. (You can find word families in Appendix B.) Write the word on the chalkboard, a piece of chart paper, or an overhead transparency. Then form the word with manipulatives such as letter cards or tiles. Display the word for the children.

2. Read the word aloud. Say the word slowly and deliberately. Then have the children say the word with you. Repeat the word several times.

3. Tell children that you will make a new word from the first word by changing one letter. Break the word apart by scrambling the letter cards or tiles. Replace a letter from the word. For example, if your first word was *book* and you changed the first letter to *l,* you would have the word *look.* If the first word was *can* and you changed the last letter to *t,* the new word would be *cat.* Say the words as you change them. Have the children say the new words with you. Explain that some words are different only in one sound and that children need to listen to words carefully to distinguish between the sounds in words.

4. Invite children to participate in the Break and Make strategy using various word families.

Ideas and Activities to Develop Rhyme

1. Read rhyming books or nursery rhymes to children every day. Reread many of the children's favorites several times. As children become familiar with specific rhymes, have them say the rhymes along with you as you read.

2. Call on children whose names have many rhyming words such as *Mike* and *Pam*. Say a word that rhymes with one of the names. Have children repeat the word along with the name that rhymes with it as in *Mike* and *spike*.

3. Tell children that you are going to say three rhyming words. Say three words that rhyme such as *run, fun,* and *bun*. Tell children that you want them to listen carefully to the words and then think of more words that rhyme with the words that you said. For example, children could say the words *sun* and *spun*. If children make up a word, tell them that they need to think of words that everyone knows. Repeat this activity several times each week with different rhyming words.

4. Help children hear the difference between words that rhyme and words that do not rhyme. Say three words, two of which rhyme. For example, say *sail, mail,* and *made*. Have children say the three words with you. Then ask children which two words rhyme.

5. Sing or chant songs that contain rhyming words. Some songs that work well are *Five Little Monkeys, The Wheels on the Bus, The Name Game, A Hunting We Will Go, This Old Man,* and *The Ants Go Marching*. Sing or chant songs several times a day. After singing, point out some of the rhyming words.

6. Have a group of children act out their favorite nursery rhyme. Have the other children guess the name of the rhyme. Then have all of the children say the rhyme aloud.

7. Say a word that has many rhyming words such as *day*. Have children brainstorm words that rhyme with the original word such as *may, say, ray,* and *pay*. When possible, have children draw pictures of several of the words that rhyme with the original word.

8. Have children create silly rhyming names for characters in their favorite books or for their pets. For example, Clifford the Big Red Dog could be named Bifford. Encourage children to have fun with rhymes.

9. Have children sit in a circle. Say a rhyming word such as *spin*. Throw a soft ball to one of the children. The child who catches the ball should say a word that rhymes with *spin* such as *win*. That child should toss the ball to another child or back to you. The person who has the ball should think of another rhyme. Continue until no one can think of additional words that rhyme with the original word. Then begin with a new word.

Ideas and Activities for Sound Blending

1. Tell the children that you are thinking of an animal. Give them a sound clue, segmenting each of the sounds of the word and saying the sounds slowly and deliberately. If the animal is a wolf, for example, say the sounds /w/ /o/ /l/ /f/. Ask children to blend the sounds together to tell you the name of the animal. Then repeat the process with the name of another animal.

2. Read a rhyming book to the children. After reading a rhyme, read a pair of rhyming words. Segment the words between the onset and rime and have the children blend the words together.

3. Collect pictures from magazines that have a subject that is identifiable to children. For example, a picture of a dog would be one that children could identify. Cut the picture into the number of sounds in the word. For example, cut the picture of the dog into three pieces. Have children put the picture puzzle together saying the sounds of the subject of the picture.

4. Tell children that you will be saying the sounds of a word and they will need to guess the word and draw a picture of it. Give children paper and crayons. Then say a word that can easily be drawn such as *bat*. Say the sounds in the word *bat*, /b/ /a/ /t/. Have children draw a bat. Repeat this activity with other words.

5. When you have an extra minute between activities or when your class is lining up to leave the room, say the sounds of a word that you have used during class. If you have been discussing wind in a lesson on the weather, for example, say the sounds /w/ /i/ /n/ /d/. Have the children blend the sounds to form the word *wind*.

6. Sing or chant songs that could be adapted as a blending activity. For example, adapt the song *Bingo* (Ericson & Juliebo, 1998). Sing or chant the song using the sounds of the child's name. Then repeat the name you used in the song. Tell children that the sounds can be put together to make a name. Repeat with another child's name. An example of the song follows.

   There was a teacher
   who had a student
   And Maria was her name
   /M/ /ar/ /i/ /a/, /M/ /ar/ /i/ /a/, /M/ /ar/ /i/ /a/
   And Maria was her name.

7. Say word parts of compound words such as *base* and *ball* for *baseball*. Have two children stand in front of the room. Tell the children that baseball has two word parts. Have the first child say the first word, *base,* and the second child say the second word, *ball.* Tell children that some words have two words in them and that they should listen for words within other words.

8. Place several objects in a bag or a box. Select one object. Say the name of the object and say, "I see a carrot." Say the word in its syllables or individual sounds. Have the children blend the sounds of the word together and say the word.

Ideas and Activities for Sound Isolation

1. Say a child's name. Have the children repeat the name with you clapping with the number of syllables. For example, say the name *Kristen*. Clap two times, one for each syllable. Say the names of other children who have two-syllable names. Have children clap with you as you say the names. Repeat with names of one syllable, three syllables, and so on.

2. Ask children to listen to you saying three words: *kite, kitten,* and *Ken*. Tell children that these words begin with the same sound, the sound /k/. Tell children that you will be saying three more words and that they should listen for the beginning sound. Say three more words and have children tell you the sound that they hear. As children become proficient at hearing beginning sounds, repeat the activity using ending sounds.

3. Tell children that you will be saying a sound and that they should think of as many words that begin (or end) with that sound as they can. Say a sound (not a letter) such as /s/ for the letter *s*. Have children think of words that begin with that sound.

4. Say words that have parts that are the same or different such as the words *ball* and *tall*. Have children say the words with you. Ask children which parts of the words are the same and which parts are different. Guide children to understand that the sounds /b/ and /t/ are different but the sound /all/ is the same in both words. Repeat using other pairs of words.

5. Read books of rhymes to children. After reading, say two of the rhyming words. Have children say the rhyming words with you several times. After children have said the rhymes, ask them which of the sounds are alike in the rhymes and which are different.

6. Sing the song "What's the Sound?" to the tune of "Old MacDonald Had A Farm" (Yopp, 1992). Use different sounds each time you sing the song. An example of a verse follows.

What's the sound that starts these words:
baby, ball, and bed?
/b/ is the sound that starts these words:
baby, ball, and bed.
With a /b/ /b/ here, and a /b/ /b/ there,
here a /b/, there a /b/, everywhere a /b/ /b/.
/b/ is the sound that starts these words:
baby, ball, and bed.

Ideas and Activities for Sound Substitution

1. Have children select a sound of the day, such as the sound /m/, and then say each of their names with that sound in place of the first sound (Yopp, 1992). Children should say Mina for Gina, Merry for Jerry, and so on.

2. Write the letters of the alphabet on large index cards and place them on a table. Say a word such as *turtle.* Have a child choose a letter from the stack on the table. Say the word *turtle,* beginning with the letter sound the child has chosen. Enjoy the fun of creating nonsense words. Repeat the activity with a new letter sound.

3. Have children create a page for a picture book with words that rhyme. For example, say the word *clown* and have children draw a picture of a *clown.* Then say the word *town* and have children draw a picture of a *town.* Repeat with other rhyming words as in *down* and *frown.* Have children read their books of rhyming words. Point out that the rhyming words have different beginning sounds but the same ending sounds. Create other pages with different rhyming words.

4. Play a consonant riddle game. Say a word such as bunny. Then present the riddle by saying, "What rhymes with bunny but starts with an /f/?" Have children guess what the word is.

5. Tell children that you want them to listen to the sounds in the words that you say. Tell them that you'll be switching one of the sounds. Say a pair of words with one sound switched. You might switch the beginning consonants as in *hill* and *Bill,* you might switch the vowels such as *ball* and *bell,* or you might switch the ending sounds as in *game* and *gate.* After saying the new words, have the children say them with you. Continue with several pairs of words.

6. Tell children that you will be singing a song that they know but that you will be changing some of the words (Yopp, 1992). Write a section of a song on the chalkboard or an overhead transparency. Sing or chant the song as it was written. Then suggest a new sound to use to sing the song. Sing the song with the new sound. Repeat with additional verses. The following song is sung to the tune of *Someone's in the Kitchen with Dinah.*

I have a song that we can sing
I have a song I know.
I have a song that we can sing
Strumming on the old banjo.

Fe-Fi-Fiddly-i-o
Fe-Fi-Fiddly-i-o
Fe-Fi-Fiddly-i-o
Strumming on the old banjo.

Ke-Ki-Kiddly-i-o
Ke-Ki-Kiddly-i-o
Ke-Ki-Kiddly-i-o
Strumming on the old banjo.

Books of Nursery Rhymes

dePaola, T. (1985). *Tomie dePaola's Mother Goose.* New York: Putnam.

Lansky, B. (1993). *The new adventures of Mother Goose: Gentle rhymes for happy times.* Deerhaven, MN: Meadowbrook.

Lobel, A. (1986). *The Random House book of Mother Goose.* New York: Random House.

Prelutsky, J. (1986). *Read-aloud rhymes for the very young.* New York: Alfred A. Knopf.

Provenson, A., & Provenson, M. (1977). *Old Mother Hubbard.* New York: Random House.

Watson, C. (1971). *Father Fox's penny rhymes.* New York: Thomas Y. Crowell.

Media and Technology

A Silly, Noisy House CD-ROM (animated toy box with sound effects, songs, and rhymes). UPDATA (800-882-2844)

Allie's Playhouse CD-ROM (learning activities including 16 sing-along nursery rhymes). UPDATA (800-882-2844)

Children's Treasury of Stories, Nursery Rhymes, and Songs CD-ROM (interactive multimedia collection of stories, nursery rhymes, and songs). UPDATA (800-882-2844)

Professional Resources

Adams, M.J., Foorman, B.R., Lundberg, I., & Beeler, T. (1998). *Phonemic awareness in young children: A classroom curriculum.* Baltimore, MD: Paul H. Brookes.

Catts, H., & Vartiainen, T. (1993). *Sounds abound.* East Moline, IL: Lingui Systems.

Dowell, R.I. (1992). *Let's talk: Performance rhymes.* Terre Haute, IN: Pollyanna Productions.

Ericson, L., & Juliebo, M.F. (1998). *The phonological awareness handbook for kindergarten and primary teachers.* Newark, DE: International Reading Association.

Yopp, H.K., & Yopp, R.H. (1997). *Oo-pples and Boo-noo-noos: Songs and activities for phonemic awareness.* Orlando, FL: Harcourt Brace.

3.7	**Alphabet Knowledge**

Goal To help children learn the names of the letters of the alphabet.

Assessments Alphabet Knowledge 2.7 and 4.7

BACKGROUND

Children learn much about reading through oral language activities. They learn the sounds of the language and how words form sentences. Children can even read some familiar words before learning the individual letters of the alphabet. As children learn about written language, they learn that language is made up of sounds, words, and sentences. Consider the young child who can identify a stop sign without knowing the names of the individual letters. Environmental print such as a stop sign is familiar to children. When children see words repeatedly, they can learn the words, even though they don't know the names of the letters in the words.

As children learn about the nature of language, however, they need to be directed to learn the names of the letters of the alphabet and to distinguish one letter from another. Learning the names of the letters of the alphabet is a developmental process. Children first need to understand about the sounds of language before they are ready to learn the alphabet. Letter names have little meaning to children before they possess some knowledge about language (Morrow, 1997).

Children need to know the letters of the alphabet to become independent readers (Ehri, 1987). As children progress beyond becoming aware of the sounds of language such as rhyming words, they need to be able to distinguish among the letters so that they can learn how to read unknown words. It is unrealistic to think that a young reader could learn enough sight words to be able to read a new story. Therefore, children need to learn that words are made up of letters, and they need to learn the names of the letters of the alphabet.

There are many approaches to teaching the alphabet. Some teachers introduce a letter a week throughout the school year. Others teach letters in the context of words and stories. There is not one right way to teach the alphabet, although some experts believe that teaching the letters of the alphabet in context is more meaningful for children (Morrow, 1997). The following teaching strategies, activities, and ideas will assist your teaching the letters of the alphabet.

TEACHING STRATEGY 1	**Using Alphabet Books**

Alphabet books are books that have letters arranged in sequential order from A through Z. There are many attractive alphabet books available on a large number of topics. Reading alphabet books to children helps them become familiar with the names of the letters in alphabetical order. Alphabet books also provide a wide range of words that start with each letter in the alphabet, which helps children learn how to associate a letter with a number of words.

DIRECTIONS

1. Choose an alphabet book to read to children. Most libraries have a large collection of alphabet books. A short list of alphabet books can be found in the Selected Resources: Alphabet Knowledge. For a more complete listing of over 100 alphabet books, refer to Appendix B in Johns and Lenski (1997).

2. Show the children the cover of the book and read the title to them. Tell them that this book will have the letters of the alphabet and that it will be about a specific topic. Tell them what the topic of the book is. For example, *Alphabears* (Hague, 1984) is a book that shows different bears with names that begin with the letters of the alphabet in alphabetical order.

3. Before reading, invite children to recite the letters of the alphabet with you.

4. Read the alphabet book, making note of any special features. Point out that each page has a letter of the alphabet in alphabetical order.

5. After reading the book, have children recite the letters of the alphabet in order. Provide assistance as needed.

6. After reading the book several times, have children read along with you.

7. Tape record the book and place the book and the tape in a listening center for children to listen to during free time.

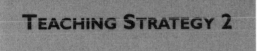

| TEACHING STRATEGY 2 | Letter Actions |

Young children tend to be very active, so the strategy Letter Actions (Cunningham, 1995) has great appeal for most children. The strategy Letter Actions entails identifying an action word that begins with a specific letter and associating that letter with the action. When children are able to associate an action with the name of a letter, they more readily learn the letters of the alphabet.

DIRECTIONS

1. Identify the name of a letter that you want to teach. Write the name of a letter on one side of a large index card.

2. For each letter, think of an action that students could perform in your classroom or outside. List the action on the reverse side of the index card. For example, if you wanted to teach the letter *n*, you could write *nod* on the reverse side of the card.

3. Show students the side of the card that has the name of the letter written on it. Say the name of the letter. Have the children repeat the letter name.

4. Tell students that they will be performing an action that begins with that letter. Show them the side of the card with the action written on it. Read the action.

5. Have the children perform the action while saying the name of the letter. Reinforce the association by repeating the same action card more than once.

6. After the children have learned several letters and actions, have a child choose a card and lead the class in performing the action.

7. The following is a sample list of actions that can be used in conjunction with Letter Actions.

argue	itch	run
bounce	jump	sit
catch	kick	talk
dance	laugh	unbend
eat	march	vacuum
fall	nod	walk
gallop	open	xylophone (play)
hop	paint	yawn
	quack	zip

TEACHING STRATEGY 3 — Identifying Letters

Children need to learn the letters of the alphabet in proper order, and they also need to learn how to identify letters in the context of words. Some children will have difficulty making the link from saying the letters of the alphabet to identifying letters in combination with other letters to form words. To help them learn letters in the context of words, point out letters in Big Books, the Morning Message, or their names. Guiding children to identify letters in print will help them learn how to read.

DIRECTIONS

1. Choose a story, morning message, or one of the children's names to teach children how to identify letters. The story can be one that you read to the children, a dictated story, or a Big Book with which the children are familiar.

2. Read the story, message, or name aloud to the children. Then have the children read it with you.

3. Place letter cards on the table in front of you. Have a child choose a letter from the stack.

4. Have the child identify the letter. If the letter is a *d*, for example, the child should say *d*.

5. Ask the children to locate any letter in the story that matches the letter chosen by the child. In this case, children should look for the letter *d*. Have one child at a time come up to point out examples of the letter in the story. If the story does not have that particular letter, the child should replace the letter in the stack and choose another letter.

6. Repeat until most of the letters of the alphabet have been chosen.

Ideas and Activities

1. Teach children the alphabet song. Sing the song several times each day. As you sing, point to the letters in the alphabet. The letters could be on a wall chart, on the chalkboard, or in an alphabet book. As children become familiar with the alphabet song, invite a child to help you point to each letter as you sing.

2. Place a layer of sand in a small container. Have children trace the letters of the alphabet in the sand.

3. Play Letter Bingo. Give each child a card filled with letters of the alphabet and markers to cover the letters. Call a letter and hold up a card with the letter on it. Have children find the letter on their Bingo card. The first child to cover a row gets Bingo.

4. Create an alphabet path on the floor of your room. Write each letter of the alphabet on a large piece of construction paper. Laminate the pieces of paper, weave them around your room, and tape them to the floor. Have students walk on the alphabet path saying the letters of the alphabet as they walk.

5. Distribute alphabet cards to each child. Give each child one card. Call out a letter. Ask the child holding that letter to stand and repeat the name of the letter. Then ask children to say a word that begins with that letter.

6. Provide the children with letter snacks. As you introduce a letter, give children a snack whose name begins with that letter. For example, when you teach the letter A, provide each child with a piece of apple.

7. Place a handful of alphabet cereal on a napkin on each child's desk. Have students sort the cereal letters in alphabetical order. Give children plain round or square cereal to mark the place of letters that are not in the cereal pile. Tell children that if they have more than one of the same letter, they should place the duplicate letters in a row.

8. Write the name of a letter on the chalkboard with a wet sponge or paintbrush. Have children call out the name of the letter before the water evaporates and the letter disappears.

9. Distribute copies of newspapers or pages from magazines to each child. Identify a letter and have children circle the letter wherever they find it on a particular part of the page.

10. Give children a journal that has a letter of the alphabet on each page. After introducing a letter, have children practice writing the letter on that page. Have children frequently page through the book saying the letters of the alphabet.

11. Spell out a child's name with letter cards or plastic letters. Use all upper case letters. Have the child use lower case letters to match the upper case letters. Scramble the top row and have the child unscramble the letters to form the correct spelling of the name.

12. Create letter posters by brainstorming words that start with a specific letter. After introducing a letter, have children think of words that start with that letter. If children are unable to correctly identify words beginning with that letter, provide several words for them. Write the words with different color markers or crayons. Display the posters in the classroom or bind them into a class alphabet book.

13. Create an alphabet center in your classroom. Stock the center with plastic letters for word building, letters to trace, alphabet puzzles and games, alphabet books, alphabet stamps, and alphabet flash cards. Allow children time to use the materials in the center on a regular basis.

14. Place a set of five to seven pairs of alphabet cards face down on a table. You should have two cards for each letter. Have children turn over two cards at a time saying the names of the letters. If the cards match, children keep them. If the cards do not match, have children replace the cards. The object is to match pairs of alphabet cards.

Alphabet Books

Agard, J. (1989). *The calypso alphabet.* New York: Henry Holt.

Aylesworth, J. (1992). *Old black fly.* New York: Henry Holt.

Base, G. (1986). *Animalia.* New York: Harry N. Abrams.

Calmenson, S. (1994). *It begins with an A.* New York: Hyperion.

Ehlert, L. (1989). *Eating the alphabet: Fruits and vegetables from A to Z.* San Diego, CA: Harcourt.

Hague, K. (1984). *Alphabears: An ABC book.* New York: Henry Holt.

Lear, E. (1992). *A was once an apple.* Cambridge, MA: Candlewick Press.

Lobel, A. (1994). *Away from home.* New York: Greenwillow.

Murphy, C. (1997). *Alphabet magic.* New York: Simon & Schuster.

Palolotta, J. (1990). *The frog alphabet book.* Chicago: Children's Press.

Park, J. (1995). *My first alphabet.* New York: Oxford Children's Press.

Shannon, G. (1996). *Tomorrow's alphabet.* New York: Greenwillow.

Viorst, J. (1994). *The alphabet from Z to A.* New York: Atheneum.

Media and Technology

Animal Alphabet CD-ROM (cartoon animation of alphabet).
UPDATA (800-882-2844)

Curious George Learns the Alphabet CD-ROM (animated letters with Curious George).
UPDATA (800-882-2844)

Letters of the Alphabet Program (Big Books, audiotapes, alphabet strips).
Phoenix Learning Resources (800-221-1274)

The Big Bug Alphabet Book CD-ROM (children learn the ABCs at a circus).
UPDATA (800-882-2844)

Professional Resources

Cunningham, P.M., & Allington, R.L. (1994). *Classrooms that work: They all can read & write.* New York: HarperCollins.

Sorrow, B.H., & Lumpkin, B.S. (1996). *CD-ROMs for librarians and educators: A guide to over 800 instructional resources* (2nd ed.). Jefferson, NC: McFarland.

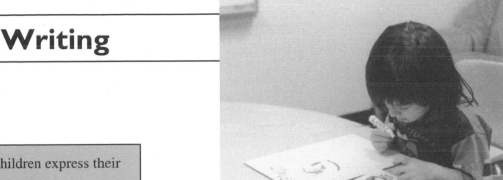

3.8 Writing

Goal   To help children express their
ideas in writing.

Assessments   Writing 2.9 and 4.9

BACKGROUND

Young children learn to write as they read, write, and explore language and writing materials. Scribbles and drawing are a child's first venture into writing, and they serve as an important foundation for later writing development (Calkins, 1986). Young children need the opportunity to explore, scribble, pretend to write, invent messages, copy important words, write labels, and write messages for their own purposes (Clay, 1975). Exploration is essential for young children to develop an understanding and awareness of writing and its forms and uses. Wide reading is also an important component of early writing development because it helps children learn about language, story structure, and print conventions in meaningful contexts. Children also learn a great deal about letter-sound associations in conjunction with their attempts at writing (Strickland, 1998). As children gain more experience with writing, they will begin to write in different forms, and their spelling development will also progress from developmental toward conventional spelling (Vacca, Vacca, & Gove, 1995).

Writing is a process that involves children in a variety of activities. Graves (1983) describes writing as a series of recursive steps that children cycle through while writing. The steps include prewriting, drafting, revising, editing, and publishing. Because writing is a recursive process, children will not necessarily progress through each step of the process in order. Furthermore, young children may only engage in limited work with certain steps such as revising and editing.

Teachers can create classroom environments that support writing development by providing opportunities for children to write on a regular basis, to choose their own personal writing topics, to have easy access to writing materials, to engage in sharing time, to receive responses to their writing, and to engage in wide reading. The following strategies and activities provide suggestions for creating a classroom environment and program that support young children's writing development.

TEACHING STRATEGY 1	Shared Writing

Shared writing provides a framework for children and teachers to compose collaboratively. The teacher acts as the scribe and expert, and the children serve as the apprentices (Routman, 1991). In shared writing, teachers demonstrate writing conventions, think aloud regarding processes they use to write, and invite children to become actively involved in the writing process.

DIRECTIONS

1. Select a predictable story to read to the children. Read and discuss the story.

2. Explain to the children that you will be composing a new version of the story.

3. Invite the children to offer suggestions and ideas for the new version of the book. Record the children's ideas on the chalkboard, an overhead transparency, or a piece of chart paper.

4. Offer prompts to guide the children's thinking and composing. For example, you might say, "I think we need to tell what the boy does next. I will write, *Then the boy.* . . ." Offer these prompts as necessary throughout the shared writing activity.

5. Model use of appropriate writing conventions by using a think-aloud procedure. For example, if you want children to remember to use a capital letter to begin each sentence, you might say, "I'm starting a new sentence. I need to use a capital letter here."

6. Once the children have shared their ideas, engage them in reading the new version of the story.

7. Discuss what revisions need to be made to improve the story. If necessary, use a think-aloud procedure to guide the children in discovering areas for revision and editing. For example, you might ask, "Does this make sense, or do we need to add something here?" or "What do we need to put at the end of a sentence?"

8. Make revisions to the story. Reread the story with the children.

9. Copy the final story onto chart paper and ask the children to illustrate the story. Bind the story and illustrations into a Big Book. Place the Big Book in the classroom library or encourage the children to take it home to share with their parents.

TEACHING STRATEGY 2	Text Tapping

Text Tapping provides a format for helping children write in a specific genre or format. Text Tapping uses children's background knowledge and previous experiences with reading and writing (Turbill, Butler, Cambourne, & Langton, 1991). Children draw on their knowledge about specific genres and language styles to help them write in various formats and styles.

DIRECTIONS

1. Select a familiar nursery rhyme such as "Jack and Jill." Read the nursery rhyme to the children. Discuss it with the children.

2. Write the nursery rhyme on the chalkboard, an overhead transparency, or a piece of chart paper. Read and reread the nursery rhyme with the children.

3. Inform the children that they will be writing their own versions of "Jack and Jill."

4. Provide a frame for "Jack and Jill" with several pieces of text deleted. For example, you may present children with the following frame.

    Jack and Jill went up the hill to fetch _____.

    Jack fell down and _____.

    And Jill came tumbling after.

5. Invite several children to share their ideas.

6. Provide time for children to complete their own versions of "Jack and Jill." Invite children to share their writing. Ask children to illustrate their writing. Display the children's writing on a bulletin board or in the classroom writing center.

7. Provide regular opportunities for children to engage in Text Tapping activities.

Ideas and Activities

1. Use a message board in the classroom to provide meaningful opportunities for children to draw or write to you and to their peers. Consider creating a classroom post office to encourage children to write letters to one another.

2. Provide literacy play centers that involve writing (e.g., restaurant, office, post office, and grocery story). See suggestions for creating literacy play centers in 3.1.

3. Invite children to create "All About Me" books that contain pictures, words, and sentences about themselves. Have children bind the books and share them with their classmates and parents.

4. Create a classroom writing center that contains a variety of writing materials. Provide daily time for children to visit the writing center. A list of suggested materials for a writing center follows.

   ☞ **Suggested Materials for Writing Center**

lined paper	picture dictionaries
unlined paper	children's writing samples
construction paper	binding supplies
pencils	letter stamps
markers	ink pads
pens	interesting pictures
crayons	list of writing topics
note cards	posters with steps in the writing process
stationery	access to word wall words
envelopes	message board
children's typewriter	computer with children's word processing program
rubber stamps	

5. Use a morning sign-in procedure to engage children in daily writing (Richgels, Poremba, & McGee, 1996). For example, at the beginning of the year, children may just sign their names on the sign-in sheet. As their writing develops, you may pose a question for them to answer, such as "Are you going to order hot lunch today?" As the year progresses, you may pose more complex questions that require more detailed responses.

6. Implement journal writing to provide children with meaningful opportunities to write each day. Suggestions for implementing personal journals follow.

   ☞ **Suggestions for Implementing Personal Journals**

   Children record and reflect on personal events and experiences. They may use writing, drawing, or a combination of the two to record their ideas. The purpose of personal journals is to engage children in personally meaningful writing. Some suggestions for implementing personal journals are shared below.

   1. Use a spiral notebook so all entries are kept together. Provide time for children to decorate the covers of their journals to establish ownership.

   2. Provide daily time for personal journal writing/drawing. Younger children will need 5 to 10 minutes, and older children will need 10 to 15 minutes for writing/drawing.

3. While children write/draw in their journals, the teacher should write in a journal to model the importance of journaling.

4. Encourage children to develop their own ideas for journal entries. If children are unable to think of ideas to write about, consult the list of journal prompts provided below.

5. Provide time for children to share their journals if they would like to do so.

7. Help children identify topics for their journals by using open-ended prompts that relate to the children's lives and experiences. A list of suggested journal prompts is provided.

✏️ Journal Prompts

If I had three wishes . . .	The best present I ever got . . .
If I could trade places with the teacher . . .	My favorite food is . . . because . . .
If I could trade places with the principal . . .	My favorite book is . . . because . . .
I laughed so hard when . . .	My favorite animal is . . . because . . .
I felt so sad when . . .	When I grow up, I want to . . .
I felt so nervous when . . .	When I was little, I . . .
I was so excited when . . .	If I could go anywhere I would . . .
I felt so silly when . . .	If I had a million dollars, I would . . .

8. Invite children to make signs, labels, and informative posters for the classroom. Post these materials in the classroom.

9. Establish a cross-age writing project with older children who will assist the younger children with writing and binding books. The older children can take dictation for younger children who are not writing on their own yet.

10. Use shared writing to send letters, thank you notes, and invitations to classroom visitors, guest speakers, parents, and school personnel. A classroom newsletter can also be written using a shared writing format. For more details about using shared writing, consult Teaching Strategy 1 in 3.8.

11. Establish an author's chair so children can share their writing. A rocking chair, tall stool, or other special chair works well for this purpose. When children are ready to share their writing, they should sit in the author's chair while the other children and the teacher gather around to listen.

12. Develop an "Author of the Week" bulletin board to display and celebrate children's writing. Rotate this honor throughout the classroom during the year.

13. Invite children into writing by presenting them with wordless picture books. Ask them to dictate or write the story or a portion of the story told by the pictures. Display their stories with the book. For a list of wordless picture books, see Selected Resources: Sense of Story (at the end of 3.4).

14. Implement a pen-pal program or E-mail key-pal program so children can exchange letters with other children or adults. Internet addresses for identifying E-mail key pals are provided in the following list.

📠 Key-Pal Resources

http://www.siec.k12.in.us/~west/edu/keypal.htm

This site provides detailed directions and links for locating key pals for children. Internet safety tips related to key pals are also provided. By having children connect with key pals, they will practice their reading and writing skills in a meaningful way.

http://www.iwaynet.net/~jwolve/school.html#AAA

This site is the home of the School Pen Pal Exchange. Tips and connections for locating key pals are provided at this site.

15. Engage children in author studies to learn about how and why their favorite authors write. Helpful resources for implementing author studies are provided in Selected Resources: Writing.

16. Provide creative opportunities for children to publish their writing. Possible ideas for publishing children's writing are listed in the box.

Publishing Ideas for Children's Writing

Class books
Class big books
Individual books
Classroom newsletter
Posters
Display in classroom writing center
Classroom bulletin boards
Performances such as plays or puppet shows

Author's chair
Sharing with other classrooms
Intercom reading of children's writing
Mailing letters, cards, and invitations
Posting children's writing on classroom
  or school internet web site
Display in school library
Display in classroom library

Selected Resources
WRITING

Children's Books That Invite Children to Write and Text Tap

Guarino, D. (1989). *Is your mama a llama?* New York: Scholastic.

Numeroff, L.J. (1991). *If you give a moose a muffin.* New York: HarperCollins.

Numeroff, L.J. (1985). *If you give a mouse a cookie.* New York: Harper and Row.

Sendak, M. (1962). *Chicken soup with rice.* New York: Holt, Rinehart and Winston.

Wescott, N.B. (1988). *The lady with the alligator purse.* Boston: Little Brown.

Williams, S. (1990). *I went walking.* San Diego: Harcourt Brace Jovanovich.

Wood, A. (1984). *The napping house.* San Diego: Harcourt Brace Jovanovich.

Media and Technology

Creativity Workshop CD-ROM (word processing and painting program for young children). Arkose (888-389-5500)

Kid Works 2 CD-ROM (word processing, paint program with text-to-speech features). UPDATA (800-882-2844)

Professional Resources

Graves, D. (1994). *A fresh look at writing.* Portsmouth, NH: Heinemann.

Hill, S. (1994). *Books alive!* Winnipeg, Manitoba: Peguis.

Kotch, L., & Zackman, L. (1995). *The author studies handbook.* New York: Scholastic Professional Books.

Kovacs, D., & Preller, J. (1991). *Meet the authors and illustrators* (Vol. 1). New York: Scholastic Professional Books.

Silvey, A. (Ed.). (1995). *Children's books and their creators.* Boston: Houghton Mifflin.

Sunflower, C. (1993). *75 creative ways to publish students' writing.* New York: Scholastic Professional Books.

3.9 Spelling

Goal To help children move from developmental to conventional spelling.

Assessments Writing 2.9 and 4.9; Developmental Spelling 2.10 and 4.10

BACKGROUND

Spelling words correctly is a challenge in any language, but spelling in English is more difficult than in many other languages. English is not a purely phonetic language; there are 26 letters in the English alphabet and 44 sounds (Tompkins, 1998). That means that words are not always spelled the way they sound. There are many historical reasons why English has evolved to become a semiphonetic language. One reason is because English is made up of words from many different languages with different spelling rules. As a result, many English words are difficult to spell correctly.

Even though English is not a completely phonetic language, there are rules, patterns, and relationships that govern the spelling of many of the words. Children need to learn about how letters form words so that they can learn to spell words correctly. A good way for children to learn how to spell is for them to practice spelling through writing.

When young children write, they create or invent their own spellings of words (Read, 1986). For example, when young children write *I love you,* they spell the words using what they know at that time about language. The word *love* is often spelled *l, lv,* or *luv* by young children. This developmental spelling is part of the learning process that children go through as they become conventional spellers.

Developmental spelling is an important part of a child's literacy development. As children experiment with spelling, they are learning how words in English are spelled. There are five stages that children may go through as they use developmental spelling and become conventional spellers (Gentry, 1981). The stages are listed below.

- **Precommunicative spelling**
  Children string letters, numbers, scribbles, and forms together but do not associate the marks with any letter sounds (e.g., *ggh4kesos* for *puppy*).

- **Semiphonetic spelling**
  Children begin to represent letter sounds in words with the appropriate letters. They may have one or two letters correct in a word (e.g., *DG* for *dog*).

- **Phonetic spelling**
  Children spell words as they sound (e.g., *sokar* for *soccer*).

- **Transitional spelling**
  Children use a high percentage of correctly spelled words and the remaining words are spelled using some type of spelling generalization (e.g., *afternewn* for *afternoon*).

- **Conventional spelling**

  Children apply the basic rules of English to spelling and correctly spell 90% of the words they write.

The goal of spelling programs is to give young children practice spelling words and to help children use conventional spelling as soon as possible. With practice spelling and instruction, children should become conventional spellers by the time they reach third or fourth grade (Tompkins, 1998). There are many teaching strategies, ideas, and activities that help children become conventional spellers. A number of them are described below.

TEACHING STRATEGY 1	Have-A-Go

The Have-A-Go Strategy was adapted by Routman (1994) from a spelling strategy used in Australia. Have-A-Go encourages children to identify words that they have written with developmental spelling and to learn how to write those words with conventional spelling. The process children use with the Have-A-Go strategy mirrors the thinking processes writers use as they write with conventional spelling. Writers first spell a word using the best information they have available, determine whether the word is spelled correctly, or try various letter patterns until the word looks correct. Have-a-Go is an ideal strategy for children using developmental spelling or for children who spell most words correctly.

DIRECTIONS

1. Have children write a story using the best spelling they can. Encourage children to spell words using the letters and sounds that they know, even if the word is not spelled correctly.

2. After children have finished writing, distribute Have-A-Go sheets similar to the example that follows.

Have-A-Go Spelling

Original Spelling	First Try	Second Try	Conventional Spelling

3. Ask children to identify three words from their story that they think might not be spelled with conventional spelling. In the first column, have children write the words the way they spelled them in their writing. Move about the group and look at the words the children have selected. Place a checkmark above each letter that is correct in the words the children have written. An example follows.

Have-A-Go Spelling

Original Spelling	First Try	Second Try	Conventional Spelling
✓ ✓ feed			
✓✓ ✓ gonna			
✓✓✓ spais			

4. Have children try to spell the word in the second column, writing the letters that were correct and trying other letter combinations for the word. Move about the group and place checkmarks above the letters in the first try that are correct. If the word is not spelled correctly, have children try to spell the word a second time. If children do not spell the word correctly the second time, write the conventional spelling in the last column. For words that are spelled correctly, congratulate children on spelling with conventional spelling and have them write the word again in the last column. An example follows.

Have-A-Go Spelling

Original Spelling	First Try	Second Try	Conventional Spelling
feed	✓✓ ✓✓✓ freend	✓✓✓✓✓ frend	friend
gonna	✓✓✓ ✓✓ gon to	✓✓✓✓✓ ✓✓ going to	going to
spais	✓✓✓ spas	✓✓✓ ✓ spase	space

5. Have children write the words they have chosen in their spelling dictionary, in a spelling journal, or on a piece of paper for the Word Wall. Tell children that they should try to spell those words with conventional spelling in their writing.

TEACHING STRATEGY 2	Directed Spelling Thinking Activity (DSTA)

The Directed Spelling Thinking Activity (DSTA) (Zutell, 1996) is a strategy that helps children understand some of the patterns in the spelling of words. The underlying belief supporting the DSTA is that children learn how to spell not by memorizing the spelling of words but by learning the concepts of how letters are combined to form words. For example, the concept behind the spelling of the word *bite* is that a word with a long vowel often has a silent *e* at the end of the word. There are other generalizations for long vowels, of course, and children who learn many of the concepts that govern spelling will be able to use these concepts to spell words correctly.

DIRECTIONS

1. Gather a small group of children who have nearly the same spelling ability.

2. Identify words and word patterns that these children may be using but have not mastered. For example, you may find that children do not add a second consonant when adding -*ing* to a word such as *running*.

3. Select a set of 15 to 20 words that have the word pattern that the children need to learn or that are in contrast to the word pattern. In the example of the word *running,* a contrasting word would be *jumping*. When adding -*ing* to the word *jump,* you do not need to double the consonant.

4. Give the children a spelling test on the list of words. Most likely, some of the children will miss several of the words.

5. Identify several words that most of the children spelled incorrectly. Ask the children why they spelled the words as they did and why they thought the words were spelled that way. Allow several minutes for discussion.

6. Using the pattern, show children how to spell the words correctly. After showing two or three examples, encourage children to use the pattern for other words on the list.

7. After children understand the pattern, give them letter cards for two or three of the words on the list. Say one word at a time giving children time to make the words from letter cards.

8. Have children write the words and the word pattern in their spelling journals.

| **TEACHING STRATEGY 3** | **Spelling Workshop** |

Many teachers have implemented reading and writing workshops in their classrooms. The principles behind using a workshop approach toward reading and writing also hold true for spelling (Gentry & Gillet, 1993). Spelling workshops are based on the belief that if children are in control of their learning, they will become more motivated to learn. Spelling workshops can motivate children to learn how to spell and to use conventional spelling in their writing.

DIRECTIONS

1. Have children select their own words to study for a week. These words may be selected from their writing, or they may be words that the children want to learn how to spell. Children in the primary grades should select from four to nine words for the week.

2. After children have selected words to study, add one or two words to their lists that are connected to topics or themes about which the children will be learning that week.

3. Have children list their spelling words in a spelling book or journal.

4. Conduct a focus lesson about ways to learn spelling words. You might introduce various spelling strategies from the Ideas and Activities section.

5. Introduce or review the look-cover-write-check strategy. Have children look at one spelling word at a time, cover the word, and write it on a piece of paper or on a slate. After children have written one word, have them check the correct spelling with their spelling list. If they have spelled the word incorrectly, they should practice writing the word correctly.

6. Have children give each other a final spelling test. Although there are disadvantages to having children give a test, the advantages outweigh the disadvantages for most children. Having children give each other the test frees the teacher from having to give multiple spelling tests. It also makes the children more responsible for their own work. Finally, it gives young readers the opportunity to read a classmate's list of words.

7. Tell children that the words they have chosen and learned should be written correctly in their writing. Encourage children to use their individual spelling lists as they write.

Ideas and Activities

1. Develop a Words-for-Free Chart. Choose five or six words that children frequently use but spell incorrectly. Write the words on a chart and post it on the wall. Add one or two words to the chart each week. As children write or try to spell words, remind them to look on the Words-for-Free Chart.

2. Encourage children to create their own personal spelling dictionary. Have children self-select spelling words that they have learned how to spell. Ask children to review frequently the words they have selected.

3. Use sentences with lined blanks to enhance children's use of spelling strategies (Snowball, 1997). Identify words that children want to learn to spell. Choose one of the words. Write a sentence using the word, but leave a blank where the word would fit. For example, write *The _____ forest is the home of many birds.* Ask children to guess which word would fit in the blank. Have children try to spell the missing

word by using spelling strategies such as sounding, thinking of word patterns, and using memory. After children have correctly spelled the word, use word patterns to spell similar words. For example, the word that fits the sentence, *rain,* has several rhyming words: *Spain, main, pain.*

4. Read rhyming books to children. Words that rhyme often have the same spelling pattern. Point out the words that have similar spelling. Have children practice the new spelling words by writing them in their spelling dictionary.

5. Help children analyze spelling patterns by giving them word clues (Gaskin, Ehri, Cress, O'Hara, & Donnelly, 1997). Identify a spelling word to teach. Write the word on a large index card. On the back of the index card, list spelling clues. Spelling clues could include:

   * The word has _____ sounds.
   * The word has _____ letters.
   * The vowel makes the same sound that you hear in _____.
   * The word begins with the same letter as the word _____.
   * The spelling pattern of the word is _____.

   Say the word and give one clue at a time until children have spelled the word. After children are familiar with the game, develop Word Clue Cards for children to use during independent learning time.

6. Provide children with the opportunity to make their spelling words or word families with letters cut from sandpaper, textured wallpaper, or felt. (See Appendix B for word families.) After they have made the words, have them trace the letters with their hands to get the feel of the spelling.

7. Create a spelling center for your classroom (Gentry, 1998). Include the following items in the spelling center: several books that have repeated spelling patterns, charts of previously taught words, reusable game mats and letter tiles, erasable markers, letter cards, writing journals, student dictionaries, paper, and gold stars. Display on a chart target words that you want children to learn to spell. Have children look for the target words in their writing journals. Tell them to circle all the target words they have found. For every circled word that is spelled correctly, reward children with a gold star. Have children find the words in other books in the spelling center. Then have children practice spelling target words with letter tiles, markers, or letter cards.

8. Play Back Spelling. Have children choose a word from their list of spelling words or from the words on the Word Wall. Have the children get in groups of two. Have one child "write" the spelling word with a finger on the back of the other child. The second child should try to guess the word. Then tell the children to change roles so that the first child can write a spelling word on the back of the second child.

9. Have children try to memorize the spelling of words. Identify a word that you want children to spell. Write the word on a large index card. Tell children that you will show them the word for five seconds and then ask them to write the word. Show children the spelling words and count silently to five. Then ask children to write the word on the chalkboard, a slate, or a piece of paper. After children are finished writing, show them the spelling word again. Ask children to compare the word they wrote with the correct spelling. Repeat using the same word if necessary or use a new word.

10. Play Spelling Bingo. Give each child a card filled with spelling words and markers to cover the words. Call a word and hold up a card with the word on it. Have children find the word on their Bingo card. The first child to cover a row gets Bingo.

11. Play Spelling Concentration. Place a set of five to seven pairs of spelling words face down on a table. You should have two cards for each word. Have children turn over two cards at a time. If the cards match, children keep them and spell the words without looking at them. If the cards do not match, have children replace the cards. The object is to match pairs of spelling words.

12. Reinforce the spelling of words children have learned with the following game. Have children form a circle. Say a spelling word that children have learned. Point to a child to say the word. Ask the child to

the right of the first child to say the first letter in the word. The next child says the next letter and so on until the word is spelled. If a child says an incorrect letter, quietly say the correct letter and give the child a chance to say the next one. Repeat with several spelling words.

13. Play the following game to practice spelling words. Identify 10 to 12 spelling words that children need to learn. Write the letters of each word on individual index cards or use preprinted letter cards. Scramble the letters of all of the words face down on a table. Have the children line up as in a relay race. Say one spelling word. The first child in the line should walk quickly to the table, find the first letter, turn it over, place the letter on the ledge of the chalkboard, and walk back to the line. The second child should find the second letter and so on until the word is spelled. Repeat with all of the spelling words.

14. Create a Word Wall in your classroom (Cunningham, 1995). Identify key words that you want children to spell correctly. You may choose words that are frequently misspelled such as *they,* or you may want to include words from your science or social studies lessons. Write the words on large pieces of paper and hang them on the wall. Tell children that these words are a part of the Word Wall and that they should refer to the Word Wall when they have questions about the spelling of a word. Review the spelling of three or four words every day. It takes several teaching lessons for most children to remember how to spell some of the difficult words in English.

Selected Resources
SPELLING

Children's Books with Repeated Word Patterns

Brown, M.W. (1993). *Four fur feet*. New York: Doubleday.

Bunting, E. (1994). *Flower garden*. San Diego: Harcourt Brace.

Cole, J. (1989). *Anna Banana: 101 jump rope rhymes*. New York: William Morrow.

Deming, A.G. (1994). *Who's tapping at my window?* New York: Penguin.

Fleming, D. (1993). *In the small, small pond*. New York: Henry Holt.

Gelman, R.G. (1984). *The biggest sandwich ever*. New York: Scholastic.

Lewison, W. (1992). *Buzz said the bee*. New York: Scholastic.

Ochs, C.P. (1991). *Moose on the loose*. Minneapolis: Carolrhoda Books.

Patz, N. (1983). *Moses supposes his toeses are roses*. San Diego: Harcourt Brace.

Seuss, Dr. (1965). *Fox in socks*. New York: Random House.

Media and Technology

Reader Rabbit 1 CD-ROM (letter recognition and spelling activities).
UPDATA (800-882-2844)

Reading Blaster: Invasion of the Word Snatchers CD-ROM (spelling activities and online tips for parents and teachers).
UPDATA (800-882-2844)

Spellbound CD-ROM (digitized spoken words with spelling activities).
UPDATA (800-882-2844)

The Reading Carnival CD-ROM (spelling games and reading puzzles).
UPDATA (800-882-2844)

Professional Resources

Bolton, F., & Snowball, D. (1993). *Teaching spelling: A practical resource*. Portsmouth, NH: Heinemann.

Gentry, J.R., & Gillet, J.W. (1993). *Teaching kids to spell*. Portsmouth, NH: Heinemann.

Phenix, J., & Scott-Dunne, D. (1994). *Spelling for parents*. Bothell, WA: The Wright Group.

Phenix, J., & Scott-Dunne, D. (1991). *Spelling instruction that makes sense*. Bothell, WA: The Wright Group.

3.10 Phonics

Goal To help children develop phonics skills.

Assessments Auditory Discrimination 2.5 and 4.5; Consonant Phonic Elements 2.11 and 4.11; Decoding 2.12 and 4.12

BACKGROUND

Phonics is not a method of teaching reading (Heilman, 1998); rather, it is an important tool for decoding unfamiliar words and making sense of what is read. Many different teaching methods and approaches include instruction on phonics. What these methods and approaches have in common is their focus on teaching children the letter-sound associations in our language (Strickland, 1998). Because approximately 84% of the words in the English language are phonetically regular, instruction in phonics is essential in helping beginning readers break the code and make sense of reading (Anderson, Hiebert, Scott, & Wilkinson, 1985).

Reading is a complex process, and children use many tools and techniques to construct meaning. Phonics is one of the cueing systems that children use when they encounter unknown words. The other cueing systems focus on semantics (meaning) and syntax (structure of language). Effective readers use these cueing systems flexibly and in combination as they attempt to construct meaning from printed materials. While phonics is an important part of beginning reading instruction, it is not the only component (Cunningham, 1995). Within a sound reading program, teachers provide instruction on the various components of word identification: structural analysis, use of context, sight vocabulary, and phonics.

The following teaching strategies and activities offer a wide variety of suggestions for helping emergent readers develop phonics skills. Some of the strategies and activities provide explicit instruction of phonics, and other ideas focus on more contextualized approaches to phonics instruction. By using a variety of approaches and strategies, you will be able to help more children develop the necessary phonics skills to progress in reading.

TEACHING STRATEGY 1	Making Words

Making Words is a hands-on phonics strategy that helps children see patterns in words as they manipulate letter cards or tiles (Cunningham & Hall, 1994). This strategy helps children understand letter and sound associations as they work with word families or onsets and rimes. An onset is the beginning part of a word that comes before the vowel. For example, in the word *cat,* the onset is *c.* A rime is the part of the word from the vowel to the end. For example, in the word *cat,* the rime is *at.* Rimes are sometimes referred to as phonograms, spelling patterns, or word families. In the Making Words strategy, children manipulate letter cards or tiles to build words that start out small and get longer as the lesson progresses. Typically, a Making Words lesson focuses on one or more rimes or spelling patterns that the children are learning. Refer to Appendix B for a list of rimes or word families. For lists of words and sample lessons for the Making Words strategy, consult Cunningham and Hall (1994).

DIRECTIONS

1. Choose the word that will be the last word made in the lesson (e.g., splash).

2. Make a list of other words that can be made using the letters in the word *splash*. Arrange these words to show how changing letter order or adding a new letter can form a new word. For example:

   a
   Al
   as
   has
   ash
   lash
   splash

3. Select the words you will include in your lesson. Consider the patterns and words that can be made by rearranging letters in a previous word. Proper nouns can be included to help children learn about using capital letters correctly.

4. Make letter cards on large index cards for each letter needed for the lesson. Write each word for the lesson on a small index card. Place the large letter cards in a pocket chart.

5. Make individual letter cards for each child. This can be done by writing letters on index cards or small squares of paper. Letter tiles can also be used.

6. Distribute a set of letters to each child. Provide a few minutes for the children to explore the letters and words they can make with their letter cards.

7. Say, "Use two letters to make the word *as*. I am as tall as Bill."

8. Pause for a moment while the children make the word with their letter cards. Ask for a volunteer to come to the front of the class and make the word using the large letter cards in the pocket chart. Provide time for the children to self-check the words they made.

9. Say, "Add one letter and make the word *has*. He has a pet dog."

10. Ask for a volunteer to make the word in the pocket chart. Have children self-check their own words.

11. Continue the lesson using the same steps with the other words.

12. When you have used all of the words on your list except the last word (splash), challenge the children by saying, "See what word you can make using all of your letters."

TEACHING STRATEGY 2	Whole-Part-Whole Phonics

Whole-Part-Whole Phonics focuses on teaching phonics within the context of meaningful text. This approach allows children to see the use of phonics skills in real reading situations. Typically, a Big Book is used as the focus of this strategy.

DIRECTIONS

1. Select a story or Big Book that contains a phonic element you want to emphasize. For example, you might use the Big Book *I Went Walking* (Williams, 1989) to teach the initial /w/ sound.

2. Read the story aloud to the children. Discuss the story.

3. Write several sentences from the story or Big Book that contain words with the target phonic element. For example, you might show the children the following sentence and question:

I went walking.
What did you see?

4. Read the sentences to the children. Invite the children to reread the sentences with you.

5. Point out the words with the target phonic element. Ask the children to read these words with you. For example, you might draw the children's attention to the following words:

went
walking
what

6. Ask the children to figure out what these words have in common. Lead the children to discover that the words contain the same letter and sound.

7. Ask the children to brainstorm other words that have the target letter and sound.

8. Reread the sentences containing the target words.

9. Return to the story or Big Book and ask the children to read along with you as you reread the story.

| **TEACHING STRATEGY 3** | **Phonics in Context** |

Phonics in Context stresses teaching target words in the context of sentences and passages. In this approach, consonants are generally not isolated but taught within the context of whole words. This approach is very common in many basal anthology programs (Gunning, 1992).

DIRECTIONS

1. Make a list of words that contain the target phonic element. Limit your list to four or five words. For example, you might teach the initial /d/ sound using the following words:

dad
door
dog
do

2. Write one sentence for each word on the chalkboard . Try to make the sentences link together to form a short story or passage. For the target words listed above, you might use the following sentences.

My <u>dad</u> came home from work.
We ran to the <u>door</u>.
He had a big <u>dog</u> with him.
"<u>Do</u> we get to keep him?" we asked.

3. Underline the target words.

4. Read the sentences aloud to the children.

5. Have the children echo read the sentences with you. To do this, you read the sentence first, and the children read the sentence immediately after you.

6.   Have the children read each target word after you read it aloud.

7.   Ask the children what letter or letters all of the target words have in common. Discuss their responses.

8.   Say the target words again and ask the children to listen carefully to determine what sound or sounds the words have in common. Discuss their responses.

9.   Ask the children to brainstorm other words that have the same sound or sounds in them. Write these words on the chalkboard.

10. Ask the children to make the sound that all of the target words contain. Then ask them what letter or letters make that sound. Invite the children to state the generalization they learned (e.g., the letter *d* makes the /d/ sound).

11. Return to the sentences and ask the children to read them chorally.

TEACHING STRATEGY 4	Explicit Phonics

Explicit Phonics focuses on teaching phonics one element at a time, building systematically from individual elements to larger pieces of text. Children first learn letters and sounds, then blend words, and then read these components in connected text. Some children who have difficulty learning from more indirect methods benefit from the explicit nature of this type of phonics instruction (Adams, 1990).

DIRECTIONS

1.   Select a letter, digraph, or other phonic element to be taught.

2.   Present the phonic element by writing it on the chalkboard (e.g., /sh/).

3.   Tell the children, "The letters *sh* stand for the /sh/ sound."

4.   Ask the children to make the /sh/ sound as you point to the letters.

5.   Have the children write the letters *sh* on their papers. Ask them to say the sound as they point to the letters.

6.   Present the children with several words that contain the target phonic element. Have the children sound out the words and say them together. Emphasize the target phonic element. For example, you might use the following words for the /sh/ sound:

shoe
sheep
she

7.   This type of lesson can be extended to include writing sentences for the words, reading the words in other materials, or playing a word game.

Ideas and Activities

1.   Teach common spelling patterns or rimes to the children. Use the list of rimes in the box on the next page for this activity. Present a rime to the children and then have them list other words that use the same rime. For example, for the rime *an*, the children might list *ban, can, fun, mun, pun,* and so on. Underline the rime in each word. Guide the children to notice that the words all have the same rime or spelling pattern. Post the lists in the classroom. Add new words to the lists as children discover them in their reading and writing.

Common Rimes

ack	all	ain	ake	ale	ame	an	ank	ap	ash
at	ate	aw	ay	eat	ell	est	ice	ick	ide
ight	ill	in	ine	ing	ink	ip	ir	ock	oke
op	ore	or	uck	ug	ump	unk			

Wylie and Durrell (1970) identified this list of 37 rimes which can be used to form over 500 primary-level words.

---

2. Use word sorts to guide children to sort words according to phonic elements. Write words on index cards and ask children to sort the words according to a specific phonic element such as short *a* words and long *a* words.

3. Use poetry to teach common rimes and other target phonic elements. Read the poem first for enjoyment. Then direct the children's attention to the rime or phonic element you want to teach. Ask the children to say the sound with you. Invite the children to identify words in the poem that contain the rime or sound. Make a list of the words and underline the rime or target phonic element. Brainstorm other words that also contain the rime or sound.

4. Engage the children in shared reading of Big Books or other enlarged texts such as chart stories. After reading the texts for enjoyment and meaning, direct the children's attention to specific phonic elements. Ask the children to identify words from the text that contain that element.

5. Use shared writing to model phonics strategies to children. For example, as you are writing a list in front of the class, think aloud as you use phonics strategies to spell a word. You might say, "I need to make a list of things to buy at the store. First I need to get milk. How does *milk* begin? It sounds like the beginning of *money* and *Mark*. That means I need to use the letter *m*." Continue with this pattern for the remainder of the word. Model this type of sounding out strategy frequently for children through shared writing.

6. Write letters or spelling patterns you want to review on large note cards or pieces of tagboard. Give one card to each child. Have several children stand in front of the class and ask them to sequence themselves in an order that spells a word. For example, if you gave the children *c, a,* and *t* cards, they could spell the word *cat*. Ask the children how they can change one letter and make a new word. For example, the *c* can be changed to an *h* to form *hat*, a *b* to form *bat*, and an *r* to form *rat*. Continue forming new words until you have run out of words. Then introduce a new spelling pattern or rime.

7. Write an incomplete sentence on the chalkboard, a sheet of chart paper, or an overhead transparency. For example, you might write, "I like to play _____." Then write a word that is one letter away from being correct. For example, you might write *hall*. Ask the children to change a letter to form a word that makes sense in the sentence. Have a child write the correct word *ball* in the blank. Continue this pattern with additional sentences.

8. Have children play sound bingo to practice their phonics skills. Using pieces of tagboard or large index cards as the bingo game board, divide the board into five rows and five columns. Write one letter in each box. Put the letters in different order on each card. Use picture cards or a word list to call out words. Ask the children to listen for the beginning sound of the word. If the children's game board contains the beginning letter of the word, they should cover the letter on the game board. When a child has a vertical, horizontal, or diagonal row covered, the child must read the covered letters and their sounds to verify that he or she has bingo. Variations of this game can focus on ending sounds, vowel sounds, or blends.

9. Play sound hunt with the children. Divide the class into small groups and assign each group a letter or spelling pattern that you want to review. Then ask the children to search for objects in the classroom that

contain the sound represented by the letter or spelling pattern. Have children make lists of the objects they find. Provide time for groups to share their findings.

10. Use word ladders (Blevins, 1998) to help children see how changing one letter can change a word. Draw a word ladder on the chalkboard, a piece of chart paper, or an overhead transparency. Write a word on the bottom rung of the word ladder. Say the word with the children. Ask if the children can change one letter to form a new word. Write the new word on the second rung. Continue until the ladder is full. A sample word ladder is shown below.

```
| sun |
| gun |
| fun |
| run |
```

11. Display a picture of an animal or object. Write its name on the chalkboard, leaving out one letter. For example, show a picture of a dog and write d __ g on the chalkboard. Ask the children what is missing. Write the missing letter in the space. Continue with other picture and word combinations. You can use this activity to focus on beginning, ending, or vowel sounds.

12. Teach children to play sound checkers to reinforce specific phonic elements. Write a word on each square of an old checkerboard. The game is played like checkers, but the children must read the words on each space they land on. If they cannot read the words correctly, they must return to their original space.

13. Use the children's names to point out similarities and differences in the way the names look and sound. Invite children to notice the sounds with which their names begin and end. For example, you might say, "Natalie's name begins with the /n/ sound. It is written with the letter *n*. Who else has a name that begins with the /n/ sound?"

14. Use children's books to teach vowel sounds. Share the book, discuss the vowel sound, and ask children to identify examples of the vowel sound. See the following boxes for recommended children's books for teaching short and long vowel sounds.

Children's Books with
SPECIFIC SHORT VOWEL SOUNDS

Short *a*

Griffith, H. (1982). *Alex and the cat.* New York: Greenwillow.

Kent, J. (1970). *The fat cat.* New York: Scholastic.

Most, B. (1980). *There's an ant in Anthony.* New York: Morrow.

Short e

Ets, M.H. (1972). *Elephant in a well.* Bergenfield, NJ: Viking.

Galdone, P. (1973). *The little red hen.* New York: Scholastic.

Lionni, L. (1994). *An extraordinary egg.* New York: Knopf.

Short *i*

Lankford, M.D. (1991). *Is it dark? Is it light?* New York: Knopf.

McPhair, D. (1984). *Fix-it.* Bergenfield, NJ: Viking.

Sanfield, S. (1995). *Bit by bit.* East Rutherford, NJ: Viking.

Short o

Anholt, C., & Anholt, L. (1992). *All about you.* Bergenfield, NJ: Viking.

Freeman, D. (1955). *Mop top.* Bergenfield, NJ: Viking.

Seuss, Dr. (1965). *Fox in socks.* New York: Random House.

Short *u*

Marshall, J. (1984). *The cut-ups.* Bergenfield, NJ: Viking.

Seuss, Dr. (1982). *Hunches and bunches.* New York: Random House.

Udry, J.M. (1981). *Thump and plunk.* New York: Harper & Row.

Children's Books with SPECIFIC LONG VOWEL SOUNDS

Long *a*

Aardema, V. (1981). *Bringing the rain to Kapiti Plain.* New York: Dial.

Henkes, K. (1987). *Sheila Rae, the brave.* New York: Greenwillow.

Munsch, R. (1987). *Moira's birthday.* Ontario: Firefly.

Long *e*

Chardiet, B., & Maccarone, G. (1992). *We scream for ice-cream.* New York: Scholastic.

Cowley, J. (1994). *The screaming mean machine.* New York: Scholastic.

Keller, H. (1983). *Ten sleepy sheep.* New York: Greenwillow.

Long *i*

Cameron, J. (1979). *If mice could fly.* Riverside, NJ: Atheneum.

Gelman, R. (1979). *Why can't I fly?* New York: Scholastic.

Minarik, E.E. (1978). *No fighting! No biting.* New York: Harper Collins.

Long o

Buller, J., & Schade. S. (1992). *Toad on the road.* New York: Random House.

Johnston, T. (1972). *The adventures of Mole and Troll.* East Rutherford, NJ: Viking.

Wild, M. (1994). *Going home.* New York: Scholastic.

Long *u*

Lobel, A. (1966). *The troll music.* New York: Harper & Row.

Segal, L. (1977). *Tell me a Trudy.* New York: Farrar, Straus & Giroux.

Slobodkin, L. (1959). *Excuse me—certainly!* New York: Vanguard Press.

Guidelines for
TEACHING PHONIC ELEMENTS

General Guidelines

- Teach common consonant sounds first.

- Teach short vowel sounds before long vowel sounds.

- Teach consonants and short vowels in combination so words can be made as soon as possible.

- Use a sequence in which the most words can be generated. Teach higher-frequency, sound-spelling relationships before less-frequent ones.

- Progress from simple to more complex sound-spellings.

Recommended Phonic Skills for Grades K-2

Kindergarten
phonemic awareness
alphabet recognition
consonants

Grade 1
phonemic awareness
blending and word building
short vowels (CVC pattern)
consonants
final e (CVCe pattern)
long vowel digraphs (ai, ay, ae, ee, oa, ow, etc.)
consonant clusters (br, cl, st, etc.)
other vowels such as oo, ou, ow, oi, oy

Grade 2
grade 1 skills review
more complex vowel spellings
structural analysis (compound words, common prefixes, common suffixes)
multisyllable words

Selected Resources
PHONICS

Media and Technology

Amusement Park Phonics and Reading (amusement park rides for practicing phonics skills).
T.S. Dennison (800-443-2976)

County Fair Phonics (fair games for practicing phonics skills).
T.S. Dennison (800-443-2976)

Kid Phonics (letter-sound correspondence activities using songs and a personalized dictionary).
UPDATA (800-882-2844)

Sound It Out Land (theme park games focusing on phonics and spelling).
UPDATA (800-882-2844)

Sound It Out Land 2 (theme park games focusing on consonant blends).
UPDATA (800-882-2844)

Professional Resources

Baer, G.T. (1999). *Self-paced phonics: A text for education* (2nd ed.). Upper Saddle River, NJ: Prentice Hall.

Bear, D.R., Invernizzi, M., Templeton, S., & Johnston, F. (1996). *Words their way.* Upper Saddle River, NJ: Prentice Hall.

Blevins, W. (1998). *Phonics from A to Z: A practical guide.* New York: Scholastic Professional Books.

Cunningham, P.M., & Hall, D.P. (1997). *Making more words: Multilevel, hands-on phonics and spelling activities.* Parsippany, NJ: Good Apple.

Cunningham, P.M., & Hall, D.P. (1994). *Making words: Multilevel, hands-on, developmentally appropriate spelling and phonics activities.* Parsippany, NJ: Good Apple.

Eldredge, J.L. (1999). *Phonics for teachers: Self instruction, methods, and activities.* Upper Saddle River, NJ: Prentice Hall.

Strickland, D.S. (1998). *Teaching phonics today: A primer for educators.* Newark, DE: International Reading Association.

3.11 Sight Words

Goal To help children learn words by sight.

Assessments Basic Sight Word Knowledge 2.14 and 4.14; Passage Reading 2.15 and 4.15

BACKGROUND

The ability to identify words is the foundation of the reading process (Stanovich, 1991). Teaching children common sight words will greatly enhance their reading development. There are some words that you want children to know by sight in their reading and writing. Approximately 50% of the words children read and write come from a list of the 100 most frequently used words (Fry, Fountoukidis, & Polk, 1985). Furthermore, the following 13 words account for almost 25% of the words children encounter in their school texts (Adams, 1990; Johns & Lenski, 1997):

a   and   for   he   in   is   it   of   that   the   to   was   you

In addition to the 13 basic sight words, there are more words that children need to learn by sight. Among these words are color words, words related to holidays and units, and words that are commonly used in children's books.

Children need to learn to automatically read and write these words for two major reasons. First, by knowing these words on sight, children can devote their attention to decoding less common words and focusing on the meaning of what they are reading and writing. Second, because many of these basic sight words are not pronounced or spelled in predictable ways, decoding them can be difficult and confusing. Since children will see these words in their reading and use them in their writing often, they will benefit greatly from knowing them automatically (Cunningham, 1995). The teaching strategies, ideas, and activities described below include a range of options from literature-based instruction to explicit instruction of sight words. By balancing these various techniques for teaching sight words, you will be able to assist a wide range of children in developing their sight word knowledge (Cunningham, 1995). Appendix C contains several sight word lists.

TEACHING STRATEGY 1	Pattern Books

Pattern Books provide a meaningful way to teach children sight words in the context of real text. By connecting sight word instruction and children's literature, children are able to see the words in the story, understand how they are used, and practice identifying the words in a meaningful context. The following strategy can be used with any pattern book, and it serves as an excellent introduction to teaching sight words to young children (May, 1998).

1. Prior to beginning the lesson, select a pattern book that emphasizes the targeted sight word(s). For very young children, you will want to select one word for study. For older children, three to five different words can be targeted.

2. Prepare teacher-made charts that contain the text but not pictures from the book.

3. Write target word(s) on chart paper. Prepare sight word cards.

4. To teach the lesson, read the book aloud to the children. Read the book again, inviting the children to chime in when they can predict what comes next.

5. Invite the children to take turns with echo reading. For echo reading, the teacher reads a line or phrase, and then the children echo it back.

6. Provide opportunities for the children to engage in choral reading of the story. For choral reading, have a group of children read a section of text in unison. You can provide support by reading along with the children and then fading your voice at the points in the text when they are able to take on more of the reading responsibility. Use a pointer to point to each word during choral reading to help children track the words as they read them.

7. Next, have children read the text from teacher-made charts that do not contain pictures.

8. Invite children to engage in echo and choral reading of the text as described above in steps 5 and 6.

9. Next, show children the targeted sight word(s) on index cards and read them with the children.

10. Ask children to place matching word cards on the charts. Have children say each word as they match their cards with the words on the chart paper. This can be done by taping the word cards to the chart paper, using a pocket chart, or using magnets on a magnetic chalkboard.

11. After placing word cards on the chart paper, read the entire text chorally with the children.

12. Next, place the word cards in random order and invite children to match the cards to the text on the chart paper. Have children say the words as they match them to the text.

13. Discuss the new words the children learned during the activity.

14. Have the children add the sight words to their word banks or personal Word Walls. You can also post the targeted word(s) on the classroom Word Wall.

TEACHING STRATEGY 2	Explicit Instruction

Explicit Instruction of sight words allows teachers to help children learn important sight words in an efficient manner. By providing focused instruction on targeted sight words, children can learn to read, spell, and write the words in a relatively short period of time. In addition, by directing children's attention to the use, spelling, and special features of sight words, you can make certain that children are aware of this important information about common sight words.

DIRECTIONS

1. Select several targeted sight words. Several lists of sight words are provided in Appendix C.

2. Say the word aloud and use it in a sentence.

3. Write the sentence on the chalkboard and underline the sight word.

4. Discuss the word's use and special features.

5. Ask children to spell the word aloud as you point to each letter. Then invite children to spell the word in the air with their fingers as they recite the spelling aloud. Next, have children write the word on paper and spell it aloud as they write.

6. Have children chant the spelling of the word as they point to each letter.

7. Finally, ask children to write the word on a note card and place it in their word banks or on their personal Word Walls.

8. Continue with this pattern for the remaining targeted sight words.

TEACHING STRATEGY 3	Associative Learning

Associative Learning for high frequency words is a strategy designed for use with children who have difficulty learning high frequency words because the words lack meaning clues for the children. The associative learning technique helps children develop concrete associations for abstract high frequency words such as *for*, *of*, and *the* (Cunningham, 1995).

DIRECTIONS

1. Select targeted sight word(s) for this strategy. Present a targeted sight word by using it in a phrase accompanied by an illustration. For example, to teach the word *of*, you could make a picture of a bowl of apples with the phrase *bowl of apples* written below the illustration. The word *of* should also be underlined and written in red ink to draw the children's attention to the word.

2. Next, have children brainstorm other uses for the word *of*. Have children create their own picture card and label. Ask children to write the targeted sight word in red ink and underline it.

3. Provide time for children to share their picture cards with other children. Have children place their picture cards in their word banks or on their personal Word Walls.

4. Continue with this pattern for other targeted sight words.

TEACHING STRATEGY 4	Word Wall

The Word Wall strategy is helpful for teaching high frequency words. The words are taught to children, and then they are posted on the Word Wall for future reference. A variety of hands-on activities are also incorporated into Word Wall instruction to help children learn and remember the high frequency words (Cunningham, 1995). Typically, teachers will spend a few minutes each day teaching and reviewing new Word Wall words over the course of a week. The following directions provide suggestions for teaching Word Wall words over a period of several days.

DIRECTIONS

1. Select up to five target high frequency words to teach in a week. Word lists, the children's spelling errors, and grade-level curriculum are sources for words for the Word Wall.

2. Introduce each word to students by writing it on an index card and using the word in a sentence. Write the sentence on the chalkboard and underline the Word Wall word.

3. Ask children to suggest other sentences that use the Word Wall word. Discuss the meaning or use of the word.

4. Point to each letter of the word as you spell it aloud. Invite children to spell the word with you as you point to each letter.

5. Trace around the configuration of the word using another color of chalk. Discuss the shape of the word.

6. Follow this pattern for each of the new Word Wall words. Place the index cards for the five new words on the Word Wall. Arrange the words alphabetically and use a different color of index card or ink for each new word.

7. Engage children in the Clap, Chant, and Write activity. Ask children to number a piece of scratch paper from one to five. Say each word, using it in a sentence. Ask children to write each word on their paper. Then have children clap and chant the spelling of each word as you lead the process. Ask children to correct their own spellings.

8. On another day, ask children to review rhymes using the Word Wall. Have children number a sheet of scratch paper from one to five. Ask them to write a Word Wall word that rhymes with the word you give to them. Give children the rhyming word and the first letter as clues. For example, you might say the word begins with *m* and rhymes with *by*. Continue this pattern for all five Word Wall words.

9. Guide children to check their own words. Ask them to say the word they wrote and to spell it aloud when you call each number and restate the clues. For example, after you say, "Number 1. The word begins with /m/ and rhymes with *by*," children should respond, "My, m-y." Continue with this pattern until all five words have been checked. Ask children to correct their work as you go through this step.

10. On another day, engage children in a cross-checking activity with the Word Wall words. Tell the children that they will need to select the Word Wall word that makes sense in a sentence and begins with a certain letter. For example, tell the children, "The word begins with *t* and fits in the sentence I went to _____ store yesterday." Continue with this pattern with all five Word Wall words.

11. Have children check their own words by reading each sentence again and restating the beginning letter of the word. Ask children to chant the word and then the spelling for each of the five Word Wall words.

12. Remind children that the Word Wall is an important resource to help them with their reading, writing, and spelling. For additional Word Wall activities, consult Cunningham (1995).

Ideas and Activities

1. Tell children that they will learn sight words best if they practice them in many different ways. Use the See, Write, Point, Say, and Spell cycle to help children practice new sight words. Guide the children through the following steps.

   - See the word in your head. Visualize what it looks like.

   - Write the word on paper; write it again using different colors; write it in different sizes; write it in the air with your finger; and write it on a friend's back using your pointing finger.

   - Point to the word and say it. Point to the word and spell it aloud, then silently.

2. Help children create personal Word Walls using file folders. Draw a grid on the file folder and label each section with a letter of the alphabet. Have children add high frequency words to their personal Word Walls. Children can use these resources at their desks or at home as they read and write (Cunningham, 1995).

3. Wordo is a variation of Bingo that focuses on practicing high frequency words. For young children, divide the Wordo card into 9 blocks, and for older children use 25 blocks. You will also need to supply plastic counters, beans, or other small objects to be used to cover words as the children fill in their blocks. Make a list of high frequency words to practice, write each word on an index card, and call out the words one at a time. Have the children chant the spelling of each word and cover it with a counter.

The first child to cover an entire row of words is the winner of the game. Ask the winner to read the words aloud to check that the words have been called. The winner can then serve as the caller. Continue the game for several rounds to provide additional practice with the high frequency words. A sample Wordo card is shown below.

Wordo

and	for	in
that	it	you
was	to	is

4. Select a children's book, poem, or chart story that contains a sight word you have been teaching. Using small sticky notes or removable correction tape, cover the sight word in the text. Present the book, poem, or story to the children. When you reach the covered word, ask the children what would make sense in the blank. Reveal the first letter of the covered word. Ask the children which of their guesses will still work. Continue this pattern until all letters of the word are revealed.

5. Play word games and puzzles such as hang-man, concentration, and go fish to provide opportunities for children to practice sight words.

6. Use the language experience approach (LEA) to teach sight words in children's spoken vocabulary. The LEA is discussed in detail in 3.3, Teaching Strategy 1. Draw children's attention to specific sight words in the text they dictated. Have children read the sight words, spell them, and discuss the word meanings or functions in that context.

7. Trace words in salt trays, sand trays, or shaving cream to help children get multiple opportunities to write, see, and remember sight words.

8. Wide reading of easy texts supports sight word development because children have many opportunities to see sight words used in meaningful contexts. Provide daily time for children to read from self-selected materials.

9. Make sight words in clay or play dough to allow students to feel the words and letters as they shape the clay or play dough. Ask children to point to each letter as they chant the spellings aloud. Pretzel dough or cookie dough can also be used so children can eat their baked sight words when the activity is over.

10. Go on a sight words hunt in the classroom or school. Ask children to identify target sight words as you tour the classroom or school. Discuss how the words are used and spelled. Discuss the importance of children knowing sight words in their daily lives.

11. Play the grab bag game with children to reinforce sight word knowledge. Write sight words on cards and place them in a bag. Have the children take turns selecting a card, reading it aloud, chanting the spelling, and using the word in a sentence. If the child is correct, he or she gets to keep the card. The winner has the most cards.

12. Scrambled words provide children with an opportunity to manipulate letter cards to spell high frequency words. Write words to be practiced on different colors of construction paper or index cards. Use one word per color. For each word, have the children arrange the letters in proper order, chant the spelling, read the word, and use it in a sentence.

Selected Resources
SIGHT WORDS

Children's Literature for Teaching Sight Words

Baker, K. (1990). *Who is this beast?* New York: Harcourt Brace.

Cameron, A. (1994). *The cat sat on the mat.* Boston: Houghton Mifflin.

Christelow, E. (1989). *Five little monkeys jumping on the bed.* New York: Trumpet.

Dobeck, J. (1996). *Stop that!* Parsippany, NJ: Modern Curriculum Press.

Grejniec, M. (1992). *What do you like?* New York: North-South Books.

Hill, E. (1980). *Where's Spot?* New York: Putnam.

Hoberman, M.A. (1982). *A house is a house for me.* New York: Penguin.

Shapiro, A. (1991). *Who says that?* New York: Dutton.

Tolstoi, A. (1968). *The great big enormous turnip.* New York: Watts.

Media and Technology

Early Learning Center CD-ROM (interactive programs that teach word skills and sight words). UPDATA (800-882-2844)

Word Tales CD-ROM (word games with sound effects and music). UPDATA (800-882-2844)

Professional Resources

Cunningham, P.M. (1995). *Phonics they use: Words for reading and writing* (2nd ed.). New York: HarperCollins.

Eldridge, J.L. (1995). *Teaching decoding in holistic classrooms.* Englewood Cliffs, NJ: Prentice Hall.

Fry, E.B., Fountoukidis, D.L., & Polk, J.K. (1985). *The new reading teachers' book of lists.* Upper Saddle River, NJ: Merrill/Prentice Hall.

Holley, C. (1997). *Warming up to big books.* Bothell, WA: The Wright Group.

3.12 Reading Comprehension

Goal To help children understand what they read.

Assessments Passage Reading 2.15 and 4.15

BACKGROUND

Reading is the process of comprehending text. As children read, they construct meaning from texts or passages. The meaning each child constructs is typically a bit different from the way other readers understand the story. That's because there is not one single, correct interpretation of any story. Comprehension is based on a number of factors, one of which is prior knowledge. As a result, no two readers will produce the same meaning from a text, and no reader's understanding of a text will exactly match what the author had in mind while writing (Goodman, 1996).

As children read, they rely on their background knowledge to make sense of the ideas and concepts of the story. Children also use their knowledge of word identification strategies to pronounce the words of the text. As they read, children set purposes for reading and monitor their reading progress. Finally, children summarize what they have read and apply those summaries to other situations (Flood & Lapp, 1990). The result of these mental activities is a construction of meaning of the passage.

As you can see, comprehending text is a complex thinking process. Because comprehension is so individual, children will vary in their ability to comprehend different stories. For example, children with a great interest in and knowledge about dogs may closely attend to the Clifford books and read with rich comprehension. Other children may not have that interest and may not comprehend Clifford stories as easily.

The way children apply strategies as they process text also has an impact on reading comprehension. Children who apply many strategies will probably have rich comprehension. Children who do not apply the reading strategies they have learned may not have as deep an understanding of the story. Therefore, you need to teach children how to use thinking strategies to comprehend the stories and books they read. Several teaching strategies, ideas, and activities follow that can help you teach children how to construct meaning as they read.

TEACHING STRATEGY I	Think Aloud

Since reading comprehension is an internal act, some children have difficulty understanding what you mean when you say, "Make a prediction." Children often do not know the meaning of the language we use in schools (Johns, 1980). To help them understand the meaning of abstract strategies, conduct a Think Aloud. When you conduct a Think Aloud, children are able to understand better how to use comprehension strategies during reading.

1. Select a passage from a story or informational article that contains a few sentences that are difficult for the children. Read the story aloud, thinking aloud as you read. As you read, insert the following phrases where appropriate and say what you are thinking.

Strategy	Think Aloud Prompts
Previewing	When I look over this passage, I can see . . . The pictures tell me that . . .
Accessing background knowledge	I know some things about . . . This story reminds me of . . .
Setting a purpose	I want to find out about . . . I'm reading this because . . .
Predicting	From the title I can tell . . . I can guess what will happen next. Next, . . .
Creating visual images	The picture I have in my mind is . . .
Identifying new words	This word must mean . . . I've seen a word like this one before. It's . . .
Thinking through a confusing point	This might mean . . . I'm not sure I understand this because . . .
Checking for understanding	So far, the story is about . . . This means . . .
Using fix-up strategies	I need to reread the part about . . . I need help with . . .
Summarizing the story	The story was about . . . The story means . . .

2. Model thinking aloud frequently, emphasizing different components of reading comprehension. For example, during one reading you might stress making predictions. At another time, you might stress summarizing. Each type of thinking strategy should be modeled many times.

TEACHING STRATEGY 2

Directed Reading-Thinking Activity (DR-TA)

The Directed Reading-Thinking Activity (DR-TA) (Stauffer, 1969) is a strategy that mirrors the thinking processes good readers use as they construct meaning from texts. The DR-TA can be applied to fiction and nonfiction materials. The strategy encourages making predictions and monitoring reading comprehension.

DIRECTIONS

1. Select a story or a passage to read aloud to children. Read the title aloud. Then ask the children to predict the contents of the story by saying, "What do you think the story will be about?" Encourage children to suggest many ideas.

2. Read the first few paragraphs or pages. Stop reading after you have introduced a few ideas or events. Ask children to monitor their comprehension by saying, "What just happened in the story?" Tie in their predictions about the title of the story by asking, "Was your first prediction about the story correct?" Allow

children time to think; then have them volunteer their answers. If children give a misinterpretation, you may choose to correct them, or you may decide to reread the first passage and ask again.

3. After children have a clear understanding of the story thus far, encourage predictions by asking them the following question, "What do you think will happen next?" Allow children to predict many options. After each prediction, ask the follow-up question, "Why do you think so?"

4. After children have made several predictions, tell children that you will continue to read the story and that they should listen to find out if their predictions were correct.

5. Read several more paragraphs or pages. Stop once more and ask children to monitor their comprehension and to make predictions. Use the same questions you asked previously. Allow children time to discuss the story thus far and make additional predictions.

6. Read the rest of the story and ask children to retell the entire story. You may choose to have children retell the story to a partner, to you, or by writing in their journals.

7. Repeat the DR-TA questions frequently to encourage children to ask the same questions as they read independently. Also, use the DR-TA during guided reading lessons. The basic DR-TA questions are listed below.

DR-TA Questions

What do you think the story will be about?

What just happened?

What do you think will happen next? Why do you think so?

TEACHING STRATEGY 3	Story Frame

A Story Frame is a summary outline of an entire story. After reading a story, children can fill in the blanks of a Story Frame to improve their comprehension (Fowler, 1982). You can create a general Story Frame as in the example below or write one specifically for a story or passage.

DIRECTIONS

1. Identify a story or a passage that has a plot that children can easily identify. Read the story aloud or have the children read it independently or with partners.

2. Encourage children to construct meaning from the story by reminding them to use comprehension monitoring strategies. For example, have them read and monitor their comprehension using the DR-TA. (See Teaching Strategy 2 in 3.12.) Remind them to use fix-up strategies if they lose track of the story's plot.

3. After the children have finished reading, remind them of the elements of the story. Explain that every story has a problem but that the "problem" might be something the main character wants done. For example, the "problem" in the story *Rainy Day Fun* (Palazzo, 1988) is that the children are trying to think of what they could do on a rainy day. Explain that this is the "problem" of the story and that events will happen through the story to solve the problem. Have children identify the solution to the problem. In *Rainy Day Fun* (Palazzo, 1988), the children decided to put on a play.

4. After children have identified the problem in the story, remind them that stories are told by events in sequential order. Have them identify the events in the story they have read.

5. Ask children to retell the story they read. Remind them to state the problem of the story, the events in the plot, and how the problem was solved. If they forget any part of the plot, direct the children to reread that portion of the story.

6. Provide children with a copy of a Story Frame. Tell them that they should fill in the blanks so that the entire paragraph tells part of the story. Children can work with a partner or independently.

7. Identify one of the children's Story Frames that correctly tells the story. Read it aloud to the children. Have children check their Story Frames to determine if they understood the story. A copy of a Story Frame is on the following page.

Story Frame

In this story, the problem starts when _____

_____ .

After that, _____

_____ .

Next, _____

_____ .

Then, _____

_____ .

The problem is finally solved when _____

_____ .

The story ends_____

_____ .

Idea-Mapping

Idea-Mapping (Armbruster, 1986) is a visual picture of how ideas are organized in informational texts. As children read nonfiction material or content area textbooks such as social studies or science books, they need to understand how text is organized in order to understand it fully. Idea-Maps help children identify important information, understand the relationship among the ideas, and improve their comprehension of the passages.

DIRECTIONS

1. Select a passage from an informational book such as a science text that is organized so that the main idea comes first and the details follow. An example adapted from *Whales: A First Discovery Book* (Jeunesse, Delafosse, Fuhr, & Sautai, 1991) follows.

   > There are two kinds of whales—toothed whales and baleen whales. Baleen whales have big mouths and no teeth. Instead, they have baleens. Baleens look like the teeth of a comb, hanging from the upper jaw. With their baleens, the biggest animals in the ocean catch the tiniest animals in the ocean. There are four kinds of baleen whales. They are blue whales, right whales, humpback whales, and gray whales.

2. Write the passage on the chalkboard, a piece of chart paper, or an overhead transparency. Have children read the passage independently or with a partner. After children have read the passage, ask them to tell their partner what they have learned.

3. Explain that sometimes books are not written as a story with a plot, setting, and characters but that they are providing information. Ask children to name additional informational books they have read or heard. If children do not mention school textbooks such as their science book, remind children that their science book also gives information.

4. Tell children that informational books are written in many different ways. Tell them that one of the ways authors of informational books organize their facts is by giving a main idea first, then writing details that fit the main idea. Ask children to identify the topic of the passage they have read. If they have difficulty identifying the topic, tell them that the topic in this passage is a description of a baleen whale.

5. Distribute copies of the Idea-Map. A sample Idea-Map follows.

Idea-Map
Main Idea:
Detail:
Detail:
Detail:
Detail:
Main Idea Sentence:

6. Have children write the topic of the passage on the first line. The topic they write should be baleen whales.

7. Ask children what they learned about baleen whales from the passage. Tell them that even though they may know other information about baleen whales, they should identify only things they have read in this particular passage. Give children a few minutes to identify the details. Then have them write the details on the next several lines. Tell them that they do not need to fill in every line but that they should list as many details as they find in the passage.

8. Finally, have children create a sentence that combines the topic and the details. Have children reread their Idea-Map, turn it face down on their desks, and tell their partner what the passage was about. Guide children to understand that the main idea sentence should be something like the following one: Baleen whales are the four kinds of whales that eat using baleens.

9. Have children write their main idea sentence on the final line of the Idea-Map. Allow children to write different main idea sentences.

10. Repeat this activity several times, each time giving children more independence until they can use the Idea-Map on their own.

Ideas and Activities

1. Have children read a story independently. They may read silently, with a partner, or out loud. After they have finished reading the story, ask one child to begin to retell the story. Encourage the first child to retell only one or two sentences. Write the sentences on the chalkboard or on an overhead transparency. Then invite another child to continue retelling the story. Write that child's retelling and continue until the story is completed. Read the retold story aloud inviting children to read with you. Explain that after readers finish reading a passage they should retell the story to themselves to help them remember it.

2. Have children create a literature time line after reading a story. Tell children that as they are reading the story they should pay particular attention to the events in the story. After children have finished reading, have them draw a horizontal line at the center of a long piece of paper. Under the line, they should write information about the time the event took place. They may have information about days of the week, months, seasons, or years. Above the time, they can draw a picture of the event that took place. Display the literature time lines around the room.

3. Encourage children to read books in a series. After they begin a series, have children write journal entries that record the main events of the story and other particulars about the main characters. As they get to know characters that are repeated in series books, children can begin writing questions to the characters. Another child reading the same series can answer the questions.

4. Help children identify the main idea of a story. Cut passages from old books or articles that are at a variety of reading levels. Fasten the passages to index cards. On the back of each card write several possible phrases or sentences that describe the main idea. Have children read the passage, write their answer on a separate sheet of paper, and then compare them with the answers on the back of the cards.

5. Before children read a story, list several words from the passage on the chalkboard or an overhead transparency. Add other words to the list that are not included in the story. For example, if you were reading *Sam's Sandwich* (Pelham, 1990), you might include the following words: *horse, lettuce, cake, picnic, cucumber, salami, ants, swim,* and *ketchup.* Before children read the story, have them predict what words they think they will encounter as they read. Ask children for reasons for their choices. As children read, have them write down the words that they found in the text. After children read, encourage them to retell the story using the words that were part of the original list.

6. Trace the outline of a doorknob on tagboard and cut it out. At the bottom of the sheet, attach a piece of paper. Have children read and retell a story in their own words and write it on the paper. Then have them hang the doorknob retelling on a door and invite others to read the retelling.

7. Encourage children to think deeply about characters in stories by having them create a character web. To create a character web, place the name of the character in the center of a circle. Then have children brainstorm qualities of the character. Since children often have difficulty thinking of character traits, you might also volunteer some ideas. Then write the characteristics of the story character on lines radiating out from the circle.

8. To foster personal responses to reading, have children use the Catch a Rainbow strategy (Richek, 1995). Tell children that they will be drawing a picture after reading a story or poem. Explain that they should not draw anything that someone else could recognize but that they should draw abstract art. When using the Catch a Rainbow strategy, children can draw a response to a story without having to be concerned about drawing ability.

9. Have children act out a story after reading with a tableau (Purves, Rogers, & Soter, 1990). Tell children that they will be creating a tableau, or a frozen scene, from a story they have read. Explain that a tableau is a scene much like a photograph. A tableau captures a scene and, unlike a videotape, it does not show movement. Explain that to create a tableau children will have to discuss which event they want to portray. Then have children decide how to arrange themselves and their props so that the audience will understand the event. Have children practice creating the tableau several times before presenting it to an audience.

10. Help children form mental images as they read by asking them to describe images as they are reading. For example, if children are reading a Curious George story, have them describe what George is seeing and what George is doing. Then have them draw a picture of a scene from the story. Explain that when readers are reading, they try to picture what they are reading.

11. Encourage children to identify sequence as they read. Explain that stories have a beginning, a middle, and an end and that the events are in a specific order. To reinforce the concept of sequence, gather several comic strips that children can read independently. Cut the comic strips into their sections. Scramble the order of the frames and have children put them in order.

12. Have children write Prove-It Prompts (May, 1998). Have children identify a section in their story to predict. Before children read, have them write what they think the passage will be about. Then have them write why they think so. After that, have children read that section of the story. After children read, have them write whether their prediction was correct and what happened in the story that proved the outcome of their prediction.

Prove-It Prompt

Name _____

Pages _____ to _____

BEFORE YOU READ: What do you think this section will be about?

_____

Why do you think so?

_____

AFTER YOU READ: Prove you were right or wrong.

_____

Series Books

Amelia Bedelia Series by P. Parish (New York: Scholastic).
Amelia Bedelia, Amelia Bedelia goes camping, Amelia Bedelia's family album.

Boxcar Children Series by G. C. Warner (New York: Albert Whitman).
*Boxcar children: Bicycle mystery, Boxcar children: Camp-out mystery, Boxcar children: Snowbound
mystery.*

Cam Jansen Series by D.A. Adler (New York: Puffin).
Cam Jansen and the mystery at the monkey house, Cam Jansen and the mystery of the gold coins.

Corduroy Series by D. Freeman (New York: Viking).
Corduroy, Corduroy's party, Corduroy's toys.

Curious George Series by H.A. Rey (Boston: Houghton Mifflin).
Curious George, Curious George flies a kite, Curious George goes to the circus.

Frog and toad Series by A. Lobel (New York: Harper & Row).
Frog and toad are friends, Frog and toad all year, Frog and toad together.

Madeline Series by L. Bemelmans (New York: Puffin).
Madeline, Madeline and the gypsies, Madeline in London.

Mr. Putter and Tabby Series by C. Rylant (Orlando, FL: Harcourt Brace).
Mr. Putter and Tabby bake the cake, Mr. Putter and Tabby pour the tea.

Nate the Great Series by S.M. Weinman (New York: Dell).
Nate the Great, Nate the Great and the lost list, Nate the Great and the snowy trail.

Pee Wee Scout Series by J. Delton (New York: Dell).
Pee Wee Scouts: Cookies and crutches, Pee Wee's on first, Pee Wee's on parade.

Media and Technology

Primary steps to comprehension CD-ROM (reading passages with questions).
Educational Resources (800-624-2926)

Reader Rabbit's Interactive Reading Journey CD-ROM (interactive trip through 40 stories).
UPDATA (800-882-2844)

3.13   Cross Checking

Goal   To help children use various strategies to cross check for meaning.

Assessments   Passage Reading 2.15 and 4.15

BACKGROUND

While reading, children check one kind of information against another, or cross check, to make sense of the words (Goodman, 1965). To use cross checking as a strategy, readers use four cues, three from print and one from their background knowledge. The cues that readers use are graphophonic (phonics) cues, semantic (context) cues, syntactic (language) cues, and background knowledge (May, 1998).

When children do not recognize a word in a passage automatically, they must stop to figure out the word. They can use graphophonic cues by matching sounds with letters or letter combinations; they can use semantic cues by trying to figure out what word would make sense in the sentences; they can use syntactic cues by deciding what word fits the structure and language of the sentence; and they use their background knowledge to make sense of the sentences together. These four cues are used simultaneously so that a child can pronounce an unknown word while comprehending the passage (Rumelhart, 1985).

To use cross checking as a strategy while they read, children need instruction on ways to use each of the language cues separately, and they also need instruction and practice using the language cues together. To know what cues children are using and what instruction they need, you will need to listen to children read on a regular basis. When you listen to children read, you will hear the types of miscues children make. Miscues are the errors children make when reading aloud. Miscues are not considered mistakes but are a window into children's reading processes (Goodman, 1965). When children make miscues, you learn which language cues they are using and which ones they need to strengthen.

For children to become proficient readers, they need a great deal of practice reading materials at their independent and instructional levels. It is through such practice that children can become competent using the four language cues. Furthermore, when children use materials that they can read easily, their reading achievement will have a greater likelihood of improving (Adams, 1990). The books children read independently need to be easy enough so that they do not miss more than one or two words per hundred. At the instructional level, students will not miss more than five or six words per hundred (Johns, 1997). When children read books that are more difficult, they have to rely more on their background knowledge and are less able to use the language cues from the print. Strategies, activities, and ideas to guide children in cross checking as they learn to read follow.

As children read, they continually use the Predict-Sample-Confirm cycle (Weaver, 1994). When children come to a word they don't know, they make a prediction about the word. While making the prediction, they sample possible words based on the letters of the word, the meaning needed in the sentence, and the type of word that fits the structure of the sentence. From the sampling, children narrow their prediction to a few words. Then children decide which word to try to confirm that prediction, or they change the word. The process of Predict-Sample-Confirm is simultaneous and ongoing. Because this strategy is a key component of reading, it should be explicitly taught to children as in the following example.

DIRECTIONS

1. Tell children that you will be modeling or showing them an important strategy that they will be using as they read. Choose a story from a Big Book or a story that children can read and place it on the chalkboard or on chart paper. Cover several of the important words with tape or with sticky notes. A one-sentence example follows.

    When we went to the apple _____, we saw four types of apple trees.

2. Begin reading the story. When you come to a word that is covered, tell children that you will be making a prediction about the word. Write the word *prediction* on the chalkboard or on chart paper. Ask children for predictions for the covered word. Under the word *prediction,* write the words the children suggested. Explain that when you come to a word you don't know, you make many predictions about what the word could be.

    Predictions
    farm
    orchard
    place
    pie
    yard

3. Tell children that you will choose one of the predicted words to place in the sentence. Choose a word that is not the correct word for the sentence. For example, using the word *farm,* read the sentence to the children.

    When we went to the apple *farm,* we saw four types of apple trees.

4. Tell children that this word may make sense, but you need to confirm its accuracy by looking at the letters of the word. Uncover the first letter in the word *orchard.* Ask children if *farm* could be the correct word and invite a child to explain. Then ask children which word they think fits the sentence based on the first letter. Most children will say the correct word, *orchard.* Explain that if the word didn't fit, you would have to continue predicting more words, sampling the words, and confirming their accuracy.

5. Repeat with additional covered words. Then encourage children to try the Predict-Sample-Confirm strategy while reading independently.

TEACHING STRATEGY 2   **Cue Questioning**

As children use cross checking, they ask themselves questions about the language cues in the sentences. Since most primary-grade children have had limited experience reading independently, they may not know the

Teaching children about the kinds of questions to ask and providing them with ideas for Cue Questioning help them as they use cross checking during reading.

DIRECTIONS

1. Identify three or four of the questions from the list on the next page and write them on the chalkboard, a piece of chart paper, or an overhead transparency. Tell children that the questions are ones they should use as they make predictions of words while they read.

2. Ask children to take out their independent reading book and read until they come to a word that is unfamiliar. Give children several minutes to read.

3. Divide the class into groups of two or three children. Tell children that they should ask each other questions about the words. Have one child read a sentence and say "blank" in place of the unknown word. Have the other children in the group ask questions until they can figure out the missing word.

4. Repeat this strategy often using a variety of Cue Questions. Tell children that they should begin asking themselves the same questions when they read and come across an unknown word.

Cue Questions

Questions for meaning cues

- Did that make sense?

- You said _____. What does that mean?

- Have your heard a word like that before?

- What would make sense here?

- What is happening in the story? Does this word make sense in the story?

Questions for syntax cues

- Did that sound right?

- Can you say it that way?

- Would it be correct to say _____?

- Can you think of a better word that fits?

- What word would sound right?

Questions for visual cues

- Did that look right?

- Do you know a word that looks like that?

- What do you notice about that word?

- Do you notice something familiar about that word?

- Do you see a part of the word you know?

Questions for self-correction

- Were you right?

- Why did you stop?

- What did you notice?

- What else could you try?

- What else do you know that could help you?

Ideas and Activities

1. In order for children to be able to use cross checking strategies, they need to read materials that are at their independent and instructional reading levels. Reading levels change at different rates for different children. Therefore, make frequent assessment decisions about children's reading levels. (See Passage Reading in Sections 2 and 4.)

2. Provide children with many opportunities to read books independently. Young children do not have attention spans that allow for long periods of reading. Therefore, provide children with five to eight minutes to read books at their own reading level at least twice a day.

3. When children read independently, they often choose books that are too difficult. Divide the books in your classroom into reading levels and mark the books with a colored sticker. For example, you might have the easiest books marked with a red sticker, the books that are closer to grade level with a blue sticker, the books at grade level with a green sticker, and the books that are above grade level with an orange sticker.

4. Young children can read many books during an independent reading period because many grade-level books are short with few words. Divide the class into groups of children who read at the same level. Provide each group of children with a small basket of books that are appropriate for the children's reading ability. Tell children that as soon as they finish reading one book they should read another one.

5. Create a strategy bookmark for children to use independently. Identify five or six questions from Cue Questioning (see Teaching Strategy 2 in 3.13) that are most appropriate for your children. Write or print the questions as statements on a bookmark. Give a bookmark to each child in your class and have the children decorate their bookmarks. After bookmarks are decorated, laminate the bookmarks so they are more durable. Give the bookmarks back to the children and tell them that they can use the bookmarks to remind them of cross checking strategies to use while they are reading independently.

    ☞ **Sample Fix-up Strategies for Bookmarks**

    1. Think of a word that makes sense.

    2. Look at the picture.

    3. Reread the sentence.

    4. Read on and then go back.

    5. Look for word chunks you know.

    6. Sound out the word.

6. Tell children that all readers use cross checking as they read. Model reading an unknown passage. Read it out loud to children, thinking aloud as you come to words that you don't know. Identify the strategies you use as you read difficult passages.

7. Have children share a word they are unable to figure out and read the word in the context in which it is found. If the child is unable to share his or her strategies, model how a combination of strategies might be used to figure out the unknown word. Help children refine the effectiveness of their strategies.

8. Have children keep a log in which they record unfamiliar words, the context, and the strategies used to pronounce the words and determine their meanings. Provide opportunities for small group sharing.

9. Provide plenty of time for reading, reading, and more reading!

Leveled Book Series

Beginning Readers
Scholastic (800-325-6149)

Heath Little Readers
D.C. Heath (800-334-3284)

Literacy 2000
Rigby (800-822-8661)

Little Red Readers
Sundance (508-486-9201)

Ready to Read
Richard C. Owen (800-336-5588)

First Start
Troll (800-526-5289)

Learn to Read
Creative Teaching Press (714-995-7888)

Little Celebrations
Scott Foresman (800-792-0550)

Reading Corners
Dominie Press (800-232-4570)

Sunshine Books
Wright Group (800-523-2371)

Media and Technology

Discus Books CD-ROM (interactive books).
Discus Knowledge Research (800-567-4321)

Reading Blaster CD-ROM (early reading skills including reading short passages).
Davidson & Associates (800-545-7677)

Using Context Clues CD-ROM (practice software using context clues).
Computer Centerline (800-852-5802)

Professional Resources

Clay, M.M. (1991). *Becoming literate: The construction of inner control.* Portsmouth, NH: Heinemann.

Fountas, I.C., & Pinnell, G.S. (1996). *Guided reading: Good first teaching for all children.* Portsmouth, NH: Heinemann.

Goodman, Y.M., & Marek, A.M. (1996). *Retrospective miscue analysis: Revaluing readers and reading.* Katonah, NY: Richard C. Owen.

Goodman, Y.M., Watson, D.J., & Burke, C.L. (1987). *Reading miscue inventory: Alternative procedures.* Katonah, NY: Richard C. Owen.

3.14 Fluency

Goal   To help children read smoothly and easily.

Assessments Passage Reading 2.15 and 4.15

BACKGROUND

Good readers are fluent readers. When you listen to children read orally, you can spot the fluent readers. Fluent readers are able to read text in a normal speaking voice with appropriate intonation and inflection. Fluent readers are able to read texts smoothly and easily using various strategies to construct meaning from print (Duffy & Roehler, 1989). They use their knowledge of word decoding, their knowledge of stories, and their knowledge of the world to understand the meaning of new texts. A goal of reading instruction in the primary grades is for students to read fluently with good comprehension.

Many times young children are not fluent readers. Think about the children you teach. Some children may be choppy readers, reading with many stops, starts, and hesitations. They may be monotonous readers who read with little or no expression. Or children may be hasty readers and race through the passage ignoring phrasing and punctuation. When children are choppy, monotonous, or hasty readers, they are not reading fluently (Wilson, 1988).

Primary-grade children need to learn how to read fluently while they are learning other reading skills. But you need to remember that developing fluency takes time and practice. While children are building fluency, they are also expanding their sight vocabulary, learning word-identification strategies, and learning how to use their background knowledge to construct meaning from new texts. As children become proficient with these reading strategies, they are able to read the words in a passage more automatically. As children read words more automatically, they can pay closer attention to reading texts smoothly and easily.

Teaching children how to read fluently also enables them to read with better comprehension. When children learn how to read in a way that mirrors spoken language, as fluent readers do, they are better able to understand the meaning of texts (Rasinski, 1989). It is important, therefore, to teach children how to read fluently as they are learning how to read. The following strategies, ideas, and activities support the teaching of fluent reading.

| TEACHING STRATEGY 1 | Teacher-Assisted Reading (Neurological Impress Method) |

For children to learn how to read fluently, they need to hear and practice fluent reading. Sometimes beginning readers can identify fluent reading, but they are unable to produce it. To help students learn how to read fluently, you can use Teacher-Assisted Reading, or the Neurological Impress Method (Heckleman, 1966). The Neurological Impress Method is a technique in which the teacher and child simultaneously read aloud from the same book. The teacher reads slightly faster than the child in order to keep the child reading at a fluent pace. The child hears the reading and tries to read with the same pace and expression. The Neurological Impress Method is a useful strategy when you are helping one child or a small group of children improve fluency.

DIRECTIONS

1. Identify an interesting short book or passage that is below the child's reading level. You might identify several books and ask the child to choose one for the lesson.

2. Have the child sit slightly in front of you so that your voice is close to the child's ear.

3. Tell the child to follow your voice during the reading.

4. Read the material out loud with the child, but a little louder and faster than the child. Read only a short passage.

5. Run your finger under the words being read.

6. Reread the same passage several times. Drop your voice behind the child's as the child begins to read fluently. Place the child's hand on your hand so that both of you can use your fingers to follow the lines of print.

7. As the child reads, do not correct any miscues. Your goal is to help the child build fluency. You can work on word-identification strategies at another time.

8. Have the child read alone while the child follows the print with a finger. Support the child's reading as needed by saying the words aloud.

9. Read the passage with the child once more, speeding up the pace. Encourage the child to read fluently at a faster pace.

10. Use this strategy several times each week. Plan on guiding reading fluency for several months. Fluency needs to be developed over a long period of time.

TEACHING STRATEGY 2 — Choral Reading

Choral reading occurs when children read poetry or other short passages together or in groups. Choral reading facilitates fluency because children are able to read print along with other children. When reading in groups, children who have trouble reading fluently are carried along with the pace and expression of the other readers. All of the readers are able to read more smoothly and easily because they are able to listen to more proficient readers as they match speech and print in a smooth, steady reading pace.

DIRECTIONS

1. Identify a poem, a short book, or a passage that would be of interest to the children who will be choral reading.

2. Note words that may be new to the children or that the children may have difficulty reading. Write the words on the chalkboard or on chart paper. Read the difficult words to the class paying special attention to sounds or patterns in the words that the children have learned.

3. Have the entire group read the passage silently.

4. Read the passage aloud or ask one of the children to read it aloud. As you read, track the print with a pointer or your hand.

5. Discuss the passage, asking children to retell the poem or story.

6. Decide on the method of choral reading. The following varieties of choral reading have been suggested by Trousdale and Harris (1993).

   - Two-part arrangement. One group of voices reads alternately with another group.
   - Soloist and chorus. One voice reads and the rest of the group joins in on the refrain.
   - Line-a-child. One child or a pair read alone. Then the next child reads the next line, and so on.
   - Increasing or decreasing volume. Voices are added or subtracted, building up to and moving away from the high point of the story.
   - Increasing or decreasing tempo. The rate of reading is increased or decreased as the passage is read.
   - Unison. The whole group reads as one.
   - Accompaniment by music, movement, or sound effects. The reading is accompanied by instruments, hand motions, or sound effects such as snapping fingers.
   - Combination. A combination of any of the above ideas.

7. Experiment with volume, tempo, and expression. Have fun.

8. Perform the choral reading for an audience. Have a leader read the title and give the first beat so the group begins together. Tape record or videotape the performance and replay it, listening for fluent reading.

TEACHING STRATEGY 3	Multipaired Simultaneous Oral Reading

At least once a week most primary-grade children will need to practice reading fluently. Some children are naturally fluent readers, but most are not. Most children need guidance and practice in order to read smoothly and easily. Because almost all of the children you teach will need practice reading fluently, all of the children can practice at once with Multipaired Simultaneous Oral Reading (Poc, 1986). During Multipaired Simultaneous Oral Reading, the group is divided into pairs. Each child takes turns reading to a partner. After one child reads, the partners switch roles so that all children practice reading fluently.

DIRECTIONS

1. Identify a passage of a story that would lend itself to building fluency. For older readers, select a passage from a chapter book that has dialogue in it. Write the page number of the passage on the chalkboard or on an overhead transparency.

2. Tell children that they will be reading the passage to a partner. Explain that the goal of their reading will be to read fluently with a steady pace and good expression.

3. Model reading the passage with fluency. Read the passage expressively at a pace that moves quickly.

4. Ask children to read the passage with you. If there are any challenging sections containing dialect or difficult words, help the children say the difficult words.

5. Have children choose a partner for reading or choose partners for the children. Each time you use this strategy, have children choose different partners so that no one becomes dependent on another reader. At times, have children of the same reading ability work together. At other times, pair children of differing abilities. If a pair does not work well together, ask the children to change partners.

6. Let the pairs of children set their own rules about how much each child will read—one page, one paragraph, two paragraphs, and so on—before switching to the second reader.

7. Have children read the selection aloud. Monitor the activity and provide guidance as needed.

8. When a pair finishes reading, give each child a silent activity to complete.

9. After everyone has completed the paired oral reading, discuss the children's success at reading fluently. Occasionally, have one or more than one child volunteer to read a passage to the class. Congratulate all children on learning to read more smoothly.

Ideas and Activities

1. Recognize that reading is a developmental process and that fluency will develop as children increase their sight vocabularies and acquire a repertoire of word-identification strategies. Children in the primary grades generally will increase fluency as they gain more experience reading.

2. Encourage the repeated readings of pattern books. Pattern books are books that have repetitive phrases like "Brown Bear, Brown Bear, what do you see?" When children read books with repetition, they quickly become familiar with the repeated phrases, making the book easier to read with fluency. See Selected Resources: Fluency for a short list of pattern books or Appendix C in Johns and Lenski (1997) for a longer list.

3. Model good reading fluency by reading aloud to children. Occasionally point out that when you read books to the class, you are reading in a way that is similar to the language children hear. Tell children that good readers try to read so that reading sounds like talking.

4. Encourage frequent reading of easy books. Children have a difficult time reading fluently when they are trying to read books that are difficult for them. If a book is difficult, children have to devote attention to word identification and can't put as much effort into fluent reading. Try to have children read easy books several times each week.

5. Use flashlight reading of Big Books (Rennick & Williams, 1995). Place a Big Book on a chalkboard ledge or a tray. Tell children that you will be shining a flashlight on the words and that the children should read along with the flashlight. Move the flashlight along the sentences at a smooth, steady pace. Invite children to read the words as the flashlight shines on them.

6. Use echo reading with the class or with small groups of children. In echo reading, you read a phrase or sentence from a Big Book and the children repeat it after you. When you read, model appropriate reading pace and expression. As children repeat the phrase or sentence, they should try to "echo" your phrasing and intonation.

7. Provide opportunities for children to listen to talking books on audiotapes or to use computer programs with sound. Capitalize on children's interests when a particularly popular book is played repeatedly by allowing children to listen and read their favorite books again and again.

8. Use daily dictated stories for fluency practice. Have children dictate one or more sentences that you write on the chalkboard or on chart paper. Read the sentences to the class. Then have the class read along with you. Tell children that you want them to read with expression.

9. Make a videotape or audiotape of yourself reading an easy book. Send the book and the tape home with the children to practice reading outside of school. You could also ask other adults who are familiar to children to participate in videotape or audiotape reading. A school principal, a head teacher, a librarian, a crossing guard, a bus driver, and a lunchroom worker are all adults that children see on a regular basis and would be good role models for reading. You may have to supervise the reading of other adults so that their reading is a good example for the children, but having a variety of reading models is worth the extra time.

10. Develop a reading pals program with older children: students in intermediate grades, middle schools, high schools, or colleges. Suggest books for the reading pals to read with your children. Ask the pals to practice reading the books several times and to aim for fluent, conversational reading. Have the reading pals read the books to your children; then have the children read along with their reading pals.

11. List common phrases on sentence strips and place them in a pocket chart. Some examples of common phrases for children in day care or schools are "in the lunchroom," "on the playground," and "to the bus." Have children practice these phrases that encourage the use of smooth, fluent reading.

12. Identify songs and poems that children enjoy. Print the songs or poems on the chalkboard or on chart paper. Read or sing them with the children. Repeat the process several times a day. Encourage children to practice independently so they can read the words fluently.

13. Have children read fluently by performing Readers' Theater scripts. Readers' Theater scripts are similar to play scripts except they do not have stage directions. Children read the lines while sitting or standing rather than acting. When asking children to perform a Readers' Theater script, assign lines; then have children read their lines several times. Children should practice their lines aloud several times. After children have practiced their lines, they can read the script for an audience.

14. Provide children with many opportunities to read to an audience. Have children identify favorite passages of books, practice them, and read them to the class. Use a small microphone to encourage fluent reading. Inexpensive microphones can be purchased at many toy stores.

Selected Resources
FLUENCY

Pattern Books

Carle, E. (1985). *The very busy spider.* New York: Philomel.

Cowley, J. (1987). *Mrs. Wishy-Washy.* Bothell, WA: The Wright Group.

Galdone, P. (1973). *The little red hen.* New York: Scholastic.

Mandel, P. (1994). *Red cat, white cat.* New York: Henry Holt.

Martin, B. (1990). *Polar bear, polar bear, what do you hear?* New York: Holt.

Numeroff, L.J. (1991). *If you give a moose a muffin.* New York: HarperCollins.

Rosen, M. (1989). *We're going on a bear hunt.* New York: Macmillan.

Shaw, N. (1992). *Sheep out to eat.* Boston: Houghton Mifflin.

Stickland, P., & Strickland, H. (1994). *Dinosaur roar!* New York: Dutton.

Viorst, J. (1972). *Alexander and the terrible, horrible, no good, very bad day.* New York: Atheneum.

Media and Technology

Failure Free Reading (talking software program).
(800-542-2170)

Interactive Reading Resources (enjoyable songs on tape that tell a story).
(847-658-5851)

Listening Library (books on tapes).
(800-243-4504)

Reading Plus System (computer program to develop fluency).
(800-732-3758)

Professional Books

Morrow, L. M. (1997). *Literacy development in the early years* (3rd ed.). Boston: Allyn and Bacon.

Olson, M.W., & Homan, S.P. (Eds.). (1993). *Teacher to teacher: Strategies for the elementary classroom.* Newark, DE: International Reading Association.

3.15 Monitoring Reading

Goal To help children monitor their reading.

Assessments Interviews about Reading 2.1 and 4.1; Passage Reading 2.15 and 4.15

BACKGROUND

Effective readers monitor their reading to ensure that what they are reading makes sense. One of the keys to becoming an independent reader is the ability to identify and correct one's comprehension problems (Paris, Lipson, & Wixon, 1994). Effective readers ask themselves, "Do I understand what I'm reading?" They also make pictures in their minds, predict from the text, and ask themselves questions as they read. When effective readers detect that what they are reading does not make sense, they realize this and apply appropriate correction or "fix-up" strategies. For example, they may look at pictures, reread to clarify ideas, look up a word in a dictionary, reread for word meaning, or ask for help (Cunningham & Allington, 1994).

Metacognition, or thinking about one's own thinking processes, is an important aspect of monitoring reading (Flavell, 1977). Baker (1991) has identified specific areas that help children develop monitoring strategies for reading. Even young readers can be taught to be on the "look-out" for the following:

- Words they don't understand.
- Information that doesn't connect with what they already know.
- Ideas that don't make sense.

While most young children do not automatically monitor their reading, they can be taught simple strategies to help them monitor as they read. The strategies and activities discussed below provide suggestions for teaching your students to become active readers who monitor their reading.

TEACHING STRATEGY 1   Critter

The Critter strategy helps children create a visual image to assist them with monitoring their reading (Johns & Lenski, 1997). It serves as a concrete reminder to children that they need to think while they are reading and that their reading should make sense.

DIRECTIONS

1. Draw a cartoon-like Critter and present it to the children on the chalkboard, a piece of chart paper, or an overhead transparency. A sample Critter is provided below.

2. Tell children that they can use the Critter to help them think and understand as they read.

3. Ask children to visualize a Critter that they have in their heads that helps them read. Provide time for children to share their ideas.

4. Have children draw and color their Critters.

5. Guide children to develop a list of important questions the Critter can help the children ask themselves as they read. Some possible questions include the following:

    • Do I understand what I am reading?
    • What do I already know about the topic?
    • How can I figure out this hard word?
    • Can I use a picture to help me?
    • Do I need to reread?
    • Should I look up the word in a dictionary?
    • Should I ask for help?

6. Laminate the children's Critters and mount them on their desks or reading folders. Post in the classroom the list of questions their Critters can prompt the children to ask themselves. Remind the children to use their Critters to help them think about and understand what they are reading.

TEACHING STRATEGY 2	Monitoring Think-Along

The Monitoring Think-Along strategy helps children understand the self-monitoring strategies that good readers use. The Monitoring Think-Along can be used to model many different self-monitoring strategies, such as making pictures in your mind, predicting what will come next, asking questions about the text, rereading to clarify ideas, rereading for word meanings, and connecting the text to personal experiences.

DIRECTIONS

1. Select a Big Book or other text that children will all be able to see. Tell children that you are going to show them some strategies that good readers use.

2. Point your index finger to your head to show that you are thinking. Tell children, "I am thinking about what this book might be about."

3. Read the title aloud and, using information from the title, make a comment such as, "That is the name of a girl. I think the story will be about her."

4. Tell the children, "Now, I'll look at the picture on the cover."

5. Make a comment using information from the cover illustration such as, "It looks like a birthday party. I think the book will be about the girl's birthday party."

6. Close your eyes, point your index finger to your head to show you are thinking, and say, "Now I'll try to make a picture in my mind of what might happen at the birthday party." Share with the children some of the things you are visualizing. For example, "I see presents, a chocolate birthday cake, balloons, and lots of children. It looks like everyone is having fun."

7. Begin to read the text aloud. After reading several sentences, stop and ask yourself a question about what you just read. For example, say, "Am I right that the book is about a birthday party? Do I need to change my prediction?" Share your answers with the children.

8. Continue reading the text, stopping periodically to model a monitoring strategy that good readers use. The list below contains possible strategies to model as part of the Monitoring Think-Along.

☞ **Self-Monitoring Strategies**

- Make pictures in your mind.
- Predict what will come next.
- Ask questions about the text.
- Reread to clarify ideas.
- Reread for word meanings.
- Connect the text to personal experiences.

TEACHING STRATEGY 3	Pause-Think-Retell

The Pause-Think-Retell (Robb, 1996) strategy helps children get into the habit of monitoring their comprehension while reading longer texts. This strategy focuses on having children pause at the end of a paragraph, page, or section of text, think about what they have read, and retell the important ideas to themselves. If children are unable to remember enough to retell the text to themselves, they should reread that portion of the text.

DIRECTIONS

1. Select a text that might be challenging for the children. Recopy the text onto chart paper or copy it onto overhead transparencies so all of the children will be able to see it.

2. Tell children that good readers use the Pause-Think-Retell strategy to make sure they understand what they are reading.

3. Model the strategy for children by reading the first paragraph, page, or section of text aloud. Then Pause, point to your head as you Think, and ask yourself, "Can I Retell what I just read?"

4. Retell several of the ideas from the paragraph, page, or section but leave out several important ideas.

5. Tell children, "I think I need to reread that because I can't retell all of the important ideas."

6. Reread the section aloud, emphasizing the important points. Then Pause, point to your head as you Think, and prompt yourself to Retell the important information. Tell children that because you remembered the important ideas from the section, you can go on to the next part of the text. You may also want to remind children how to distinguish among ideas; some are more important than others.

7. Continue modeling this strategy for the next paragraph, page, or section. This time, provide a complete retelling and tell children, "I remembered the important ideas so I can go on to the next part of the book."

8. Continue modeling this strategy for several paragraphs, pages, or sections.

9. Ask children to try the strategy with the next section of the text. Provide prompts such as "Stop and think," "Can you retell what you just read?" and "Did you remember all the important ideas?" to guide them through the process. If children have difficulty distinguishing between important ideas and minor details in their retellings, before conducting further retellings you may want to reinstruct students how to distinguish minor details from important ideas.

10. Display a poster that has the words Pause-Think-Retell on it. Remind children to use this strategy when they are reading independently.

Ideas and Activities

1. Implement monitoring logs to help children monitor their independent reading. Include a list of questions for them to consider. The monitoring questions should be modeled for children prior to expecting them to use a monitoring log. Provide discussion time for them to share the monitoring strategies they are using while reading. Sample monitoring questions are provided in the following list.

   ? Monitoring Questions for Logs

   Did I predict before reading?
   Did I make pictures in my head?
   Did I ask myself questions as I read?
   Did I understand what I read?
   Did I reread when I didn't understand?
   What did I do when I came to unknown words?
   Can I retell what I read?
   Can I tell which ideas stand out or are more important than others?
   What else did I do to monitor my reading?

2. Make bookmarks that include monitoring strategies and questions. Provide copies for home and school reading.

3. Develop an I-Need-Help Procedure for children to use when they realize their reading doesn't make sense and their strategies are not working. Have children copy the I-Need-Help Procedure on the cover of their

reading folder or on a bookmark. Also display the I-Need-Help Procedure on a poster in the classroom. A sample I-Need-Help Procedure is listed in the box.

I-Need-Help Procedure
1. Think for a minute. Try to solve the problem yourself.
2. Use classroom resources to help you (monitoring log, monitoring posters, Word Wall).
3. Ask three students for help.
4. Ask the teacher.

4. Explain to the children that good readers create pictures in their minds as they read. Read a passage aloud and ask the children to draw what they saw in their minds. Provide time for the children to share their drawings. Compare their drawings to the text. Explain that good readers create these types of pictures in their minds while they are reading. Read another passage to the children and ask them to close their eyes and visualize a picture in their mind based on the passage. Provide sharing time. Encourage children to use visualization as they read.

5. Have children use partner questioning to support the use of monitoring strategies. Divide the class into partners and have one partner serve as the questioner and the other as the reader. The reader should read a paragraph aloud, and the questioner should ask a question about how the reader monitored his or her reading. For example, the questioner may ask, "Did that make sense to you?" or "Can you retell that in your own words?" or "What did you do when you came to the hard word?" Children can refer to the list of monitoring questions from their monitoring logs (idea 1) or the strategy picture cards (idea 6) to help them with this activity.

6. Use strategy picture cards to provide children with a visual clue regarding the monitoring strategies they can use to help them understand their reading. Post the picture cards in the classroom, provide children with their own copy for their reading folder, and send a copy home for the children and their parents to use for home reading. Sample strategy picture cards are provided in the box on the next page.

Strategy Picture Cards

Does It Make Sense?

What Do You Already Know?

Read On

Look at Word Parts and Letters

Reread

Make a Prediction

The picture makes me think of . . .

Make a Picture in Your Head

Retell in Your Own Words

In this story, the . . .

Look at Picture Clues

Ask for Help

HELP!

7. Conference with children and use a monitoring strategy checklist to assess which monitoring strategies they use as they read and which ones they still need to learn. Use this information to plan future Think-Alongs and other instructional activities. A sample monitoring strategy checklist is provided in the box.

Monitoring Strategy Checklist

Before Reading do you:

_____ Think about the title and cover?

_____ Make predictions?

_____ Think about what you know about the topic?

During Reading do you:

_____ Ask yourself if the reading makes sense?

_____ Pause-Think-Retell?

_____ Make pictures in your mind?

_____ Use strategies to figure out hard words?

_____ Reread to help yourself understand?

_____ Use pictures for clues?

_____ Ask yourself questions?

After Reading do you:

_____ Retell the story?

_____ Think about what you read?

_____ Share what you learned with someone?

_____ Think about what strategies you used to help you read?

Big Books for Demonstrating Monitoring Reading

Cowley, J. (1983). *Meanies.* San Diego: Rigby.

Ehlert, L. (1990). *Feathers for lunch.* New York: Trumpet.

Oppenheim, J. (1994). *"Not now! said the cow."* New York: Trumpet.

Peek, M. (1985). *Mary wore her red dress.* New York: Trumpet.

Wells, R. (1985). *Hazel's amazing mother.* New York: Dial.

Williams, S. (1989). *I went walking.* New York: Trumpet.

Media and Technology

Reader Rabbit's Interactive Reading Journey CD-ROM (40 storybooks can be read independently or followed as the character reads aloud).
UPDATA (800-882-2844)

Talking Classic Tales CD-ROM (interactive fairy tales for building comprehension and reading strategies).
UPDATA (800-882-2844)

The Reading Carnival CD-ROM (games and stories build comprehension and problem-solving skills).
UPDATA (800-882-2844)

Professional Resources

Baskwell, J., & Whitman, P. (1997). *Every child can read: Strategies and guidelines for helping struggling readers.* New York: Scholastic Professional Books.

Combs, M. (1996). *Developing competent readers and writers in the primary grades.* Columbus, OH: Merrill.

Glazer, S.M. (1992). *Reading comprehension: Self-monitoring strategies to develop independent readers.* New York: Scholastic Professional Books.

Robb, L. (1996). *Reading strategies that work: Teaching your students to become better readers.* New York: Scholastic Professional Books.

SECTION 4

Early Literacy Posttests

Section 4 contains 15 Early Literacy Assessments arranged the same way as the assessments in Section 2. These assessments are designed as posttests to help gauge the child's progress after instruction. The assessments are listed below along with the page where the directions and, if applicable, the child's copy can be found.

	Assessments	Directions	Child's Copy
4.1	Interviews About Reading	20	N/A*
4.2	Retelling a Story	21	N/A
4.3	Literacy Knowledge	22	*Animals* book
4.4	Wordless Picture Reading	37	207
4.5	Auditory Discrimination	39	N/A
4.6	Rhyme Detection	40	N/A
4.7	Alphabet Knowledge	41	208
4.8	Phoneme Segmentation	43	N/A
4.9	Writing	44	N/A
4.10	Developmental Spelling	45	235
4.11	Consonant Phonic Elements	47	209
4.12	Decoding	51	211
4.13	Caption Reading	53	212
4.14	Basic Sight Word Knowledge	55	213
4.15	Passage Reading	57	214

*Not Applicable

The directions for the posttests are the same as those presented in Section 2, so we did not repeat the directions here. Refer to Section 2 for administration directions. The child's copies needed for the assessments are found on the following pages. At the very end of this section is the Record Booklet (pp. 219–245) that is used to record and summarize the child's responses to the assessments administered.

These posttests permit you to maintain an ongoing record of the child's growth as a reader. Coupled with your insightful observations and the child's daily performance in your classroom, you should have a rich source of data to monitor the child's growth in literacy.

Note:
Remove and bind the following *Animals* booklet for use with the Literacy Knowledge Assessment (4.3).

Animals

by Dorie Cannon

I love animals.

They eat, sleep,

and play

every day.

Just like me!

1

Cats sleep a lot.

They play with
string and eat
fish. I like their
soft fur.

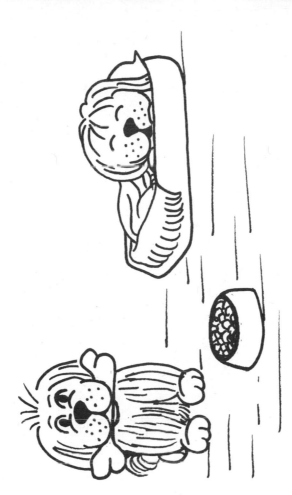

Dogs eat bones,

run, and bark.

They sleep in a bed.

I sleep in a bed, too!

Fish swim, sleep,
and eat in the
water. I like their
pretty colors.

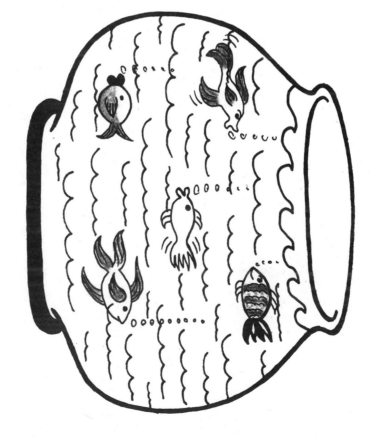

Bears eat fish and sleep in caves. They scratch their backs on trees. Ouch! That would hurt.

Elephants roll in mud
and eat tree bark.

They lie on the
ground to sleep.

How do they do that?

6

Monkeys play

and sleep in trees.

They eat bananas.

I eat bananas too!

Birds love to fly.

They eat seeds

and sleep in nests.

There's a big

nest in my tree.

8

Rabbits eat plants.

They hop and

sleep in underground

nests. I can hop like

a rabbit.

I love animals
very much.

Someday I will
work in a zoo.

I	S	K	H	Q	V	L
A	G	P	J	N	D	
T	C	Z	E	F	U	M
B	O	X	Y	R	W	

r	x	z	k	t	e	y
w	q	c	g	h	m	a
i	p	s	v	d	l	j
u	o	f	b	a	n	g

Posttest — Alphabet Knowledge — Child's Copy

o   x   d   n   k

n   d   a   g   h

f   k   r   x   t

m   s   p   t   h

l   v   t   j   n

d s r o g

h y f b c

f k g s t

w c r d n

r h j n p

Posttest — Consonant Phonic Elements — Child's Copy

210

Jay Conway

Chuck Hoke

Kimberly Blake

Homer Preston

Cindy Simpson

Chester Wright

Stanley Shaw

Glen Spencer

Flo Thorton

Grace Brewster

Ron Smitherman

Vance Middleton

Bernard Prendergraph

Source: Cunningham, P. (1990). The names test: A quick assessment of decoding ability. *The Reading Teacher, 44,* 124–129.

Posttest — Decoding — Child's Copy

1

The frog sits.

2

The frog eats.

3

The frog jumps.

4

The frog swims.

Posttest — Caption Reading — Child's Copy

1. of

2. to

3. in

4. that

5. was

6. you

7. on

8. are

9. with

10. at

Sam Likes Books

Sam likes books.

He likes big books.

He likes small books.

He likes all kinds of books.

Sam likes to read his books at home.

Ball Game

Bob went to a ball game with his dad.

They sat by first base. Dad got two hot

dogs and two cold drinks for lunch.

The ball player hit the ball. It came

to Bob. He caught the ball with his glove.

Bob jumped up and down. He was happy.

The Pet Shop

Mike ran home quickly from school. He was in a hurry to see his mom. Mike asked, "Are you ready, mom?" Mom just smiled. She was feeding the new baby. Mike jumped up and down saying, "Let's go, mom!" When mom finished, all three of them got into the car. They drove to the pet shop.

Mike looked in all the cages. He saw some brown baby dogs. He saw cats and kittens. Mike also saw birds, hamsters, and turtles. Mike wanted to choose a small pet with only two legs. He knew he would take good care of it.

Night Time Friend

"It's time to come in the house," Mother called to Joe from the kitchen. "It's getting late and will be dark soon."

Joe did not want to go inside. He sat outside waiting for his friend. Mother watched from the window.

Joe looked up into the sky. He wondered what was taking his friend so long. Then Joe saw something black glide across the night sky. He knew it was his night time friend. Joe watched as it ate insects while flying around the garden.

In the morning, his friend would hang upside down in a cave and fall asleep.

RECORD BOOKLET FOR EARLY LITERACY ASSESSMENTS

Jerry L. Johns, Susan Davis Lenski, & Laurie Elish-Piper

Child _____ Grade/Age _____ Sex M F   Date of Test _____

School _____ Examiner _____ Date of Birth _____

Profile of Emergent Reader

	Low or Not Evident	Some	High or Always Evident
4.1 Interviews About Reading Attitude and Interest	⊢────┼────┼────┼────⊣		
4.2 Retelling a Story	⊢────┼────┼────┼────⊣		
4.3 Literacy Knowledge _____ /20	⊢────┼────┼────┼────⊣		
4.4 Wordless Picture Reading	⊢────┼────┼────┼────⊣		
4.5 Auditory Discrimination _____ /12	⊢────┼────┼────┼────⊣		
4.6 Rhyme Detection _____ /10	⊢────┼────┼────┼────⊣		
4.7 Alphabet Knowledge			
_____ /26 upper case	⊢────┼────┼────┼────⊣		
_____ /28 lower case	⊢────┼────┼────┼────⊣		
4.8 Phoneme Segmentation _____ /11	⊢────┼────┼────┼────⊣		
4.9 Writing	⊢────┼────┼────┼────⊣		
4.10 Developmental Spelling	⊢────┼────┼────┼────⊣		
4.11 Consonant Phonic Elements			
_____ /15 initial	⊢────┼────┼────┼────⊣		
_____ /10 final	⊢────┼────┼────┼────⊣		
4.12 Decoding _____ /26	⊢────┼────┼────┼────⊣		
4.13 Caption Reading	⊢────┼────┼────┼────⊣		
4.14 Basic Sight Word Knowledge _____ /10	⊢────┼────┼────┼────⊣		
4.15 Passage Reading			
word recognition	⊢────┼────┼────┼────⊣		
comprehension	⊢────┼────┼────┼────⊣		

If you're interested in the child's	You might want to use assessment
oral language ability/comprehension	4.2, 4.4
general notions about reading and literacy	4.1, 4.3, 4.7, 4.9, 4.10
writing and spelling	4.9, 4.10
ability to work with sounds orally	4.5, 4.6, 4.8
phonics and decoding abilities	4.9, 4.10, 4.11, 4.12
word knowledge	4.4, 4.9, 4.10, 4.13, 4.14
story knowledge or sense of story	4.2, 4.4, 4.15
ability to read independently	4.13, 4.14, 4.15

Interviews About Reading
EMERGENT READER (PreK–K)

Teacher's Directions   20
Child's Copy   None

1. Do you like to have someone read to you? _____ Yes _____ No

   Who do you like to read to you? _____

2. What kinds of stories do you like?

   _____

3. Tell me the name of a favorite story.

   _____

4. Do you have many books at home? _____ Yes _____ No

   Where do you keep the books? _____

5. Who do you know that likes to read? _____

6. Are you learning to read? _____ Yes _____ No

   Tell me more about that. _____

7. Do you want to learn how to read better? _____ Yes _____ No

   Tell me more about that. _____

8. Do you think you will be a good reader? _____ Yes _____ No

   Tell me more about that. _____

9. What makes a person a good reader? _____

   _____

10. What is reading? _____

   _____

Qualitative Judgments
of Interviews About Reading
EMERGENT READER (PreK–K)

	Not Evident Low Seldom Weak Poor		Some		Evident High Always Strong Excellent
Overall interest in reading	├	┼	┼	┼	┤
Familiarity with specific stories	├	┼	┼	┼	┤
Availability of books	├	┼	┼	┼	┤
Knowledge of reading role models	├	┼	┼	┼	┤
Confidence in learning to read	├	┼	┼	┼	┤
Motivation to learn to read	├	┼	┼	┼	┤
Knowledge of purpose of reading	├	┼	┼	┼	┤

Observations, Comments, Notes, and Insights

From Johns, Lenski, and Elish-Piper, *Early Literacy Assessments & Teaching Strategies*

Teacher's Directions   20
Child's Copy   None

1. Do you like to have someone read to you? _____ Yes _____ No

   Who do you like to read to you? _____

2. What kinds of stories do you like? _____

   _____

3. Tell me the name of a favorite story. _____

4. Do you have many books at home? _____ Yes _____ No

   How many books do you think you have? _____

5. Who do you know that likes to read? _____

   _____

6. Do you think you are a good reader? _____ Yes _____ No

   Why or why not? _____

7. What makes a person a good reader? _____

   _____

8. When you are reading and come to a word you don't know, what do you do?

   _____

9. What do you do when you don't understand what you are reading?

   _____

10. What is reading?

   _____

Qualitative Judgments of Interviews About Reading
EARLY READER (GRADES 1–2)

	Not Evident Low Seldom Weak Poor		Some		Evident High Always Strong Excellent
Overall interest in reading	├	┼	┼	┼	┤
Familiarity with specific stories	├	┼	┼	┼	┤
Availability of books	├	┼	┼	┼	┤
Knowledge of reading role models	├	┼	┼	┼	┤
Confidence in learning to read	├	┼	┼	┼	┤
Motivation to learn to read	├	┼	┼	┼	┤
Knowledge of word-identification strategies	├	┼	┼	┼	┤
Knowledge of comprehension strategies	├	┼	┼	┼	┤
Knowledge of purpose of reading	├	┼	┼	┼	┤

Observations, Comments, Notes, and Insights

From Johns, Lenski, and Elish-Piper, *Early Literacy Assessments & Teaching Strategies*

Teacher's Directions   21
Child's Copy   None

BRIEF DIRECTIONS

Say to the child: **"I'm going to read a story to you. After I am finished reading, I will ask you to tell me the story as if you were telling it to someone who has not read the story. As you listen, try to remember as much of the story as you can."** Read an age-appropriate book that is new to the child. After reading, say, **"Now tell me as much of the story as you can."** If the child hesitates, ask probing questions such as **"What was the story about?"** or **"Who was in the story?"** or **"What happened next?"**

Qualitative Judgments of Retelling a Story

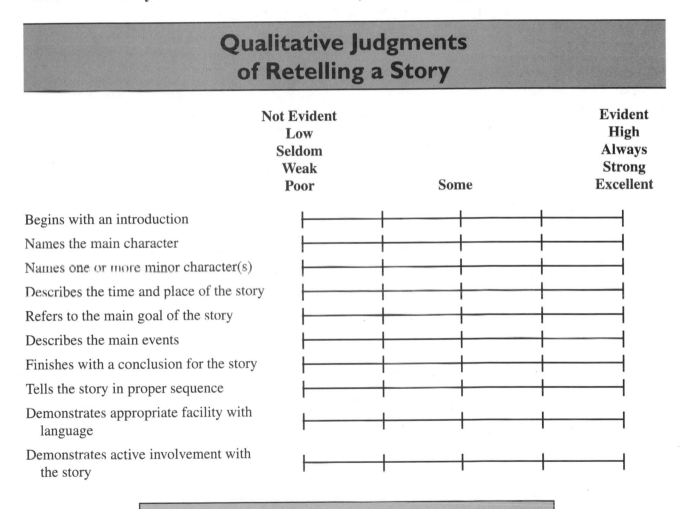

	Not Evident Low Seldom Weak Poor		Some		Evident High Always Strong Excellent
Begins with an introduction					
Names the main character					
Names one or more minor character(s)					
Describes the time and place of the story					
Refers to the main goal of the story					
Describes the main events					
Finishes with a conclusion for the story					
Tells the story in proper sequence					
Demonstrates appropriate facility with language					
Demonstrates active involvement with the story					

Observations, Comments, Notes, and Insights

From Johns, Lenski, and Elish-Piper, *Early Literacy Assessments & Teaching Strategies*

Teacher's Directions 22
Child's Copy   195–206

BRIEF DIRECTIONS

Show the book *Animals* to the child. Say, **"I'd like you to show me some of the things you know about reading. You won't have to read."** Ask the following questions as *you* read the book to the child. Circle correct (+) or incorrect (−) responses. Total correct responses.

PAGE

	+ −	1.	Hand the book to the child and say, **"Show me the front of this book."**
1	+ −	2.	Say, **"Point to where I should start reading."** *Read page 1.*
2	+ −	3.	Ask, **"Which way should I go?"** Check for knowledge of left to right. *Read first line of page 2.*
2/3	+ −	4.	Ask, **"Where should I go after that?"** Check for knowledge of a return sweep to the left. *Read rest of page 2 and page 3.*
3	+ −	5.	On page 3, point to the comma and ask, **"What's this or what's this for?"**
4	+ −	6.	*Read text on page 4.* Point to a period and ask, **"What's this or what's this for?"**
5	+ −	7.	*Read text on page 5.* Point to the exclamation mark and ask, **"What's this or what's this for?"**
6	+ −	8.	*Read text on page 6.* Point to the question mark and ask, **"What's this or what's this for?"**
6	+ −	9.	Point to a lower-case letter (w, g, c) and say, **"Find a capital letter like this, find an upper-case letter like this, or find the big one like this."**
7	+ −	10.	*Read text on page 7.* Say, **"Show me one letter."** (Two 3″ × 5″ cards may be useful for items 10–19.)
	+ −	11.	Say, **"Show me two letters."**
	+ −	12.	Say, **"Show me only one word."**
	+ −	13.	Say, **"Show me two words."**
	+ −	14.	Say, **"Show me the first letter of a word."**
	+ −	15.	Say, **"Show me the last letter of a word."**
	+ −	16.	Say, **"Show me a long word."**
	+ −	17.	Say, **"Show me a short word."**
	+ −	18.	Say, **"Show me a sentence."**
8/9	+ −	19.	*Read text on pages 8 and 9.* Point to a capital letter (B, p. 8 and R, I, p. 9) and say, **"Find a small letter like this or find a lower-case letter like this."**
10	+ −	20.	*Read text on page 10.* Close the book and hand it to the child with back cover showing and say, **"Show me the title or show me the name of the book."**

☐ **Total Correct**

Qualitative Judgments of Literacy Knowledge

	Not Evident Low Seldom Weak Poor		Some		Evident High Always Strong Excellent
Overall engagement	⊢————————	————————	————————	————————	————————⊣
Understanding of print directionality	⊢————————	————————	————————	————————	————————⊣
Knowledge of punctuation	⊢————————	————————	————————	————————	————————⊣
Correspondence of upper-case and lower-case letters	⊢————————	————————	————————	————————	————————⊣
Knowledge of letter and letters	⊢————————	————————	————————	————————	————————⊣
Knowledge of word and words	⊢————————	————————	————————	————————	————————⊣
Ability to frame a sentence	⊢————————	————————	————————	————————	————————⊣

Observations, Comments, Notes, and Insights

Teacher's Directions 37
Child's Copy 208

Qualitative Judgments of Wordless Picture Reading

	Not Evident Low Seldom Weak Poor		Some		Evident High Always Strong Excellent
Overall engagement					
Connects pictures to story					
Language use					
Sense of story					

Reading Dictation (check one if used)

_____ Child was unable to read what was dictated.

_____ Child pointed to words but only read a few words.

_____ Child pointed to words and read about half of the words.

_____ Child read what was dictated practically verbatim.

Observations, Comments, Notes, and Insights

Teacher's Directions 39
Child's Copy None

			Same	**Different**
1. debt	—	get		☐
2. tick	—	tip		☐
3. touch	—	touch	☐	
4. disk	—	desk		☐
5. mall	—	mall	☐	
6. came	—	tame		☐
7. sew	—	saw		☐
8. lass	—	laugh		☐
9. duck	—	dock		☐
10. mud	—	mug		☐
11. thing	—	thing	☐	
12. nice	—	mice		☐

Total Correct ☐

Observations, Comments, Notes, and Insights

Teacher's Directions 40
Child's Copy   None

BRIEF DIRECTIONS

Say to the child: **"I want you to tell me if two words rhyme. When words sound the same at the end, they rhyme. *Hat* rhymes with *cat*. Does *look* rhyme with *book*? Yes. Does *mat* rhyme with *bat*? Yes. But not all words rhyme. *Mice* does not rhyme with *soon* because *mice* ends with *ice* and *soon* ends with *oon*. Does *cat* rhyme with *pig*? No. Does *sick* rhyme with *pick*? Yes. Now, listen carefully. I'm going to say some words, and I want you to tell me if they rhyme."** Place a ✓ in the appropriate column, total correct responses, and record the score in the box.

		Correct	Incorrect
1. me	— he	_____	_____
2. ball	— mall	_____	_____
3. hog	— let	_____	_____
4. than	— ran	_____	_____
5. skim	— trim	_____	_____
6. rag	— men	_____	_____
7. that	— fat	_____	_____
8. green	— broom	_____	_____
9. ring	— sack	_____	_____
10. shake	— bake	_____	_____

Total Correct ☐

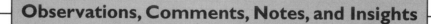

Observations, Comments, Notes, and Insights

From Johns, Lenski, and Elish-Piper, *Early Literacy Assessments & Teaching Strategies*

Teacher's Directions   41
Child's Copy   208

BRIEF DIRECTIONS

Present the alphabet sheet to the child. Use 5″ × 8″ cards to block off everything but the line being read. If necessary, point to each letter with a finger. Then say, **"Here are some letters. I want to see how many you know."** Place + above correctly identified letters. Record the child's responses for incorrect letters. Total correct responses and record the score in the boxes. Note that lower case *a* and *g* appear in both manuscript and print form.

I	S	K	H	Q	V	L
A	G	P	J	N	D	
T	C	Z	E	F	U	M
B	O	X	Y	R	W	

☐ **Total Correct**

r	x	z	k	t	e	y
w	q	c	g	h	m	a
i	p	s	v	d	l	j
u	o	f	b	a	n	g

☐ **Total Correct**

Observations, Comments, Notes, and Insights

Teacher's Directions   43
Child's Copy   None

BRIEF DIRECTIONS

Say to the child: **"Today we're going to play a word game. I'm going to say a word, and I want you to break the word apart. You are going to tell me each sound in the word in order. For example, if I say** *old,* **you should say** */o/-/l/-/d/."** (*Teacher: Be sure to say the sounds, not the letters, in the word.*) **"Let's try a few together."**

PRACTICE ITEMS

ride, go, man (*Assist the child in segmenting these items as necessary.*)

TEST ITEMS

(*Circle those items that the child correctly segments; incorrect responses may be recorded on the blank line following the item.*) The correct number of phonemes is indicated in parentheses.

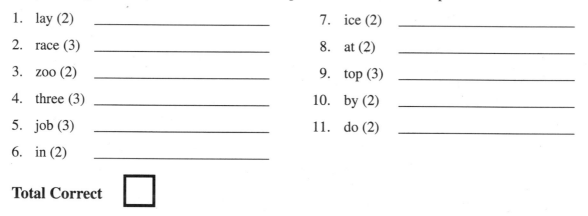

1. lay (2) _____   7. ice (2) _____

2. race (3) _____   8. at (2) _____

3. zoo (2) _____   9. top (3) _____

4. three (3) _____   10. by (2) _____

5. job (3) _____   11. do (2) _____

6. in (2) _____

Total Correct ☐

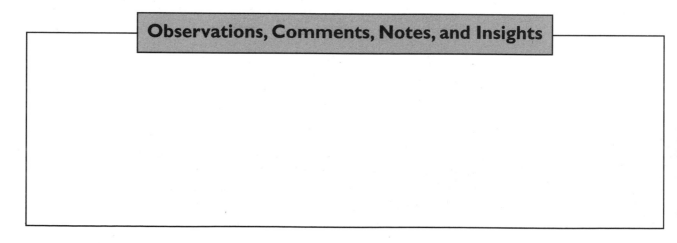

Observations, Comments, Notes, and Insights

The author, Hallie Kay Yopp, California State University, Fullerton, grants permission for this test to be reproduced. The author acknowledges the contribution of the late Harry Singer to the development of this test. Adapted from Yopp, H.K. (1995). A test for assessing phonemic awareness in young children. *The Reading Teacher, 49,* 20–29.

Teacher's Directions   44
Child's Copy   None

BRIEF DIRECTIONS

Give the child paper and pencil. Ask the child to do some writing. Record qualitative judgments, observations, and insights below.

Qualitative Judgments of Writing

	Not Evident Low Seldom Weak Poor	Some	Evident High Always Strong Excellent

Directionality

Left to right

Top to bottom

Child's Name

Knowledge of first (F) and last (L) name

Letter-Sound Relationships

Represents sounds heard at word beginnings

Represents sounds heard at word endings

Represents sounds heard in word middles

Uses vowels

Writing Conventions

Use of word boundaries

Use of punctuation

Writing (check one)

_____ Scribbles or "cursivelike" scribbles

_____ Letterlike formations

_____ Repeated letters, numbers, words

_____ Variety of letters, numbers, wordsx

Overall Message Intent (check one)

_____ Child indicated no message intent or did not communicate a message.

_____ Child talked about but did not read or pretend to read what was written.

_____ Child was able to read what was written.

Teacher could make sense of writing independently.   yes   no

Teacher's Directions 45–46
Child's Copy   235

BRIEF DIRECTIONS

Provide each child with a copy of the child's sheet. Tell the child(ren), **"Today we are going to spell some words. Some of the words will be hard, but don't worry. Just spell them the best you can by making good guesses about the sounds and letters you hear in the words."** Dictate each word and use it in a short sentence. The words are listed below. Use the Developmental Spelling Stage Scoring Chart on page 46 to analyze the child's spelling for each word. Then determine each child's general developmental spelling stage by noting the stage that appeared most frequently.

1.	drop	6.	mess
2.	faster	7.	packed
3.	liked	8.	make
4.	back	9.	earn
5.	monster	10.	greet

Circle the child's developmental spelling stage for each word.

1. **drop**	Precommunicative	Semiphonetic	Phonetic	Transitional	Conventional
2. **faster**	Precommunicative	Semiphonetic	Phonetic	Transitional	Conventional
3. **liked**	Precommunicative	Semiphonetic	Phonetic	Transitional	Conventional
4. **back**	Precommunicative	Semiphonetic	Phonetic	Transitional	Conventional
5. **monster**	Precommunicative	Semiphonetic	Phonetic	Transitional	Conventional
6. **mess**	Precommunicative	Semiphonetic	Phonetic	Transitional	Conventional
7. **packed**	Precommunicative	Semiphonetic	Phonetic	Transitional	Conventional
8. **make**	Precommunicative	Semiphonetic	Phonetic	Transitional	Conventional
9. **earn**	Precommunicative	Semiphonetic	Phonetic	Transitional	Conventional
10. **greet**	Precommunicative	Semiphonetic	Phonetic	Transitional	Conventional

GENERAL DEVELOPMENTAL SPELLING STAGE (CHECK ONE)

☐ Precommunicative   ☐ Semiphonetic   ☐ Phonetic   ☐ Transitional   ☐ Conventional

Child's Name _____

Stage

1. _____   _____

2. _____   _____

3. _____   _____

4. _____   _____

5. _____   _____

6. _____   _____

7. _____   _____

8. _____   _____

9. _____   _____

10. _____   _____

Posttest — Developmental Spelling — Child's Copy

Teacher's Directions   47
Child's Copy   209–210

INITIAL CONSONANT SOUND RECOGNITION

PART 1

1. coat	ball	**cat**	leg	wagon
2. wood	ball	cat	leg	**wagon**
3. book	**ball**	cat	leg	wagon
4. leaf	ball	cat	**leg**	wagon
5. wet	ball	cat	leg	**wagon**

PART 2

6. door	o	x	**d**	n	k
7. head	n	d	a	g	**h**
8. keep	f	**k**	r	x	t
9. mother	**m**	s	p	t	h
10. toy	l	v	**t**	j	n

PART 3

11. man	**m**	s	r	o	g
12. fork	h	y	**f**	b	c
13. giraffe	f	k	**g**	s	t
14. nose	w	c	r	d	**n**
15. pencil	r	h	j	n	**p**

Total Correct ☐

From Johns, Lenski, and Elish-Piper, *Early Literacy Assessments & Teaching Strategies*

FINAL CONSONANT SOUND RECOGNITION

PART 4

1. hat	ball	**cat**	leg	wagon
2. hen	ball	cat	leg	**wagon**
3. log	ball	cat	**leg**	wagon
4. feet	ball	**cat**	leg	wagon
5. call	**ball**	cat	leg	wagon

6. truck	o	x	d	n	**k**
7. land	n	**d**	a	g	h
8. bent	f	k	r	x	**t**
9. mouse	m	**s**	p	t	h
10. pin	l	v	t	j	**n**

Total Correct ☐

Observations, Comments, Notes, and Insights

(based on Cunningham, 1990)

Teacher's Directions 51
Child's Copy   211

BRIEF DIRECTIONS

Present the sheet with the names to the child. Say, **"I'd like you to pretend to be a teacher who must read the names of students in a class—just as I have done in our class. Do the best that you can and make a guess if you're not sure."** Use a 5″ × 8″ card to expose one name at a time and say, **"Begin with this one."** Note correct responses with a + and use phonetic spellings for names that are mispronounced. Total correct responses and record the score in the box.

	First Name	Last Name
Jay Conway	_____	_____
Chuck Hoke	_____	_____
Kimberly Blake	_____	_____
Homer Preston	_____	_____
Cindy Simpson	_____	_____
Chester Wright	_____	_____
Stanley Shaw	_____	_____
Glen Spencer	_____	_____
Flo Thorton	_____	_____
Grace Brewster	_____	_____
Ron Smitherman	_____	_____
Vance Middleton	_____	_____
Bernard Prendergraph	_____	_____

Total Correct

From Johns, Lenski, and Elish-Piper, *Early Literacy Assessments & Teaching Strategies*

Teacher's Directions 53
Child's Copy   212

The frog sits.

The frog eats.

The frog jumps.

The frog swims.

Qualitative Judgments of Caption Reading

If the child read the story, check the most characteristic statement of the child's reading.

_____ The child's reading is an exact match with the text.

_____ The child's reading closely matches the text.

_____ The child's reading is somewhat related to the text but is based on the illustrations.

_____ The child's reading is related mostly to the illustrations.

If you read the story first, check the statement most characteristic of the child's reading.

_____ The child used memory to read the text with high accuracy.

_____ The child used memory and illustrations to read the text with fair accuracy.

_____ The child did not seem to remember your reading and relied almost entirely on the illustrations to read the text.

	Not Evident Low Seldom Weak Poor		Some		Evident High Always Strong Excellent

Other Reading Behaviors

Retelling					
Reads left to right					
Reads top to bottom					
Demonstrates letter-sound relationships					
Uses monitoring (rereads, corrects)					
Points to correct words (if requested by you)					
Engagement					
Confidence as a reader					

Observations, Comments, Notes, and Insights

From Johns, Lenski, and Elish-Piper, *Early Literacy Assessments & Teaching Strategies*

Teacher's Directions 55
Child's Copy   213

BRIEF DIRECTIONS

Present the list of words for the posttest. Ask the child to identify the words. Say, **"I want you to say some words for me. Let's begin with this one."** Use a plus (+) for correct responses. Record the child's responses for incorrect words. Total correct responses and put the score in the box.

1. of _____

2. to _____

3. in _____

4. that _____

5. was _____

6. you _____

7. on _____

8. are _____

9. with _____

10. at _____

Total Correct ☐

Observations, Comments, Notes, and Insights

Teacher's Directions 57–58
Child's Copy   214

Background: Low |——|——| **High**

Sam Likes Books

Sam likes books.

He likes big books.

He likes small books.

He likes all kinds of books.

Sam likes to read his books at home.

EE (Pre-Primer) Activating Background:
Read the title to yourself and look at the pictures. Then tell me what you think this story will be about.

T   1. ___   What is the story mostly about?
(books; Sam)

F   2. ___   Who likes books?
(Sam)

F   3. ___   Where does Sam like to read?
(at home)

E   4. ___   What do you think Sam reads about?
(any logical response)

I   5. ___   Why do you think Sam likes to read?
(any logical response; it is fun)

V   6. ___   What is a book?
(any logical response; something you read)

Total Miscues [ ]   **Significant Miscues** [ ]   **Questions Missed** [ ]

Word Recognition Scoring Guide		
Total Miscues	Level	Significant Miscues
0	Independent	0
1	Ind./Inst.	—
2	Instructional	1
—	Inst./Frust.	—
3	Frustration	2

Retelling
Excellent
Satisfactory
Unsatisfactory

WPM
)1500

Comprehension Scoring Guide	
Questions Missed	Level
0	Independent
1	Ind./Inst.
1½	Instructional
2	Inst./Frust.
2½+	Frustration

Qualitative Analysis of Word Identification and Comprehension (1 = not evident; 5 = evident)											
Word Identification						**Comprehension**					
Uses graphophonic information	1	2	3	4	5	Makes predictions	1	2	3	4	5
Uses semantic information	1	2	3	4	5	Seeks to construct meaning	1	2	3	4	5
Uses syntatic information	1	2	3	4	5	Understands topic and major ideas	1	2	3	4	5
Knows basic sight words automatically	1	2	3	4	5	Remembers facts or details	1	2	3	4	5
Possesses sight vocabulary	1	2	3	4	5	Evaluates ideas from passages	1	2	3	4	5
Possesses numerous strategies	1	2	3	4	5	Makes and supports appropriate inferences	1	2	3	4	5
Uses strategies flexibly	1	2	3	4	5	Stays focused on reading	1	2	3	4	5

Teacher's Directions 57–58
Child's Copy   215

Background: Low |———|———| **High**

Ball Game

Bob went to a ball game with his dad.

They sat by first base. Dad got two hot

dogs and two cold drinks for lunch.

　　The ball player hit the ball. It came

to Bob. He caught the ball with his glove.

Bob jumped up and down. He was happy.

E (Primer) Activating Background:
Read the title to yourself and look at the picture. Then tell me what you think this story will be about.

T 　1. ___　 What is this story about?
　　　　　　　(a boy and his dad at a ball game)

F 　2. ___　 Where did Bob and his dad sit?
　　　　　　　(by first base)

F 　3. ___　 What did they eat for lunch?
　　　　　　　(hot dogs and cold drinks)

E 　4. ___　 What do you think Bob will do with the
　　　　　　　ball he caught at the game?
　　　　　　　(any logical response; keep it in a safe
　　　　　　　place; show it to his friends)

I 　5. ___　 Why do you think Bob was happy?
　　　　　　　(any logical response; he caught the ball;
　　　　　　　he sat by first base)

V 　6. ___　 What does "glove" mean?
　　　　　　　(something that goes over your hand to
　　　　　　　catch balls)

Total Miscues [ ]　　**Significant Miscues** [ ]　　**Questions Missed** [ ]

Word Recognition Scoring Guide		
Total Miscues	Level	Significant Miscues
0	Independent	0
1–2	Ind./Inst.	—
3	Instructional	1
4	Inst./Frust.	2
5+	Frustration	3

Retelling
Excellent
Satisfactory
Unsatisfactory

____ WPM

) 3000

Comprehension Scoring Guide	
Questions Missed	Level
0	Independent
1	Ind./Inst.
1½	Instructional
2	Inst./Frust.
2½+	Frustration

Qualitative Analysis of Word Identification and Comprehension (1 = not evident; 5 = evident)						
Word Identification						**Comprehension**
Uses graphophonic information	1 2 3 4 5		Makes predictions	1 2 3 4 5		
Uses semantic information	1 2 3 4 5		Seeks to construct meaning	1 2 3 4 5		
Uses syntatic information	1 2 3 4 5		Understands topic and major ideas	1 2 3 4 5		
Knows basic sight words automatically	1 2 3 4 5		Remembers facts or details	1 2 3 4 5		
Possesses sight vocabulary	1 2 3 4 5		Evaluates ideas from passages	1 2 3 4 5		
Possesses numerous strategies	1 2 3 4 5		Makes and supports appropriate inferences	1 2 3 4 5		
Uses strategies flexibly	1 2 3 4 5		Stays focused on reading	1 2 3 4 5		

Teacher's Directions 57–58
Child's Copy   216

Background: Low |———|———| **High**

The Pet Shop

Mike ran home quickly from school. He was in a hurry to see his mom. Mike asked, "Are you ready, mom?" Mom just smiled. She was feeding the new baby. Mike jumped up and down saying, "Let's go, mom!" When mom finished, all three of them got into the car. They drove to the pet shop.

Mike looked in all the cages. He saw some brown baby dogs. He saw cats and kittens. Mike also saw birds, hamsters, and turtles. Mike wanted to choose a small pet with only two legs. He knew he would take good care of it.

E 7141 (Grade 1) Activating Background:
Read the title to yourself and look at the picture. Then tell me what you think this story will be about.

T   1. ___   What is this story about?
(getting a new pet; a trip to the pet shop)

F   2. ___   How did Mike get home from school?
(he ran)

F   3. ___   Why did Mike run home from school?
(he was in a hurry to see his mom; he wanted to go to the pet shop)

F   4. ___   What was mom doing when Mike got home from school?
(feeding the baby)

F   5. ___   How did Mike get to the pet shop?
(he rode in his mom's car; mom drove the car)

F   6. ___   What animals did Mike see?
(dogs, cats, kittens, birds, hamsters, turtles [any three])

I   7. ___   Which animal do you think Mike will choose to be his pet? Why?
(a bird because it has two legs)

I   8. ___   What kind of things will Mike probably have to do to take care of his new pet?
(any logical response)

E   9. ___   What animal would you choose for a pet? Why?
(any logical response)

V 10. ___   What are "cages"?
(a place for animals to sleep; where zoo animals live)

Total Miscues [ ]   **Significant Miscues** [ ]   **Questions Missed** [ ]

Word Recognition Scoring Guide		
Total Miscues	Level	Significant Miscues
0–1	Independent	0–1
2–4	Ind./Inst.	2
5	Instructional	3
6–9	Inst./Frust.	4
10+	Frustration	5+

Retelling
Excellent
Satisfactory
Unsatisfactory
WPM
)6000

Comprehension Scoring Guide	
Questions Missed	Level
0–1	Independent
1½–2	Ind./Inst.
2½	Instructional
3–4½	Inst./Frust.
5+	Frustration

From Johns, Lenski, and Elish-Piper, *Early Literacy Assessments & Teaching Strategies*

Teacher's Directions 57–58
Child's Copy   217

Background: Low |———|———| **High**

Night Time Friend

"It's time to come in the house," Mother called to Joe from the kitchen. "It's getting late and will be dark soon."

Joe did not want to go inside. He sat outside waiting for his friend. Mother watched from the window.

Joe looked up into the sky. He wondered what was taking his friend so long. Then Joe saw something black glide across the night sky. He knew it was his night time friend. Joe watched as it ate insects while flying around the garden.

In the morning, his friend would hang upside down in a cave and fall asleep.

E 8224 (Grade 2) Activating Background:
Read the title to yourself and look at the picture. Then tell me what you think this story will be about.

T   1. ___   What is this story about?
(a boy waiting for his friend)

F   2. ___   Where was Joe?
(outside; in the yard)

F   3. ___   What did Mother want Joe to do?
(come in the house)

F   4. ___   Why did Joe want to stay outside?
(he was waiting for his friend)

F   5. ___   How did Joe's friend sleep?
(upside down)

F   6. ___   What did Joe's friend eat?
(insects)

I   7. ___   What season do you think it is in this story? Why?
(any logical response)

I   8. ___   What is Joe's friend?
(a bat)

E   9. ___   Why do you think Mother wanted Joe to come inside?
(any logical response; it was time for bed; it is dangerous to be outside after dark)

V 10. ___   What does "glide" mean?
(to move smoothly in the air)

Total Miscues [ ]   **Significant Miscues** [ ]   **Questions Missed** [ ]

Word Recognition Scoring Guide		
Total Miscues	Level	Significant Miscues
0–1	Independent	0–1
2–4	Ind./Inst.	2
5	Instructional	3
6–9	Inst./Frust.	4
10+	Frustration	5↑

Retelling
Excellent
Satisfactory
Unsatisfactory

_____ WPM
) 6000

Comprehension Scoring Guide	
Questions Missed	Level
0–1	Independent
1½–2	Ind./Inst.
2½	Instructional
3–4½	Inst./Frust.
5+	Frustration

From Johns, Lenski, and Elish-Piper, *Early Literacy Assessments & Teaching Strategies*

APPENDICES

Professional Organizations and Agencies

Association for Supervision and Curriculum
Development (ASCD)
1250 Pitt
Alexandria, VA 22314
1-800-933-ASCD
http://www.ascd.org

Association of Childhood International
17904 Georgia Ave.
Suite 215
Olney, MD 20832
1-800-423-3563
http://www.udel.edu/bateman/acei/index.html

Center for the Improvement of Early Reading
Achievement (CIERA)
University of Michigan School of Education
610 University Ave., Rm. 1600 SEB
Ann Arbor, MI 48109-1259
http://www.ciera.org

Children's Book Council
568 Broadway, Suite 404
New York, NY 10012
1-212-966-1990
http://www.cbcooks.org

Council for Exceptional Children (CEC)
1920 Association Dr.
Reston, VA 22091
1-888-CEC-SPED
http://cec.sped.org

International Reading Association (IRA)
800 Barksdale Rd.
P.O. Box 8139
Newark, DE 19714
1-800-336-READ
http://www.ira.org

National Association of the Education of Young
Children (NAEYC)
1834 Connecticut Ave., NW
Washington DC 20009
http://www.naeyc.org

National Council of Teachers of English
1111 Kenyon Rd.
Urbana, IL 61801
1-800-369-6283
http://www.ncte.org

Word Families

Short *a* Sounds

~ab	~ack	~ad	~ag	~am	~amp	~an	~and
cab	back	ad	bag	am	camp	an	and
dab	hack	bad	gag	dam	damp	ban	band
gab	jack	cad	hag	ham	lamp	can	hand
jab	pack	dad	nag	jam	champ	fan	land
lab	rack	fad	rag	clam	clamp	man	sand
nab	sack	had	sag	cram	cramp	pan	gland
tab	tack	lad	tag	slam	stamp	ran	grand
blab	black	mad	wag	swam	tramp	tan	stand
slab	slack	pad	brag			van	strand
crab	crack	sad	drag			clan	
drab	track	clad	flag			plan	
grab	shack	glad	shag			scan	
scab	whack	shad	snag			span	
stab	smack		stag			than	
	snack						
	stack						

~ang	~ank	~ap	~ash	~ast	~at	~atch
bang	bank	cap	ash	cast	at	catch
fang	rank	gap	bash	fast	bat	hatch
gang	sank	lap	cash	last	cat	latch
hang	tank	map	dash	mast	tat	match
rang	yank	nap	gash	past	hat	patch
sang	blank	rap	hash	vast	mat	thatch
tang	clank	sap	lash	blast	pat	
clang	plank	tap	mash		sat	
slang	crank	chap	rash		vat	
	drank	clap	sash		brat	
	frank	flap	clash		chat	
	spank	slap	crash		flat	
	thank	snap	smash		slat	
		trap	stash		scat	
			trash		that	

Short *e* Sounds

~eck	~ed	~eg	~ell	~en	~end	~ent
deck	bed	beg	bell	den	end	bent
heck	fed	keg	dell	hen	bend	dent
neck	led	leg	fell	men	lend	lent
peck	red	peg	sell	pen	mend	rent
check	wed		tell	ten	send	sent
speck	bled		well	glen	blend	tent
	fled		yell	then	spend	went
	sled		quell	when	trend	spent
	shed		shell			
	sped		smell			
			spell			
			swell			

~ess	~est	~et
less	best	bet
mess	nest	get
bless	pest	jet
chess	rest	let
dress	vest	met
	west	net
	chest	pet
	crest	set
	quest	wet
		vet
		fret

Short *i* Sounds

~ib	~ick	~id	~ift	~ig	~ill	~im
bib	kick	bid	gift	big	bill	dim
fib	lick	did	lift	dig	fill	him
rib	nick	hid	rift	fig	gill	rim
crib	pick	kid	sift	jig	hill	skim
	sick	lid	drift	pig	kill	slim
	tick	rid	shift	rig	mill	swim
	wick	grid	swift	wig	pill	trim
	brick	skid		brig	rill	whim
	trick	slid		swig	sill	
	chick				till	
	thick				will	
	click				chill	
	flick				drill	
	slick				grill	
	quick				quill	
	stick				spill	

~in	~ing	~ink	~ip	~ish	~lt	~itch
in	bing	ink	dip	dish	it	itch
bin	ring	pink	hip	fish	bit	ditch
din	sing	sink	lip	wish	fit	pitch
fin	wing	wink	nip	swish	hit	witch
kin	bring	blink	rip		kit	stitch
pin	fling	slink	sip		lit	switch
sin	sting	stink	tip		pit	
tin	swing	think	yip		sit	
win	thing		zip		wit	
chin			chip		grit	
shin			ship		mitt	
thin			whip		quit	
grin			flip		slit	
skin			slip		skit	
spin			grip		spit	
twin			trip		twit	
			quip			
			skip			
			snip			

Short *o* Sounds

~ob	~ock	~od	~og	~ong	~ot
cob	cock	cod	bog	bong	cot
fob	dock	hod	cog	gong	dot
gob	hock	nod	dog	long	got
job	lock	pod	fog	song	hot
rob	mock	rod	hog	tong	not
mob	pock	sod	jog	wrong	pot
sob	rock	clod	log	strong	rot
blob	sock	plod	clog		blot
slob	tock	shod	frog		clot
snob	clock		smog		plot
	flock				slot
	crock				shot
	frock				spot
	shock				trot
	smock				
	stock				

Short *u* Sounds

~ub	~uck	~ud	~uff	~ug	~ull	~um
cub	buck	bud	buff	bug	cull	bum
dub	duck	cud	cuff	dug	dull	gum
hub	luck	mud	huff	hug	gull	hum
nub	muck	stud	muff	jug	hull	mum
pub	puck	thud	puff	lug	lull	rum
rub	suck		bluff	mug	mull	sum
sub	tuck		gruff	pug	null	glum
tub	chuck		stuff	rug	skull	slum
club	shuck			tug		drum
grub	cluck			chug		scum
stub	pluck			thug		chum
	stuck			plug		
				slug		
				smug		

~ump	~un	~unch	~ung	~unk	~up	~ush
bump	bun	bunch	dung	bunk	up	gush
dump	fun	lunch	hung	dunk	cup	hush
hump	gun	punch	lung	hunk	pup	lush
jump	nun	brunch	rung	junk	sup	mush
lump	pun	crunch	sung	sunk		rush
pump	run		clung	chunk		blush
clump	sun		flung	drunk		flush
plump	shun		stung	flunk		plush
slump	spun		swung	skunk		slush
stump	stun					brush
thump						crush
						shush

~ust	~ut
bust	but
dust	cut
just	gut
must	hut
rust	jut
crust	nut
	rut
	shut

Long *a* Sounds

~ace	~ade	~age	~aid	~ail	~ain	~ale	~ame
ace	fade	age	aid	ail	gain	ale	came
face	jade	cage	laid	bail	main	dale	dame
lace	lade	page	maid	fail	pain	hale	fame
mace	made	rage	paid	hail	rain	kale	game
pace	wade	sage	raid	jail	vain	male	lame
race	blade	wage	braid	mail	brain	pale	name
brace	glade	wage		nail	drain	sale	same
place	grade	stage		pail	grain	tale	tame
space	trade			rail	train	vale	blame
	shade			sail	chain	scale	flame
	spade			tail	plain	shale	frame
				wail	slain	stale	shame
				frail	stain	whale	
				quail			
				snail			
				trail			

~ane	~ape	~aste	~ate	~ave	~ay	~aze
cane	ape	baste	ate	cave	bay	daze
lane	cape	haste	date	gave	day	gaze
mane	gape	paste	fate	nave	gay	haze
pane	nape	taste	gate	pave	hay	maze
sane	tape	chaste	hate	rave	jay	blaze
vane	drape		late	save	lay	glaze
wane	grape		rate	brave	nay	graze
crane	shape		sate	crave	pay	
			crate	grave	ray	
			grate	shave	say	
			plate	slave	way	
			skate		clay	
			slate		play	
			state		fray	
					tray	
					stay	
					sway	

Long *e* Sounds

~e	~ea	~each	~ead	~eak	~eal	~eam
be	pea	each	bead	beak	deal	beam
he	sea	beach	lead	leak	heal	ream
me	tea	peach	read	peak	meal	seam
we	flea	reach	plead	weak	peal	team
she	plea	teach		bleak	real	cream
		bleach		freak	seal	dream
				speak	veal	gleam
					zeal	
					steal	

~ean	~eat	~ee	~eed	~eek	~eel	~een
bean	eat	bee	deed	leek	eel	keen
dean	beat	fee	feed	meek	feel	seen
lean	feat	see	heed	peek	heel	teen
mean	heat	tee	need	reek	keel	green
wean	meat	wee	seed	seek	peel	queen
clean	neat	free	weed	week	reel	sheen
glean	peat	tree	bleed	cheek		
	seat	glee	breed	creek		
	cheat	thee	creed	sleek		
	cleat	three	freed			
	pleat		greed			
	treat		speed			
	wheat		steed			
			tweed			

~eep	~eet
beep	beet
deep	fleet
jeep	meet
keep	greet
peep	sheet
seep	sleet
weep	sweet
creep	tweet
sheep	
steep	
sweep	

Long *i* Sounds

~ice	~ide	~ie	~ife	~igh	~ight	~ike
lice	bide	die	knife	high	bright	bike
mice	hide	lie	life	nigh	fight	dike
nice	ride	pie	rife	sigh	flight	hike
rice	side	tie	wife	thigh	fright	like
vice	tide	vie			light	mike
slice	wide				might	pike
spice	bride				night	spike
twice	glide				plight	
	slide				right	
					sight	
					slight	
					tight	

~ild	~ile	~ime	~ind	~ine	~ipe	~ire
mild	file	dime	bind	dine	pipe	ire
wild	mile	lime	find	fine	ripe	dire
child	pile	time	hind	line	wipe	fire
	rile	chime	kind	mine	gripe	hire
	tile	crime	mind	nine	swipe	mire
	vile	grime	rind	pine		sire
	smile	slime	wind	tine		tire
	while		blind	vine		wire
			grind	shine		
				spine		
				swine		
				thine		
				twine		
				whine		

~ite	~ive
bite	dive
kite	five
mite	hive
site	live
quite	chive
spite	drive
white	

Long *o* Sounds

~o	~oad	~oam	~oan	~oast	~oat	~obe
go	goad	foam	loan	boast	oat	lobe
no	load	loam	moan	coast	boat	robe
so	road	roam	roan	roast	coat	globe
	toad		groan	toast	goat	
					moat	
					bloat	
					float	
					gloat	

~ode	~oe	~oke	~old	~ole	~olt	~ome
ode	doe	coke	old	dole	bolt	dome
bode	foe	joke	bold	hole	colt	gnome
code	hoe	poke	cold	mole	dolt	home
mode	toe	woke	fold	pole	jolt	Nome
rode	woe	yoke	gold	role	volt	
		bloke	hold	stole		
		choke	mold			
		smoke	sold			
		spoke	told			

~one	~ope	~ose	~ost	~ote	~ow
bone	cope	hose	ghost	note	bow
cone	dope	nose	host	rote	low
lone	hope	pose	most	tote	mow
pone	mope	rose	post	vote	row
tone	rope	chose		quote	sow
zone	scope	those			tow
shone	slope	close			blow
stone					flow
					glow
					slow
					crow
					grow
					show
					snow

Long *u* Sounds

~use	~ute
use	cute
fuse	mute
muse	flute

Sight Word Lists

- **Rank Order of the 50 Most Common Words**
- **Revised Dolch List**
- **Revised Dolch List (Organized by Reader Level)**

Rank Order of the 50 Most Common Words

1. the	18. with	35. when
2. of	19. be	36. an
3. and	20. his	37. their
4. to	21. at	38. there
5. a	22. or	39. her
6. in	23. from	40. can
7. is	24. had	41. we
8. that	25. I	42. what
9. it	26. not	43. about
10. was	27. have	44. up
11. for	28. this	45. said
12. you	29. but	46. out
13. he	30. by	47. if
14. on	31. were	48. some
15. as	32. one	49. would
16. are	33. all	50. so
17. they	34. she	

From Zeno, S.M., Ivens, S.H., Millard, R.T., & Duvvuri, R. (1995). *The Educator's Word Frequency Guide.* Brewster, NY: Touchstone Applied Science Associates.

Revised Dolch List

a	could	he	might	same	told
about	cut	heard	more	saw	too
across	did	help	most	say	took
after	didn't	her	much	see	toward
again	do	here	must	she	try
all	does	high	my	short	turn
always	done	him	near	should	two
am	don't	his	need	show	under
an	down	hold	never	six	up
and	draw	hot	next	small	upon
another	eat	how	new	so	us
any	enough	I	no	some	use
are	even	I'm	not	soon	very
around	every	if	now	start	walk
as	far	in	of	still	want
ask	fast	into	off	stop	warm
at	find	is	oh	take	was
away	first	it	old	tell	we
be	five	its	on	ten	well
because	for	just	once	than	went
been	found	keep	one	that	were
before	four	kind	only	the	what
began	from	know	open	their	when
best	full	last	or	them	where
better	gave	leave	other	then	which
big	get	left	our	there	while
black	give	let	out	these	white
blue	go	light	over	they	who
both	going	like	own	think	why
bring	gone	little	play	this	will
but	good	long	put	those	with
by	got	look	ran	thought	work
call	green	made	read	three	would
came	grow	make	red	through	yes
can	had	many	right	to	yet
close	hard	may	round	today	you
cold	has	me	run	together	your
come	have	mean	said		

Revised Dolch List
(Organized by Reader Level)

Jerry L. Johns

Preprimer		Primer		Grade 1		Grade 2	
a	look	about	on	after	long	across	near
and	make	all	one	again	made	always	need
are	me	around	out	am	many	because	once
at	my	ask	put	an	more	been	only
big	no	away	run	another	much	best	open
blue	not	but	saw	any	must	both	round
call	play	eat	say	as	never	close	same
can	ran	fast	she	be	next	done	short
come	red	from	show	before	off	draw	six
did	said	good	so	began	oh	enough	small
do	see	has	some	better	old	even	start
down	stop	him	soon	black	or	every	ten
for	that	his	take	bring	other	full	thought
get	the	into	then	by	our	grow	through
go	this	know	they	came	over	heard	today
green	to	let	too	cold	own	high	together
have	up	like	two	could	read	hot	toward
he	want	may	us	cut	right	I'm	turn
help	we	new	went	didn't	should	keep	upon
here	what	now	yes	does	still	leave	use
I	who	of	your	don't	tell	left	warm
in	will			far	than	mean	well
is	with			find	their	might	while
it	work			first	them	most	yet
little	you			five	there		
				found	these		
				four	think		
				gave	those		
				give	three		
				going	told		
				gone	took		
				got	try		
				had	under		
				hard	very		
				her	walk		
				hold	was		
				how	were		
				if	when		
				its	where		
				just	which		
				kind	white		
				last	why		
				light	would		

Continuum of Children's Development in Early Reading and Writing

Note: This list is intended to be illustrative, not exhaustive. Children at any grade level will function at a variety of phases along the reading/writing continuum.

Phase 1: Awareness and exploration (goals for preschool)

Children explore their environment and build the foundations for learning to read and write.

Children can

- enjoy listening to and discussing storybooks
- understand that print carries a message
- engage in reading and writing attempts
- identify labels and signs in their environment
- participate in rhyming games
- identify some letters and make some letter-sound matches
- use known letters or approximations of letters to represent written language (especially meaningful words like their name and phrases such as "I love you")

What teachers do

- share books with children, including Big Books, and model reading behaviors
- talk about letters by name and sounds
- establish a literacy-rich environment
- reread favorite stories
- engage children in language games
- promote literacy-related play activities
- encourage children to experiment with writing

What parents and family members can do

- talk with children, engage them in conversation, give names of things, show interest in what a child says
- read and reread stories with predictable texts to children

- encourage children to recount experiences and describe ideas and events that are important to them
- visit the library regularly
- provide opportunities for children to draw and print, using markers, crayons, and pencils

Phase 2: Experimental reading and writing (goals for kindergarten)

Children develop basic concepts of print and begin to engage in and experiment with reading and writing.

Kindergartners can

- enjoy being read to and themselves retell simple narrative stories or informational texts
- use descriptive language to explain and explore
- recognize letters and letter-sound matches
- show familiarity with rhyming and beginning sounds
- understand left-to-right and top-to-bottom orientation and familiar concepts of print
- match spoken words with written ones
- begin to write letters of the alphabet and some high-frequency words

What teachers do

- encourage children to talk about reading and writing experiences
- provide many opportunities for children to explore and identify sound-symbol relationships in meaningful contexts

(continued)

From Learning to read and write: Developmentally appropriate practices for young children, *The Reading Teacher, 52,* 193–216. Copyright © 1998 International Reading Association. Reprinted with permission. This is a joint position statement of the International Reading Association and the National Association for the Education of Young Children.

- help children to segment spoken words into individual sounds and blend the sounds into whole words (for example, by slowly writing a word and saying its sound)
- frequently read interesting and conceptually rich stories to children
- provide daily opportunities for children to write
- help children build a sight vocabulary
- create a literacy-rich environment for children to engage independently in reading and writing

What parents and family members can do
- daily read and reread narrative and informational stories to children
- encourage children's attempts at reading and writing
- allow children to participate in activities that involve writing and reading (for example, cooking, making grocery lists)
- play games that involve specific directions (such as "Simon Says")
- have conversations with children during mealtimes and throughout the day

Phase 3: Early reading and writing (goals for first grade)

Children begin to read simple stories and can write about a topic that is meaningful to them.

First graders can
- read and retell familiar stories
- use strategies (rereading, predicting, questioning, contextualizing) when comprehension breaks down
- use reading and writing for various purposes on their own initiative
- orally read with reasonable fluency
- use letter-sound associations, word parts, and context to identify new words
- identify an increasing number of words by sight
- sound out and represent all substantial sounds in spelling a word
- write about topics that are personally meaningful
- attempt to use some punctuation and capitalization

What teachers do
- support the development of vocabulary by reading daily to the children, transcribing their lan-

guage, and selecting materials that expand children's knowledge and language development
- model strategies and provide practice for identifying unknown words
- give children opportunities for independent reading and writing practice
- read, write, and discuss a range of different text types (poems, informational books)
- introduce new words and teach strategies for learning to spell new words
- demonstrate and model strategies to use when comprehension breaks down
- help children build lists of commonly used words from their writing

What parents and family members can do
- talk about favorite storybooks
- read to children and encourage them to read to you
- suggest that children write to friends and relatives
- bring to a parent-teacher conference evidence of what your child can do in writing and reading
- encourage children to share what they have learned about their writing and reading

Phase 4: Transitional reading and writing (goals for second grade)

Children begin to read more fluently and write various text forms using simple and more complex sentences.

Second graders can
- read with greater fluency
- use strategies more efficiently (rereading, questioning, and so on) when comprehension breaks down
- use word identification strategies with greater facility to unlock unknown words
- identify an increasing number of words by sight
- write about a range of topics to suit different audiences
- use common letter patterns and critical features to spell words
- punctuate simple sentences correctly and proofread their own work
- spend time reading daily and use reading to research topics

(continued)

What teachers do

- create a climate that fosters analytic, evaluative, and reflective thinking
- teach children to write in multiple forms (stories, information, poems)
- ensure that children read a range of texts for a variety of purposes
- teach revising, editing, and proofreading skills
- teach strategies for spelling new and difficult words
- model enjoyment of reading

What parents and family members can do

- continue to read to children and encourage them to read to you
- engage children in activities that require reading and writing
- become involved in school activities
- show children your interest in their learning by displaying their written work
- visit the library regularly
- support your child's specific hobby or interest with reading materials and references

Phase 5: Independent and productive reading and writing (goals for third grade)

Children continue to extend and refine their reading and writing to suit varying purposes and audiences.

Third graders can

- read fluently and enjoy reading
- use a range of strategies when drawing meaning from the text
- use word identification strategies appropriately and automatically when encountering unknown words
- recognize and discuss elements of different text structures
- make critical connections between texts
- write expressively in many different forms (stories, poems, reports)
- use a rich variety of vocabulary and sentences appropriate to text forms
- revise and edit their own writing during and after composing
- spell words correctly in final writing drafts

What teachers do

- provide opportunities daily for children to read, examine, and critically evaluate narrative and expository texts
- continue to create a climate that fosters critical reading and personal response
- teach children to examine ideas in texts
- encourage children to use writing as a tool for thinking and learning
- extend children's knowledge of the correct use of writing conventions
- emphasize the importance of correct spelling in finished written products
- create a climate that engages all children as a community of literacy learners

What parents and family members can do

- continue to support children's learning and interest by visiting the library and bookstores with them
- find ways to highlight children's progress in reading and writing
- stay in regular contact with your child's teachers about activities and progress in reading and writing
- encourage children to use and enjoy print for many purposes (such as recipes, directions, games, and sports)
- build a love of language in all its forms and engage children in conversation

REFERENCES

Adams, M.J. (1990). *Beginning to read: Thinking and learning about print.* Cambridge, MA: MIT Press.

Adams, M.J., Foorman, B., Lundberg, I., & Beeler, T. (1996). *Phonemic awareness in young children.* Baltimore: Brookes Publishing.

Ahlberg, J., & Ahlberg, A. (1986). *The jolly postman.* Boston, MA: Little Brown.

Anderson, R.C. (1994). Role of reader's schema in comprehension, learning, and memory. In R.B. Ruddell, M.R. Ruddell, & H. Singer (Eds.), *Theoretical models and processes of reading* (4th ed.) (pp. 469–482). Newark, DE: International Reading Association.

Anderson, R.C., Hiebert, E.H., Scott, J.A., & Wilkinson, I.A.G. (1985). *Becoming a nation of readers: The report of the Commission on Reading.* Champaign, IL: The National Academy of Education.

Armbruster, B.B. (1986). *Using frames to organize expository text.* Paper presented at the National Reading Conference, Austin, TX.

Baker, L. (1991). Metacognition, reading, and science education. In C.M. Santa & D.E. Alvermann (Eds.), *Science learning: Processes and applications* (pp. 2–13). Newark, DE: International Reading Association.

Blevins, W. (1998). *Phonics from A to Z: A practical guide.* New York: Scholastic Professional Books.

Bromley, K.D. (1998). *Language arts: Exploring connections.* Needham Heights, MA: Allyn and Bacon.

Calkins, L. (1986). *The art of teaching writing.* Portsmouth, NH: Heinemann.

Carle, E. (1969). *The very hungry caterpillar.* Cleveland, OH: Collins-World.

Chall, J.S. (1996). *Stages of reading development.* Orlando, FL: Harcourt.

Chomsky, C. (1972). Stages in language development and reading. *Harvard Education Review, 42,* 1–33.

Clay, M.M. (1985). *The early detection of reading difficulties* (3rd ed.). Portsmouth, NH: Heinemann.

Clay, M.M. (1979). *Reading: The patterning of complex behavior.* Portsmouth, NH: Heinemann.

Clay, M.M. (1975). *What did I write? Beginning writing behavior.* Exeter, NH: Heinemann.

Clay, M.M. (1966). *Emergent reading behavior.* Doctoral Dissertation, University of Auckland, New Zealand.

Cochrane, D., Cochrane, D., Scalena, D., & Buchanan, E. (1988). *Reading, writing, and caring.* Katonah, NY: Richard C. Owen.

Cullinan, B.E. (1992). *Invitations to read: More children's literature in the reading program.* Newark, DE: International Reading Association.

Cunningham, P.M. (1995). *Phonics they use: Words for reading and writing* (2nd ed.). New York: HarperCollins.

Cunningham, P.M. (1990). The names test: A quick assessment of decoding ability. *The Reading Teacher, 44,* 124–129.

Cunningham, P.M., & Allington, R.L. (1994). *Classrooms that work: They can all read and write.* New York: HarperCollins.

Cunningham, P.M., & Hall, D.P. (1994). *Making words: Multilevel, hands-on, developmentally appropriate spelling and phonics activities.* Parsippany, NJ: Good Apple.

Duffy, G.G., & Roehler, L.R. (1989). *Improving classroom reading instruction* (2nd ed.). New York: Random House.

Edwards, P.A. (1986). *Parents as partners in reading.* Chicago: Childrens Press.

Ehri, L.C. (1987). Learning to read and spell words. *Journal of Reading Behavior, 19,* 5–31.

Elkonin, D.B. (1973). USSR. In J. Downing (Ed.), *Comparative reading: Cross-national studies of behavior and processes in reading and writing* (pp. 551–579). New York: Macmillan.

Ericson, L., & Juliebo, M.F. (1998). *The phonological awareness handbook for kindergarten and primary teachers.* Newark, DE: International Reading Association.

Flavell, J.H. (1977). *Cognitive development.* Englewood Cliffs, NJ: Prentice-Hall.

Flood, J., & Lapp, D. (1990). Reading comprehension instruction for at-risk students: Research-based practices that can make a difference. *Journal of Reading, 33,* 490–496.

Fowler, G.L. (1982). Developing comprehension skills in primary students through the use of story frames. *The Reading Teacher, 36,* 176–179.

Fry, E.B., Fountoukidis, D.L., & Polk, J.K. (1985). *The new reading teacher's book of lists.* Upper Saddle River, NJ: Merrill/Prentice Hall.

Gaskin, I.W., Ehri, L.C., Cress, C., O'Hara, C., & Donnelly, K. (1997). Analyzing words. *Language Arts, 74,* 172–192.

Gentry, J.R. (1998). Spelling strategies. *Instructor, 107,* 40.

Gentry, J.R. (1981). Learning to spell developmentally. *The Reading Teacher, 34,* 378–381.

Gentry, J.R., & Gillet, J.W. (1993). *Teaching kids to spell.* Portsmouth, NH: Heinemann.

Gile, J. (1995). *Oh, how I wished I could read!* Stevens Point, WI: Worzalla.

Gillam, R.B., & van Kleeck, A. (1996). Phonological awareness training and short-term working memory: Clinical implications. *Language Disorders, 17,* 72–81.

Goodman, K.S. (1996). *On reading.* Portsmouth, NH: Heinemann.

Goodman, K.S. (1965). A linguistic study of cues and miscues in reading. *Elementary English, 42,* 639–643.

Graves, D. (1983). *Writing: Teachers and children at work.* Exeter, NH: Heinemann.

Gunning, T.G. (1992). *Creating reading instruction for all children.* Boston: Allyn and Bacon.

Heckleman, R.G. (1966). Using the neurological impress method of remedial reading instruction. *Academic Therapy Quarterly, 1,* 235–239.

Heilman, A.W. (1998). *Phonics in proper perspective* (8th ed.). Upper Saddle River, NJ: Merrill.

Huck, C.S. (1976). *Children's literature in the elementary school* (3rd ed.). New York: Holt, Rinehart and Winston.

Jeunesse, G., Delafosse, C., Fuhr, U., & Sautai, R. (1991). *Whales: A first discovery book.* New York: Scholastic.

Johns, J.L. (1997). *Basic reading inventory* (7th ed.). Dubuque, IA: Kendall/Hunt.

Johns, J.L. (1980). First graders' concepts about print. *Reading Research Quarterly, 15,* 529–549.

Johns, J.L., & Lenski, S.D. (1997). *Improving reading: A handbook of strategies* (2nd ed.). Dubuque, IA: Kendall/Hunt.

Leichter, H.P. (1984). Families as environments for literacy. In H. Goelman, A. Oberg, & F. Smith (Eds.), *Awakening to literacy* (pp. 38–50). Exeter, NH: Heinemann.

Lukens, R.J. (1995). *A critical handbook of children's literature* (5th ed.). Glenview, IL: Scott, Foresman.

Macon, J., & Macon, J. (1991). Knowledge chart. In J.M. Macon, D. Bewell, & M.E. Vogt (Eds.), *Responses to literature: Grades K–8* (pp. 13–14). Newark, DE: International Reading Association.

May, F.B. (1998). *Reading as communication: To help children write and read* (5th ed.). Upper Saddle River, NJ: Merrill.

Miles, B. (1995). *Hey, I'm reading.* New York: Scholastic.

Mooney, M.E. (1990). *Reading to, with, and by children.* Katonah, NY: Richard C. Owen.

Morrow, L.M. (1997). *Literacy development in the early years* (3rd ed.). Boston: Allyn and Bacon.

O'Donnell, M.P., & Wood, M. (1992). *Becoming a reader: A developmental approach to reading instruction.* Boston: Allyn and Bacon.

Ogle, D. (1986). K-W-L: A teaching model that develops active reading of expository text. *The Reading Teacher, 38,* 564–570.

Palazzo, J. (1988). *Rainy day fun.* Mahwah, NJ: Troll.

Paris, S.G., Lipson, M.Y., & Wixon, K.G. (1994). Becoming a strategic reader. In R.B. Ruddell, M.R. Ruddell, & H. Singer (Eds.), *Theoretical models and processes of reading* (4th ed.) (pp. 788–810). Newark, DE: International Reading Association.

Pelham, D. (1990). *Sam's sandwich.* New York: Dutton.

Perfetti, C.A., Beck, I., Bell, L., & Hughes, C. (1987). Phonemic knowledge and learning to read are reciprocal: A longitudinal study of first grade children. *Merrill-Palmer Quarterly, 33,* 283–319.

Poe, V.L. (1986). Using multipaired simultaneous oral reading. *The Reading Teacher, 40,* 239–240.

Purcell-Gates, V. (1989). What oral/written language differences can tell us about beginning instruction. *The Reading Teacher, 42,* 290–295.

Purves, A.C., Rogers, T., & Soter, A.O. (1990). *How porcupines make love II: Teaching a response-centered literature curriculum.* White Plains, NY: Longman.

Rasinski, T.V. (1989). Fluency for everyone: Incorporating fluency instruction in the classroom. *The Reading Teacher, 42,* 690–693.

Rasinski, T.V., & Padak, N.D. (1996). *Holistic reading strategies: Teaching children who find reading difficult.* Columbus, OH: Merrill.

Read, C.C. (1986). *Children's creative spelling.* London: Routledge & Kegan Paul.

Rennick, L.W., & Williams, K.M. (1995). Flashlight reading: Making the reading process concrete. *The Reading Teacher, 49,* 174.

Richek, M.A. (1995). *Reading success for at-risk children: Ideas that work.* Bellevue, WA: Bureau of Education and Research.

Richgels, D.J., Poremba, K.J., & McGee, L.M. (1996). Kindergartners talk about print: Phonemic awareness in meaningful contexts. *The Reading Teacher, 49,* 632–642.

Rob, L. (1996). *Reading strategies that work: Teaching your students to become better readers.* New York: Scholastic.

Routman, R. (1994). *Invitations: Changing as teachers and learners K–12.* Portsmouth, NH: Heinemann.

Rumelhart, D.E. (1985). Toward an interactive model of reading. In H. Singer & R.B. Ruddell (Eds.), *Theoretical models and processes of reading* (3rd ed.) (pp. 722–750). Newark, DE: International Reading Association.

Salinger, T.S. (1996). *Literacy for young children* (2nd ed.). Columbus, OH: Merrill.

Savage, J.F. (1994). *Teaching reading using literature.* Madison, WI: WCB Brown and Benchmark.

Schmidt, B., & Buckley, M. (1991). Plot relationships chart. In J.M. Macon, D. Bewell, & M. Vogt (Eds.), *Responses to literature: Grades K–8* (pp. 7–8). Newark, DE: International Reading Association.

Sendak, M. (1963). *Where the wild things are.* New York: Harper and Row.

Silvern, S.B., & Silvern, L.R. (1990). *Beginning literacy and your child* (Parent Booklets). Newark, DE: International Reading Association.

Snow, C.E., Burns, S.M., & Griffin, P. (Eds.). (1998). *Preventing reading difficulties in young children* (Prepublication Copy). Washington, DC: National Academy Press.

Snowball, D. (1997). Use sentences with word blanks to pump spelling strategies. *Instructor, 101,* 22–23.

Stanovich, K.E. (1991). Word recognition: Changing perspectives. In R. Barr, M.L. Kamil, P. Mosenthal, & P.D. Pearson (Eds.), *Handbook of reading research* (Vol. II) (pp. 418–452). New York: Longman.

Stauffer, R.G. (1970). *The language experience approach to the teaching of reading.* New York: Harper & Row.

Stauffer, R.G. (1969). *Teaching reading as a thinking process.* New York: Harper & Row.

Strickland, D.S. (1998). *Teaching phonics today: A primer for educators.* Newark, DE: International Reading Association.

Sulzby, E., & Teale, W. (1991). Emergent literacy. In R. Barr, M.L. Kamil, P. Mosenthal, & P.D. Pearson (Eds.), *Handbook of reading research* (Vol. II) (pp. 727–757). New York: Longman.

Taylor, D. (1983). *Family literacy: Young children learning to read and write.* Exeter, NH: Heinemann.

Teale, W.H., & Sulzby, E. (1989). Emerging literacy: New perspectives. In D.S. Strickland & L.M. Morrow (Eds.), *Emerging literacy: Young children learn to read and write* (pp. 1–15). Newark, DE: International Reading Association.

Tompkins, G.E. (1998). *Language arts* (4th ed.). Upper Saddle River, NJ: Prentice-Hall.

Tompkins, G.E. (1997). *Literacy for the 21st century: A balanced approach.* Columbus, OH: Merrill.

Trousdale, A., & Harris, V. (1993). Interactive storytelling: Scaffolding children's early narratives. *Language Arts, 67,* 164–173.

Turbill, J., Butler, A., Cambourne, B., & Langton, G. (1991). *Frameworks course notebook.* Stanley, NY: Wayne Finger Lakes Board of Cooperative Educational Services.

Vacca, J.L., Vacca, R.T., & Gove, M.K. (1995). *Reading and learning to read* (3rd ed.). Boston: Little Brown.

Weaver, C.A. (1994). *Reading process and practice.* Portsmouth, NH: Heinemann.

Williams, S. (1989). *I went walking.* New York: Trumpet.

Wilson, P.T. (1988). *Let's think about reading and reading instruction: A primer for tutors and teachers.* Dubuque, IA: Kendall/Hunt.

Wylie, R., & Durrell, D.D. (1970). Teaching vowels through phonograms. *Elementary English, 47,* 787–791.

Yopp, H.K. (1995). A test for assessing phonemic awareness in young children. *The Reading Teacher, 49,* 20–29.

Yopp, H.K. (1992). Developing phonemic awareness in young children. *The Reading Teacher, 45,* 696–703.

Zutell, J. (1996). The directed spelling thinking activity (DSTA): Providing an effective balance in word study instruction. *The Reading Teacher, 50,* 98–108.

INDEX

3825